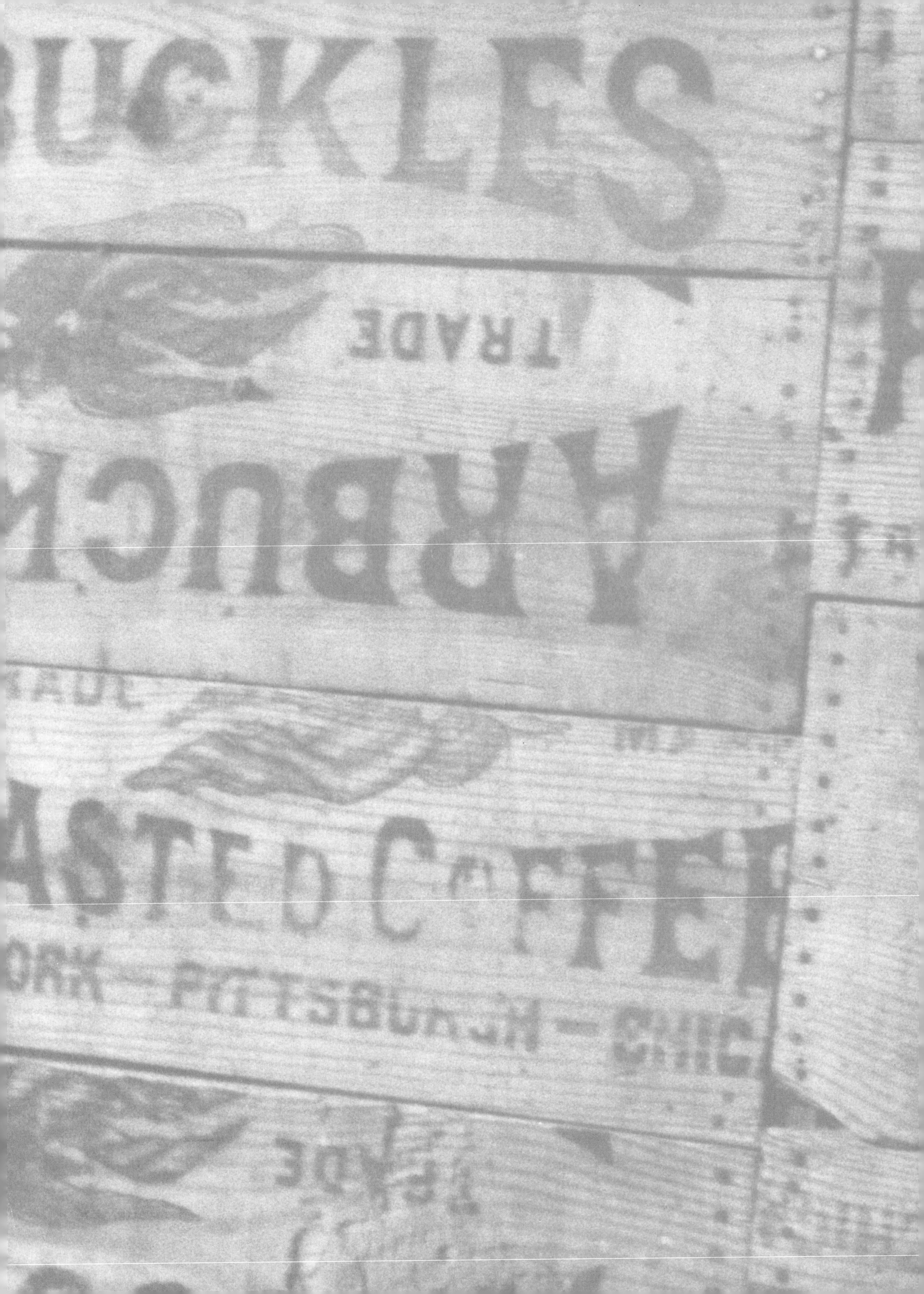
TRADE
PITTSBURGH

ARBUCKLES

THE COFFEE THAT

WON THE WEST

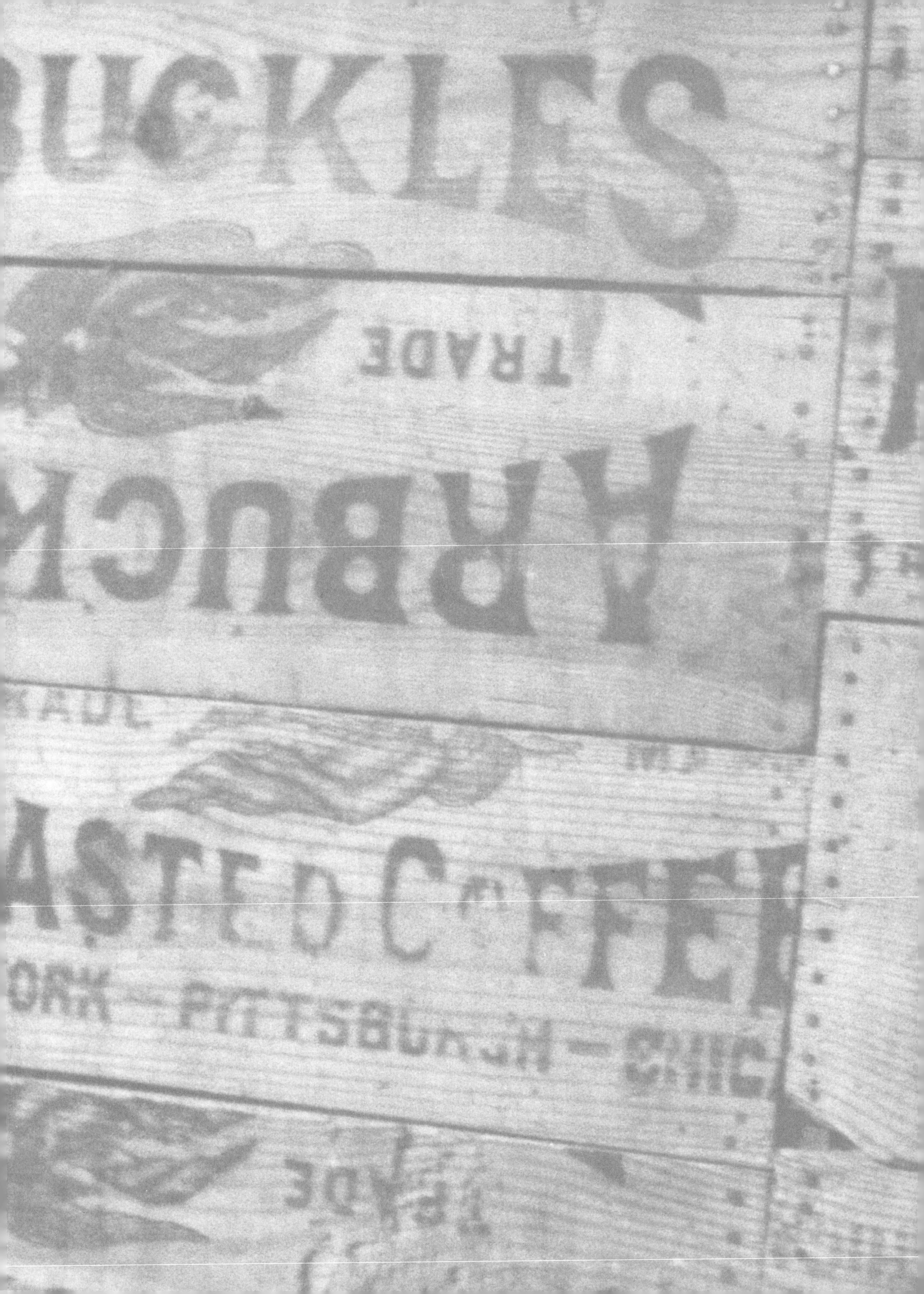
UCKLES
TRADE
ARBUCK
ASTED COFFE
ORK – PITTSBURGH – CHIC
TRADE

ARBUCKLES

THE COFFEE THAT
WON THE WEST

BY

FRANCIS L. FUGATE

Texas
Western
Press

THE UNIVERSITY OF TEXAS AT EL PASO

1994

First Edition
Library of Congress Catalog Card No. 92-062486
ISBN 0-87404-230-5

Texas Western Press books are printed on acid-free paper, meeting the
guidelines for permanence and durability of the Committee on
Production Guidelines for Book Longevity of the Council on
Library Resources.

FOR

ROBERTA

MY PARTNER AND COLLABORATOR

FOR FIFTY-TWO YEARS

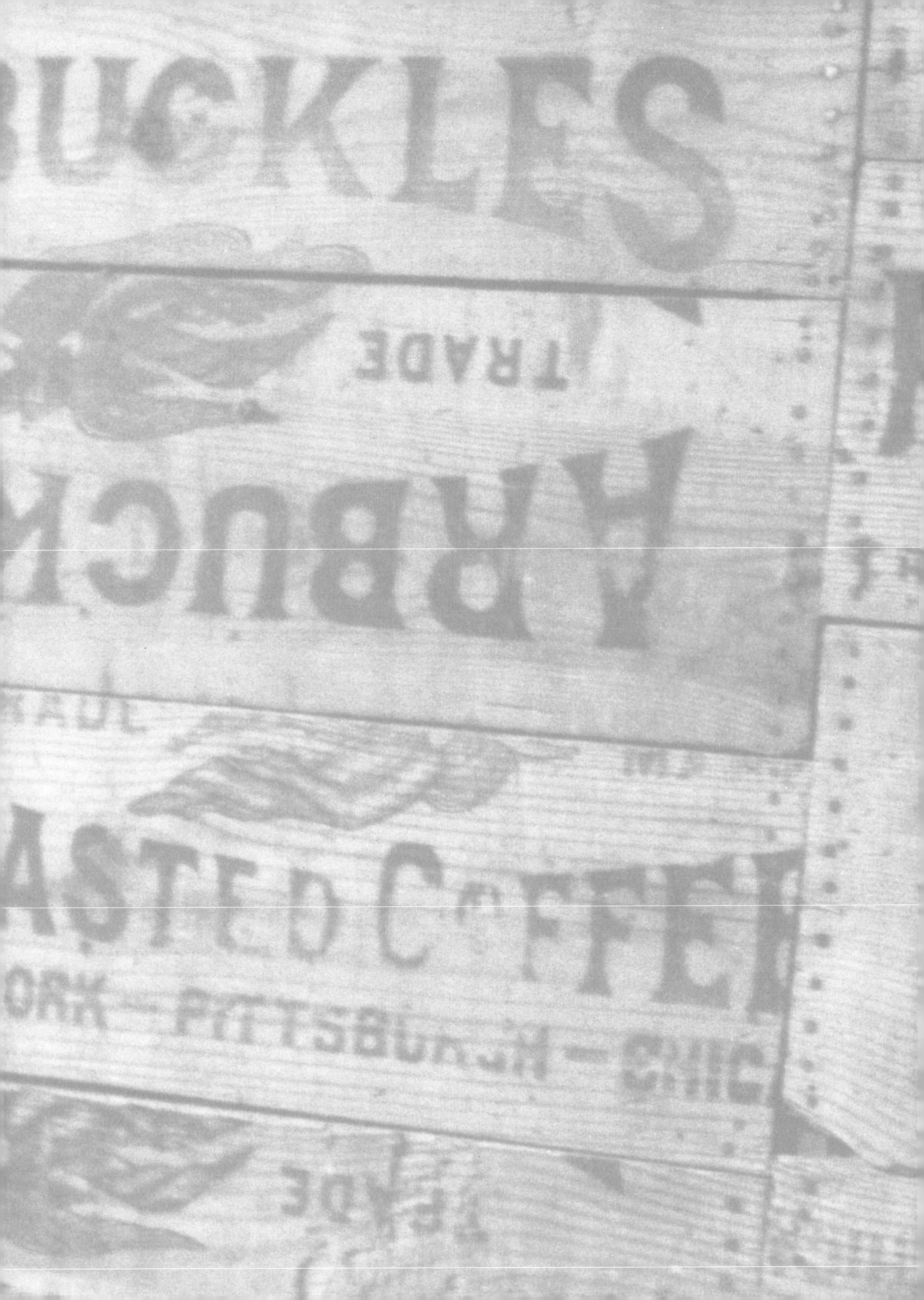

Contents

The author with a framed section of an Arbuckles Roasted Coffees crate.
(Photograph by Roberta B. Fugate)

INTRODUCTION

I set out in pursuit of Arbuckles Coffee when I was only ten years old. The boy next door had a bicycle his father had obtained with the signatures printed on Arbuckles Coffee packages, a forerunner of trading stamps. Teddy also had a collection of colorful Arbuckles' trade cards telling about various states and countries. Our teacher, Miss Cunningham, was a geography buff. Teddy included his father's Arbuckles' cards in his notebook. Teddy got a good grade, while Miss Cunningham made me stay after school to copy maps from geography books.

My family used Butternut Coffee, but I started a campaign to get them to change, unaware that Arbuckles had ceased including trade cards in the packages and doling out premiums to users.

"Butternut makes a damn good coffee," my father stubbornly maintained.

So I resorted to skullduggery. I took the tube from our percolator. Then I spit on kitchen matches, the old wooden kind that made an awful stench when they got wet. I struck the matches and dropped them, smoldering and smoking, down through the percolator tube. Dad noticed the difference right away.

"Mother, you must not be washing that damned coffeepot!"

"Why don't we change to Arbuckles ?" I suggested craftily.

"Butternut has always made damned good coffee. It's the coffeepot."

Mother washed the percolator, and I repeated the match treatment every day or so—until my father caught me. We did not change to Arbuckles'. Neither did I get a bicycle or any geography cards, but I had considerable difficulty sitting down for at least a week.

Later, as I began writing stories and articles about the West, I discovered the West's love affair with Arbuckles Coffee and launched a pursuit of the subject to obtain background material. One of my most fertile sources of information about the West was an old store in Organ, New Mexico. The proprietor was a pack rat; he saved everything: mail order catalogues, war bond posters, old advertisements. If you could name it, Mr. Bentley could find it. He wouldn't sell any of his treasures, but he would show them to you and give you a rundown on their history.

When I heard about Mr. Bentley's death, I headed for Organ. But I got there a month too late. A member of the family was in the store cleaning things out. The wonderful old posters dating back to the Spanish American War were gone from the walls.

"We threw those dusty old things out," the lady told me.

"How about all of those Montgomery Ward catalogues he had?"

"Only one of those was any good. Some fellow came through here offering a prize of five dollars for the oldest Montgomery Ward catalogue in town. We got the prize and burned the rest of them."

"How about Arbuckles Coffee? There wouldn't happen to be an old package of that around?"

"No, I don't— *Wait*!" Her eyes brightened. "Out in the chickenyard. He had a chicken coop made out of an old coffee crate. We've sold the chickens. You can go look at it if you want to."

There it was! A genuine Arbuckles shipping crate, dusty and smeared with chicken dung, but plainly emblazoned with the famous "flying angel" trademark. I carried the box into the store, wondering if I had enough money in my pocket to pay for it.

"You want to buy *that*?" the woman asked. "Would fifty cents be too much?"

I broke the speed law all the way back home to El Paso. With the crate cradled in my arms, I rang the doorbell with my elbow. Roberta opened the door.

"Look what I've got!"

Roberta's nose wrinkled. "Take that stinking thing out to the garage, and *don't* come through the house!"

She did not relent until the day we found the side of a crate, just like mine, in an antique shop—framed with a price tag of $150. It took considerable cleaning and restoration until a side of my chicken coop was ready to hang on our office wall. In the meantime, I had been surreptitiously accumulating a collection of old Arbuckles trade cards.

After Roberta quit teaching first graders to read, she joined me as a collaborator in writing about the West. One day she came out of the file closet with my secret collection of Arbuckles trade cards in her hand.

"You've got so much stuff about Arbuckles Coffee, why don't we do a book about it?"

And that was the beginning of this volume. Prior to her death, Roberta spent much of her spare time during some two years probing western source materials to unearth the facts which form the skeleton of this book.

Francis L. Fugate

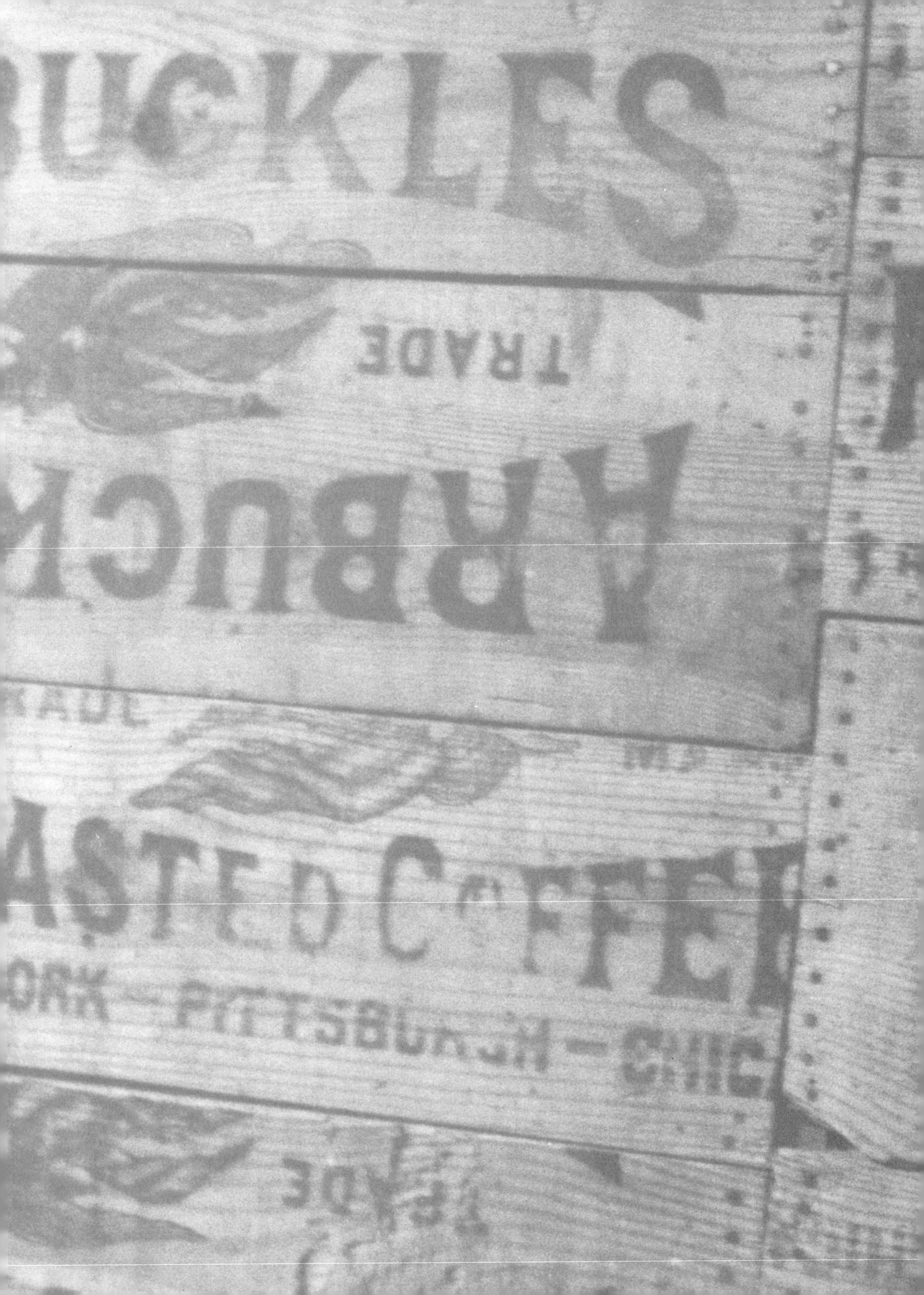

BUCKLES
TRADE
ASTED COFFE
ORK – PITTSBURGH – CHIC

ACKNOWLEDGMENTS

It would be impossible to give credit to all who have contributed to this volume, but I would be remiss not to mention substantial contributions by a number of institutions and people. Personnel at the Arizona Historical Society; Wyoming State Archives, Museums & Historical Department; Plainsman Museum, Aurora, Nebraska; and the Archives of the National Museum of American History, Smithsonian Institution, were particularly efficient and helpful.

Special thanks go to Marlene P. Ware, Hayden Library, Arizona State University; Ed Chamberlin, curator, Hubbell Trading Post National Historic Site, Ganado, Arizona and Stanislaus Skarzynski, Springfield Armory National Historic Site.

Then there was Harold R. Belsher of Scottsdale, Arizona, who toured the Indian reservations with me and enabled me to take a photograph of the "Arbuckle crate" wall at the Red Lake Trading Post. James E. Sherman, of Tucson, generously displayed and photographed his Arbuckle collection and provided helpful insights. A whopping vote of thanks goes to Jerry M. Eckhart, of Cisco, Texas, for permission to use his grandfather's ledger and letters generated while he was serving as an Arbuckle Brothers salesman in southern Oklahoma.

I deeply appreciate the hospitality of Stefanie and Albert E. Ward, of Albuquerque. They shared their home, their collections and their knowledge. Albert's corrections and suggestions wrought much improvement in the text.

Thanks to Jim Bob Tinsley's knowledge of western music, I found out about "Make Me a Cowboy Again." Al Packard, of Santa Fe, provided a photograph of his splendid "Arbuckles Flying Angel" pictorial rug. Western poet Robert Dyer gave permission to publish his poem "Arbuckle's," and Beverly Baker, of *El Palacio* magazine, provided illustrations. Ron Harris and Jack Harvey, of Old West Outfitters, filled me in on the resurrection of Arbuckles Ariosa.

David Shindo, of Darst-Ireland Photography, El Paso, must be recognized for exercising his magic to bring faded photographs back to life.

Last but by no means least, Dale L. Walker, of Texas Western Press, kept the project alive by reading the manuscript along the way and making invaluable suggestions. Without Dale and our sessions over the bottomless coffeepot at the Village Inn, this volume would not exist.

Illustrations not otherwise credited are from the author's collection.

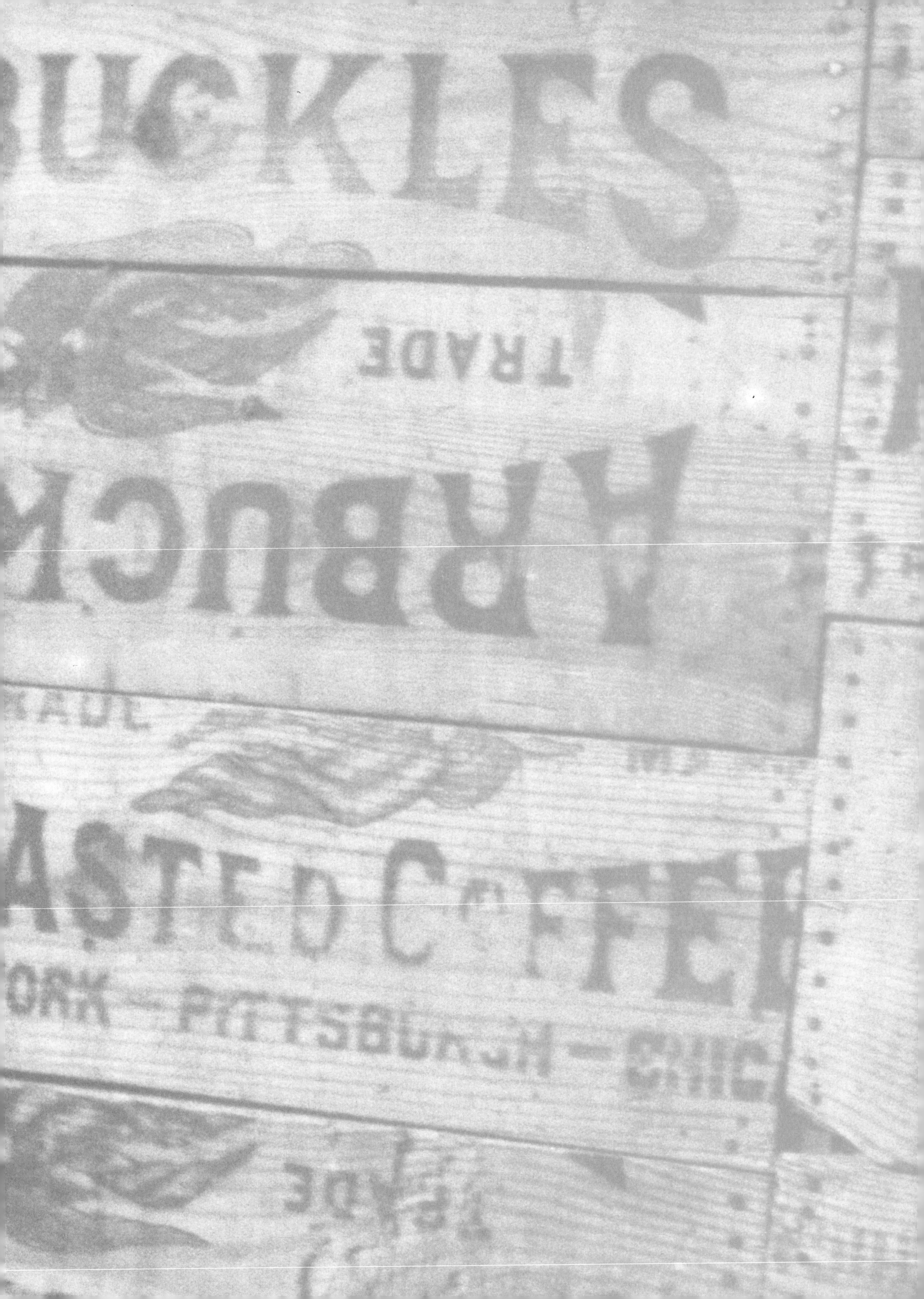
TRADE
PITTSBURGH

1
WINE OF ARABIA

The United States is the largest consumer of coffee in the world. The trend began during colonial times with the Boston Tea Party. It received impetus by way of the inventive genius and business acumen of John Arbuckle. In 1869, Arbuckle relieved coffee drinkers of the troublesome chore of roasting coffee beans before use. He followed up with manufacturing and marketing methods which spread his name and his product across the nation, particularly in the West where "Arbuckles" became a synonym for "coffee."

The origin of coffee as a beverage is obscured by misty clouds of folklore. However, use of the bean can be traced from Abyssinia (now Ethiopia) where the plants were indigenous. The warlike Gallas, formerly nomads of southern Ethiopia, crushed the caffeine-laden berries, combined them with animal fat, and rolled the mixture into balls to make travel rations, much as pemmican was used by Plains Indians and trappers in the American West.[1]

Since there was lively exchange and occasional warfare between the Abyssinians and the Greeks, knowledge of coffee reached the great medical school at Alexandria, founded soon after the death of Aristotle in 322 B.C. as the Greek center of sciences. Unfortunately, the school's library, some 700,000 volumes, was subsequently destroyed, reputed to have been used as fuel to stoke the furnaces of public baths. However, Arabian physicians had translated records from the Greek, preserving much of the medical knowledge of the day.

Discounting a couple of dubious Biblical and Homeric references,[2] the earliest surviving mention of coffee was by Rhazes, an Arabian philosopher and physician from the first quarter of the tenth century. He wrote an encyclopedic compendium of medical knowledge. He described *bunca* as being good for the stomach, discussing its healing properties in a manner indicating that it had been around for many years. His documentation pointed back to Abyssinia.[3] Avicenna, a later Arabian chronicler, noted that *bunchum* "fortifies the members, it cleans the skin and dries up the humidities that are under it, and gives an excellent smell to all the body."[4]

Coffee was first mentioned in European medical treatises late in the sixteenth century. Since that time, the magnitude of literature has swelled to formidable proportions. For example, Wolf Mueller compiled a bibliography of coffee, tea, and cocoa in medical literature prior to the beginning of the present century. His tabulation of titles of major sources up to 1900 filled a hefty 228-page volume.[5]

Coffee's emergence in Arabia as a social drink is tainted by the vagaries of folklore. The most persistent legend comes from southern Arabia and tells of Kaldi, a goatherd. One day he noticed his charges gamboling about with unusual vigor. He attributed the unaccustomed activity to something they had eaten and followed his goats as they pastured. Kaldi watched them eat red berries from a strange shrub. Kaldi tasted the berries, liked them, and after that regularly joined the goats in their eating and cavorting under the influence of the fruit.

Later, a passing Moslem holy man from a nearby monastery observed the frolicking goatherder and investigated the cause. The monk took some of the red berries back to the monastery. The priest sampled the fruit and experienced a warm and comforting glow. Naturally, anything which promoted happiness was subject to ecclesiastical suspicion, particularly since the Koran forbade intoxication. However, the priests sought Allah's guidance in the matter.

According to the story, Mohammed appeared to one of them in a dream with instructions: Boil these mysterious berries in water and drink the brew. This would keep the holy men awake and give them more time to devote to their prayers. The priest awoke and hastened to the prophet's bidding. For a time, communicants in this particular monastery logged more prayer-time than any other in Araby. Perhaps the priests made a tactical error by referring to their newfound beverage as *qahwah* ("wine"). The Moslem hierarchy ruled coffee was an intoxicant and invoked the Koran's prohibition, leaving the red berries—at least temporarily—to Kaldi and his goats.

Naturally, historians give scant credence to this oft-repeated folktale, but there seems to be little doubt that the use of coffee as a drink began in Yemen among Moslem priests of the Sufi order during the mid-1400s.[6] Coffee cultivation and use of the beverage spread northward as far as the holy city of Mecca, the birthplace of Mohammed, and aroused indictment by the Moslem hierarchy. The charge was that the idle congregated in coffee houses rather than in mosques, playing chess and other games and amusing themselves with singing, dancing, and music—contrary to the manners of strict Mohammedans. The imams took action.

The first attempt at prohibition of coffee occurred in Mecca in 1511, sparking a long controversy which waged through the Moslem world. Termed "a tool of Satan," coffee was attacked as a violation of Islamic law. Some medical authorities accused coffee of promoting impotence and causing lethargy, melancholia, and leprosy; others pointed to salutary effects. After almost a century of theological prohibition, countered by popular protest and subversive use, the advocates of coffee won.[7]

Abd al-Qadir, an Arabian lawyer-theologian and a follower of Mohammed, was eager to convince his contemporaries that coffee drinking was not incompatible with the prophet's law. His book, *Argument in Favor of the Legitimate Use of Coffee*, has been dubbed "the earliest advertisement for coffee."[8] During the persecution in Mecca, Arabian poets waxed ecstatic in praise of coffee:

> O Coffee! Thou dost dispel all cares, thou art the object of desire to the scholar.
>
> This is the beverage of the friends of God; it gives health to those in its service who strive after wisdom.
>
> Prepared from the simple shell of the berry, it has the odor of musk and the color of ink.
>
> The intelligent man who empties these cups of foaming coffee, he alone knows truth.
>
> May God deprive of this drink the foolish man who condemns it with incurable obstinacy.
>
> Coffee is our gold. Wherever it is served, one enjoys the society of the noblest and most generous men.
>
> O drink! As harmless as pure milk, which differs from it only in its blackness.[9]

Coffee houses rapidly became a firmly established social institution throughout the Middle East. Men patronized the coffee houses. The women insisted upon being supplied with coffee to drink at home. For example, in Turkey, as part of the wedding ceremony, men promised never to let their wives be without coffee. To do so was a legitimate cause for divorce.[10] In his treatise on coffee, French traveler Antoine Galland remarked that "as much money must be spent in the private families of Constantinople for coffee as for wine in Paris." On the streets of Constantinople beggars asked for money to buy coffee.[11]

Coffee cultivation increased in the Yemen district. During the mid-seventeenth century so much coffee was shipped from the port of Mocha at the mouth of the Red Sea that "mocha" became the trade name for the acidy, heavy-bodied Arabian coffee, deemed "smooth and delicious" in flavor. The Arabians guarded their newfound and lucrative industry as zealously as twentieth-century OPEC members labored to control the world's supply of oil. For a time the Arabians prevented the spread of coffee culture by permitting none of the berries to leave the country unless they were first steeped in boiling water or parched to destroy their powers of germination.

As travelers to the Middle East spread word of the stygian drink and Venetian traders exported the berries, coffee spread across the Mediterranean and over Europe, inevitably precipitating controversy along the way. Shortly after coffee reached Rome, perhaps at the instigation of wine merchants who feared competition, priests appealed to Pope Clement VIII (1535-1605) to forbid coffee's use among Christians. The Evil One himself had given this hellish black brew to the infidel Moslems. In drinking it, Christians risked falling into Satan's trap.

The pope was curious. He ordered some coffee brought to him and tried a cup. He was reported to have said: "Why, this Satan's drink is so delicious that it would be a pity to let the infidels have exclusive use of it. We shall fool Satan by baptizing it, and making it a truly Christian beverage."[12]

Coffee came to Vienna as a result of the Ottoman Empire's attempt to overrun Europe. In 1683, the Turks laid siege to Vienna. Franz Georg Kolshitsky, a Pole who had lived for many years among the Turks, volunteered to attempt to penetrate Turkish lines and contact rescuing forces. After the resulting Christian victory, when the booty was being divided up, nobody knew what to do with a mountainous pile of bags of coffee beans the fleeing Turks had left behind. Some thought they were camel fodder and began to burn the bags.

Kolshitsky knew better. As a reward for his services, he received the coffee and a building in which to open a coffee house. However, the Viennese did not take to the thick bitter brew prepared in the Turkish manner. Kolshitsky persisted. He filtered the grounds, added milk to the clarified liquid, and Vienna was on its way to becoming the "mother of cafés."[13]

During the siege, a Viennese baker made rolls in the shape of the Turkish standard, a crescent-shaped moon, as a symbol of Christian defiance—the *kipful*. Kolshitsky started serving coffee with the crescent-shaped rolls. As Paul Lunde pointed out three centuries later, "And *voilá!* The croissant—and the continental breakfast—was born."[14]

By 1839, there were eighty coffee houses in Vienna proper and fifty more in the suburbs. The grateful Coffee Makers' Guild of Vienna erected a statue of Franz Georg Kolshitsky to commemorate their hero.[15]

When coffee reached Prussia, Frederick the Great protested because its use was upsetting the balance of trade; too much money was going overseas to foreign coffee merchants. A number of German doctors abetted King Frederick's cause by urging women to abstain from drinking coffee because its use provoked sterility. In 1732, Johann Sebastian Bach struck a blow for women's rights with his *Coffee Cantata*, a musical "protest of the fair sex" against the current propaganda: "Ah! How sweet coffee tastes! Lovelier than a thousand kisses, sweeter far than muscatel wine!" proclaimed the heroine.[16]

On September 13, 1777, King Frederick issued a manifesto urging that his subjects drink beer instead of coffee.[17] When that failed, he created a government monopoly which limited the preparation of coffee to royal roasting establishments. This effectively confined use of coffee to the nobility, clergy, and government officials and turned a tidy profit to the royal coffers.

Poorer classes had to obtain coffee by stealth or fall back on substitutes such as barley, wheat, corn, chicory, and dried figs. Discharged wounded soldiers were employed to spy on people who were roasting coffee without permits. They followed their noses and became known as "coffee-smellers" by the indignant populace. German housewives gave the term "coffee klatch" to the English language to describe a casual gathering to drink coffee and converse, from German *kaffee* ("coffee") plus *klatsch* ("gossip" or "chat").[18]

In 1660, a shipload of coffee arrived in Marseilles. It was thought of as a drug until 1664 when Jean de Thévenot's widely circulated *Relation d'un voyage fait au Levant* came along. His description of the use of Turkish coffee instigated a rash of coffee houses, and vintners enlisted members of the medical profession to mount an attack on the looming threat to rout Bacchus. Monsieur Colomb, a young doctor from the faculty of the university in nearby Aix, prepared a thesis summing up the medical opposition to coffee for delivery in the town hall of Marseilles. He began:

> We note with horror that this beverage, thanks to the qualities which have been incautiously ascribed to it, has tended almost completely to disaccustom people from the enjoyment of wine— although any candid observer must admit that neither in respect of taste or smell, nor yet of colour, nor yet of any of its essential characteristics, is it worthy to be named in the same breath with fermented liquor, or wine!

After reciting a list of recriminations, Monsieur Colomb concluded:

> . . . Through the acidification of the blood, which has already assumed the condition of a river-bed at midsummer, all parts of the body are deprived of their juices, and the whole frame becomes

excessively lean.

These evils are especially noticeable in persons who are by nature of a bilious temperament, who from birth upwards have suffered from a hot liver and a hot brain; in persons whose intelligence is extremely subtle, and whose blood is already superheated. For these reasons we have to infer that the drinking and use of coffee would be injurious to the inhabitants of Marseilles.[19]

Those in opposition to coffee seized upon a familiar theme, circulating the story of a queen of Persia who was frustrated by lack of sexual satisfaction from her coffee-addicted husband. Looking out her window, she saw some men about to geld a stallion. The cruel operation was unnecessary, she declared. If they would simply feed the beast coffee, in a few days he would become as cold as the king was toward her.[20]

Other French doctors, including Philippe Sylvestre Dufour of Lyons, came to the rescue of coffee,[21] and its use gradually spread across France. In 1669, it was introduced to the salons of Paris by Soliman Aga, the Turkish ambassador from Mohammed IV to the court of Louis XIV.[22] According to Isaac Disraeli, the ambassador served it in brilliant porcelain cups with gold and silver saucers on embroidered silk doilies fringed with gold bullion. Turkish slaves knelt to present cups to Parisian dames who were seated on cushions on the ground. Coffee quickly attained fashionable status.[23]

Both Voltaire and Bernard de Fontanelle, French author and conversationalist, were habitués of Parisian coffee houses; and both have been credited with responding to the accusation that coffee was a slow poison by saying: "I think it must be, for I've been drinking it for eighty-five years and am not dead yet." It was probably Fontanelle, since he lived to be almost a hundred; Voltaire died at eighty-four.[24]

English writers and travelers of the sixteenth and seventeenth centuries told about the use of coffee in the Levant. William Parry's *Sir Antonie Sherlies Travelles*,[25] published in London in 1601, described the manners and customs of the Turks in Aleppo in less than complimentary terms. He called them "damned Infidells":

They sit at their meat (which is served to them upon the ground) as Tailers sit upon their stalls, crosse-legd; for the most part, passing the day in banqueting and carowsing, untill they surfet, drinking a certain liquor, which they do call *Coffe*, which is made of seede much like mustard seede, which will soone intoxicate the braine like our Metheglin.[26]

Other writers were more charitable, and coffee next made its way to

TRAITEZ

Nouveaux & curieux

DU CAFE',

DU THE'

ET DU

CHOCOLATE.

Ouvrage également neceffaire aux
Medecins, & à tous ceux qui
aiment leur fanté.

Par PHILIPPE SYLVESTRE DUFOUR

*A quoy on a adjouté dans cette Edition, la meil-
leure de toutes les methodes, qui manquoit
à ce Livre, pour compofer*

L'EXCELLENT CHOCOLATE.

fuivant la Copie de Lyon.

A LA HAYE,

Chez ADRIAN MOETJENS, Mar-
chand Libraire prez la Cour, à la.
Librairie Françoife.

M. DC, LXXXV,

*Title page of Philippe Sylvestre Dufour's treatise on coffee, tea, and chocolate,
published in Lyons in 1685.*

England. Dr. William Harvey, the physician who discovered the circulation of blood, was reported to have used it in his home prior to 1652. Shortly before his death in 1657, he told his solicitor: "This little bean is the source of happiness and wit!" He bequeathed fifty-six pounds of coffee to the London College of Physicians, directing that they should meet monthly and drink coffee to commemorate the day of his death.[27]

According to a recipe published in London in 1662, brewing a pot of coffee was not a simple process:

> To make the drink that is now much used called coffee. The coffee-berries are to be bought at any Druggist, about three shillings the pound; take what quantity you please, and over a charcoal fire, in an old pudding-pan or frying-pan, keep them always stirring until they be quite black, and when you crack one with your teeth that it is black within as it is without; yet if you exceed, then do you waste the Oyl, which only makes the drink; and if less, then will it not deliver its Oyl, which must make the drink; and if you should continue fire till it be white, it will then make no coffee, but only give you its salt. The Berry prepared as above, beaten and forced through a Lawn Sive, is then fit for use.
>
> Take clean water, and boil one-third of it away what quantity soever it be, and it is fit for use. Take one quart of this prepared Water, put in it one ounce of your prepared coffee, and boil it gently one-quarter of an hour, and it is fit for your use; drink one-quarter of a pint as hot as you can sip it.[28]

The first coffee house in England opened in Oxford in 1650. Two years later, Pasqua Rosée opened a coffee house in London and distributed a handbill, the first English advertisement for coffee. It would quicken the "spirits" and make the "heart lightsome." Additionally, "It is excellent to prevent and cure the Dropsy, Gout, and Scurvy. . . . It is very good to prevent Mis-carryings in Child-bearing Women. . . . It will prevent Drowsiness, and make one fit for busines, . . . you are not to Drink it after Supper, unless you intend to be watchful, for it will hinder sleep for 3 or 4 hours." (Appendix A)

The leading lights of literature and politics patronized the proliferation of coffee houses which spread across London. Matthew Green, an eighteenth-century poet, wrote in *The Spleen*:

> Or to some coffee-house I stray,
> For news, the manna of a day,
> And from the hipp'd discourses gather
> That politics go by the weather.

Illustration from Dufour's treatise on coffee, showing an Arab drinking coffee and the coffee plant.

In The Rape of the Lock (1712-14), Alexander Pope commented:

Coffee (which makes the politician wise
And see through all things with his half-shut eyes)

In coffee houses the price of coffee ranged from one to two pence per dish. London's coffee houses became known as "penny universities" because they were great schools of conversation and for only a penny one could attend and listen to debate by the greatest minds in the nation.[29]

Opposition followed a familiar pattern. A broadside was published, *The Ale-Wives' Complaint Against the Coffee Houses* for spiriting away the tavern trade. In 1674, the women of London protested because they were not allowed in the coffee houses. They issued a manifesto: *The Womens Petition against Coffee. Representing to Publick Consideration the Grand Inconveniences accruing to their Sex from the Excessive Use of that Drying, Enfeebling Liquor.* They claimed their menfolk had become addicted to coffee and were becoming "as unfruitful as the deserts, from which the unhappy berry is said to be brought." Neglected by husbands who spent all their time in coffee houses, the women allowed the whole race was in danger of extinction.[30]

By 1675, Charles II became convinced that coffee houses were "seminaries of sedition" where "divers false, malicious and scandalous reports are devised and spread abroad to the Defamation of his Majestie's Government, and to the Disturbance of the Peace and Quiet of the Realm." On December 29, 1675, the king issued "A Proclamation for the Suppression of Coffee Houses."

Public protest soon convinced Charles II that he had blundered. On January 8, 1676—only ten days later—"His Gracious Majesty" saved face by recalling the ban out of his "princely consideration and royal compassion." By 1700, there were more than 2,000 coffee houses in London alone.[31]

Toward the end of the eighteenth century, the popularity of coffee houses declined. The first step in the deterioration was precipitated by coffee house proprietors launching a newspaper in competition with newsmen and editors who gathered information in coffee houses.[32] The second cause of the decline of the coffee houses was the development of the private club as a social amenity. The crowning blow came as a result of the British government's desire to foster trade with India and China.

The British East India Company became far more interested in tea than coffee, which was imported from Dutch, French, and Arabian sources. Tea became the official court drink. Still denied access to coffee houses, disgruntled ladies furthered the British East India Company's

cause by demanding tea rather than coffee in the fashionable establishments patronized by both sexes. The coffee house was doomed. Some
became chop houses, others converted to taverns, and the rest closed
their doors.

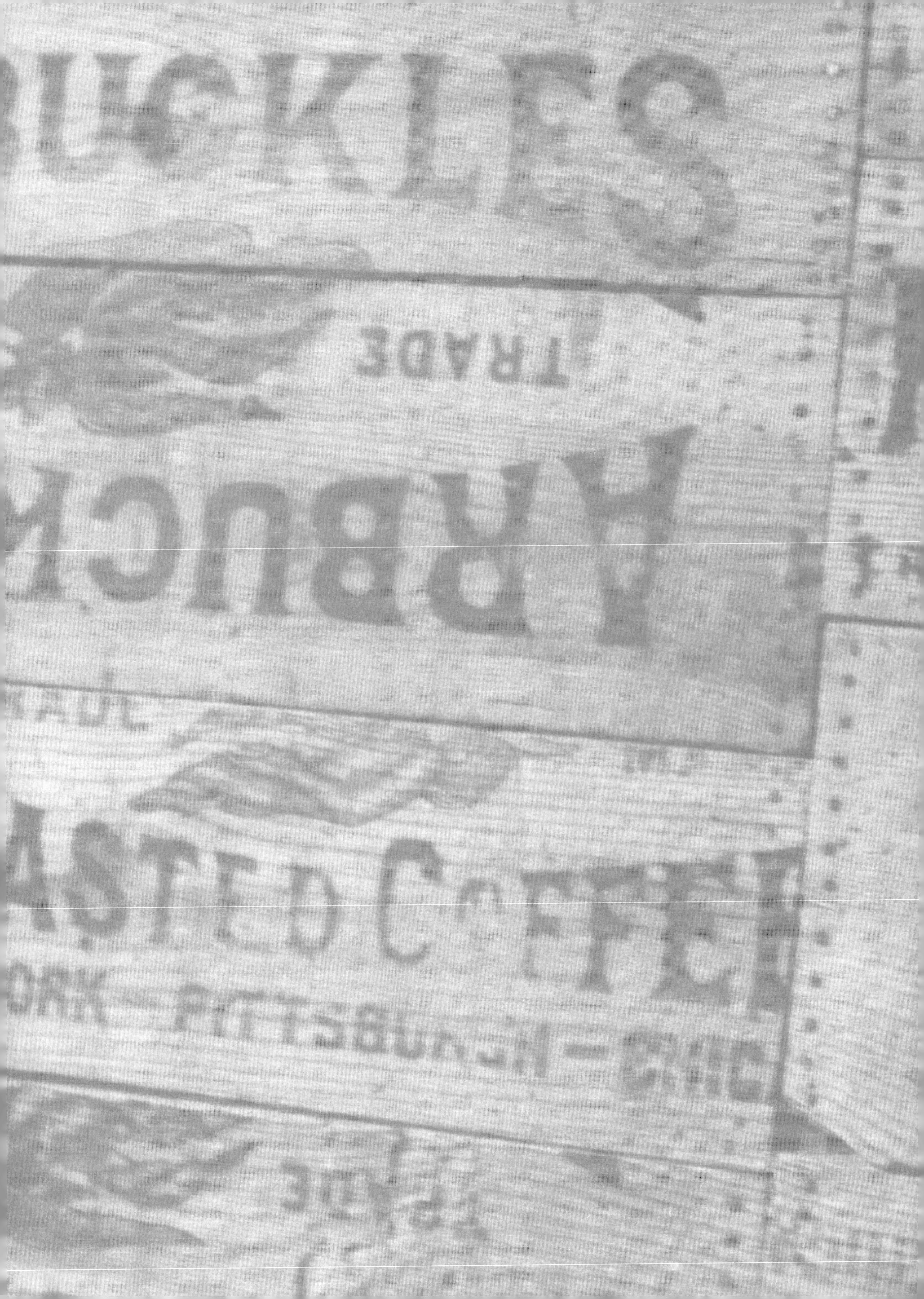
UCKLES
TRADE
ASTED COFFE
ORK – PITTSBURGH – CHIC

2
A STAPLE OF THE AMERICAN WEST

After the introduction of coffee into the New World, coffee lovers would have to wait almost two centuries for a Pittsburgh grocer named John Arbuckle to hit upon an innovation which would make roasted coffee generally available to American households. In the meantime, "this rare Arabian cordial" flowed westward across the continent, gathering devotees who would elevate the United States to first place among coffee consuming nations of the world.

Capt. John Smith, founder of the Colony of Virginia at Jamestown, brought the first knowledge of coffee to North America in 1607. Previously he had traveled in the Middle East. He wrote of the Turks: "Their best drink is *coffa* of a graine they call *coava*." But there was no written mention of the use of coffee in the Virginia colony.[1]

Neither is there a record of coffee in the cargo of the *Mayflower* in 1620, although there was a wooden mortar and pestle, later used to make "coffee powder" as ground coffee was called in those days. The earliest record of coffee in America comes from New York in 1668, when a beverage was made of roasted beans, apparently imported by the Dutch from Amsterdam, and flavored with sugar or honey and cinnamon.[2]

Coffee first appears in official records of the New England colony in 1670. In Boston, Dorothy Jones was granted a license to sell "coffee and cuchaletto," the latter being the seventeenth-century spelling for chocolate or cocoa. Since the first coffee house in Boston did not open until later, it is probable that Dorothy Jones was selling powdered coffee.[3] In 1683, the year following William Penn's settlement on the Delaware River, he was buying coffee in the New York market at eighteen shillings and nine pence per pound.[4]

Reflecting the English trend, coffee houses opened in Boston, New York,[5] and Philadelphia.[6] However, tea had made such progress in England, thanks in part to the British East India Company applying epithets such as "syrop of soot" and "essence of old shoes" to coffee,[7] that the directors moved to expand tea's use in the colonies. King George spoiled their plans with the Stamp Act of 1765, imposing taxes on paints, oils, lead, glass, and tea. When the colonists retaliated by refusing to import any goods of English make, Parliament repealed all the taxes except for that on tea.

In 1773, with the cry "no taxation without representation," a group of Boston citizens disguised themselves as Indians, boarded English ships lying in the harbor, and threw their tea cargoes into the bay. Abigail Adams called it "that bainfull weed."[8]

Thus, the die was cast to make coffee the sovereign drink of the American people. Travelers and couriers put up at coffee houses where they swapped tales, read broadsides, and exchanged newspapers brought by ship captains from overseas. Patriots and conspirators began to gather in the Green Dragon, a Boston tavern which served coffee in addition to the usual rum, gin, small beer, and metheglin, the latter a mead-like alcoholic drink made of fermented honey. Daniel Webster later was to call the Green Dragon the "headquarters of the Revolution."[9]

Apparently George Washington did not wholeheartedly join the colonial boycott against British tea.[10] A handbook published by the Mount Vernon Ladies Association of the Union reported that in October 1775, he breakfasted "on three small Indian hoe cakes and as many dishes of tea."[11] Baron von Steuben's secretary-valet noted that after Martha Washington's arrival at Valley Forge the officers' wives met at General Washington's quarters "where the evening was spent in conversation over a dish of tea or coffee."[12]

In 1774, John Adams, an inveterate tea drinker, stopped at Mrs. Huston's tavern at Falmouth, Massachusetts, en route to the first Continental Congress in Philadelphia. He asked the proprietress if a weary traveler could get a dish of tea if it had been honestly smuggled or paid no duties.

"No, sir," replied Mrs. Huston, "we have renounced all tea in this place, but I'll make you coffee."

Adams wrote his wife Abigail, "Tea must be universally renounced, and I must be weaned, and the sooner the better."[13]

On September 15, 1786, Washington recorded in his diary: "Sent my boat to Alexandria for Molasses and Coffee which had been sent me from Surinam by a Mr. Branden of that place."[14] On May 17, 1793, he made a presidential visit to a Philadelphia coffee house to assure a group of merchants and traders that peace would continue.[15]

Coffee continued to be an expensive luxury into the nineteenth century. In 1816, Reuben Woolworth was running a boarding house in Turin, New York. He had to pay an extravagant forty-four cents a pound for coffee at Roland Clapp's store. Clapp's records reveal that he sold only two or three pounds a month.[16]

Historically, military service and warfare have increased the popularity of coffee among members of the United States armed services. If Dr. Benjamin Rush—surgeon, signer of the Declaration of Independence, and member of Congress from Philadelphia— had prevailed, the trend would have started much earlier than it did.

The first Continental Army ration established by Congress on November 4, 1775, and issued by order of General Washington on December 25, contained neither coffee nor tea; there was a daily allowance of "spruce beer, cider or molasses." After demobilization following Gen. Charles Cornwallis's surrender in 1781, the ration included "one gill [four fluid ounces] of common rum" for "medicinal purposes."

Dr. Rush led a protest against "the custom of drinking spiritous liquors which prevails so generally in our Army." In 1790, Congress reduced the ration to "half a gill of rum, brandy or whiskey." In 1798, war with France threatened, and Congress sought to encourage enlistment by raising the liquor allowance to a full gill. Controversy over the use of "ardent spirits" continued for more than thirty years with much debate and little action by Congress.

On October 25, 1832, President Andrew Jackson settled the argument under his authority to prescribe components of the ration. He decreed that coffee and sugar would be substituted for the liquor allowance. Congress finally got around to confirming his order on July 5, 1838:

> And be it further enacted that the allowance of sugar and coffee to noncommissioned officers, musicians and privates in lieu of the spirit or whiskey component part of the Army ration, now directed by regulation, shall be fixed at six pounds of coffee and 12 pounds of sugar to every 100 rations, to be issued weekly where it can be done with convenience to the public service, and, when not so issued to be paid for in money.

In 1858, the director of the Medical Department of Texas felt an increase in the allowance of coffee and sugar would "greatly conduce to the interest of the services by the greatly increased health, comfort and power of endurance a liberal use of the infusion will bestow upon all who drink it." This and similar recommendations resulted in increasing the ration to ten pounds of coffee and fifteen pounds of sugar per 100 men, approved by Congress on June 21, 1860.[17]

The popularity of coffee during the Civil War is documented in many accounts of army life. The best is *Hardtack and Coffee*, written in 1888 by John D. Billings, a Massachusetts artilleryman. Doling out coffee was serious business. The regimental quartermaster usually received the ration in an oatsack. He divided it among his ten units. Then the quartermaster sergeant of a battery would apportion his allotment among the detachments in his command. The sergeant of each detachment was responsible for dividing it among his men.

Usually he laid out a rubber blanket on the ground. With members of the unit standing around watching, he measured the coffee into as many piles as there were men. He spooned out the sugar which accompanied the coffee ration on another blanket. In some cases, the sergeant would then turn his back and take out his roster. One of the men would point to a pile and call out, "Who shall have this?" and the sergeant would read a name from the roster.

In the field, preserving one's ration of coffee and sugar presented a major problem. Billings wrote that an observer could tell how long a soldier had been in the service by the way he cared for his ration of coffee and sugar:

> The manner in which each man disposed of his coffee and sugar ration after receiving it is worth noting. Every soldier of a month's experience in campaigning was provided with some sort of a bag into which he spooned his coffee; but the kind of bag he used indicated pretty accurately, in a general way, the length of time he had been in the service. For example, a raw recruit just arrived would take it up in a paper, and stow it away in that well known receptacle for all eatables, the soldier's haversack, only to find it a part of a general mixture of hardtack, salt pork, pepper, salt, knife, fork, spoon, sugar, and coffee by the time the next halt was made. A recruit of long standing, who had been through this experience and had begun to feel his wisdom-teeth coming, would take his up in a bag made of rubber blanket or a poncho; but after a few days carrying the rubber would peel off or the paint of the poncho would rub off from contact with the greasy pork or boiled meat ration which was its travelling companion, and make a black, dirty mess, besides leaving the coffee-bag unfit for further use. Now and then some young soldier, a little starchier than his fellows, would bring out an oil-silk bag lined with cloth, which his mother had made and sent him; but even oil-silk couldn't stand everything, certainly not the peculiar inside furnishings of the average soldier's haversack, so it was not long in yielding. But your plain, straight forward old veteran, who had shed all his poetry and romance, if he had ever possessed any, who had roughed it up and down "Old Virginny," man and boy, for many months, and who had tried all plans under all circumstances, took out an oblong plain cloth bag, which

looked as immaculate as the every-day shirt of a coalheaver, and into it scooped without ceremony both his sugar and coffee, and stirred them thoroughly together.

There was method in this plan. He had learned from hard experience that his sugar was a better investment thus disposed of than in any other way; for on several occasions he had eaten it with his hardtack a little at a time, had got it wet and melted in the rain, or, what happened fully as often, had sweetened his coffee to his taste when the sugar was kept separate, and in consequence had several messes of coffee to drink *without* sweetening, which was *not* to his taste. There was now and then a man who could keep the two separate, sometimes in different ends of the same bag, and serve them up proportionately.[18]

Each man carried a preserve can in which to boil his coffee; he was issued a small tin cup for drinking. Sometimes, when tired and foot-sore, a soldier would drop out of the marching column to build a small campfire and cook a mess of coffee. He would then hurry on to over-take the column. The real joy came at night when his unit reached a bivouac area. For firewood, the men requisitioned rails from the nearest fence. Billings told about it:

> Little campfires, rapidly increasing to hundreds in number, would shoot up along the hills and plains and, as if by magic, acres of territory would be luminous with them. Soon they would be surrounded by the soldiers, who made it an almost invariable rule to cook their coffee first, after which a large number, tired out with the toils of the day, would make their supper of hard-tack and coffee, and roll up in their blankets for the night. If a march was ordered at midnight, unless a surprise was intended, it must be preceded by a pot of coffee; if a halt was ordered in mid-forenoon, or afternoon, the same dish was inevitable, with hardtack accompaniment usually. It was coffee at meals and be-tween meals; and men going on guard or coming off guard drank it at all hours of the night.[19]

On June 19, 1862, Maj. Gen. George B. McClellan issued General Or-der No. 136 from headquarters of the Army of the Potomac at Camp Lincoln, Virginia:

> I. The extra issue of whisky heretofore ordered will be imme-diately discontinued.
> II. All commanding officers are enjoined strictly to enforce the existing orders directing that hot coffee be served to the troops

immediately after reveille.

A month later, Jonathan Letterman, surgeon and medical director of the Army of the Potomac, had other ideas. Obviously a believer in the medical efficacy of whisky, he wanted to brighten the troops' life with a toddy. In July 1862, he wrote General McClellan:

> GENERAL: I have the honor to submit the following extract from a report of the sick and wounded in this army, taken from the latest reports made to this office by the medical directors of corps, and to present to you certain suggestions for removing the causes of disease and improving the general condition of the men:

> . . . That when troops are to march they should have breakfast, if only a cup of coffee, before starting, and after their arrival in camp each man be given a gill of whisky in a canteen three-fourths filled with water.

Doctor Letterman finished off with a prescription for the preparation of coffee:

> Directions for cooking in camp.
> Coffee should be roasted over a slow fire, constantly stirring until it becomes of a chestnut-brown color, and not burnt, as is so commonly done. It should be boiled for twenty minutes, set to one side, sweetened, well stirred, and a little cold water added to cause the grounds to settle.[20]

Small units prepared their own meals in the field and, since bean coffee kept better than ground, there was need for a compact, highly portable coffee grinder. During the Civil War, a coffee mill was designed to fit in place of the patchbox in the butt stock of a Sharps carbine. Coffee beans were fed into a port on the bottom of the stock and ground coffee was expelled through a slot on the side of the stock opposite the detachable handle. Several carbines were fitted with grinders as an experiment toward ultimately providing one coffee mill per company, but the device was never approved as standard equipment.[21]

Prevalent usage during the Civil War had much to do with increasing the popularity of coffee in the United States, but the beverage had started its flow westward across the nation long before the Civil War. After the Revolutionary War, beginning with the earliest exploratory probings to the west, coffee quickly became a staple of the diet, particularly among those on the frontier.

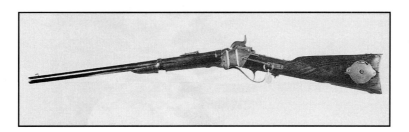

A "coffee mill" Sharps carbine in the Springfield Armory National Historic Site collection at Springfield, Massachusetts.

In 1804, the Lewis and Clark expedition's list of provisions included a fifty-pound bag. As the party started up the Missouri River on May 14, 1804, the supply of coffee was obviously carefully husbanded. On June 25, 1805, Capt. William Clark noted in his journal: "I had a little coffee for brackfast [*sic*] which was to me a necessity as I had not tasted any since last winter."[22]

Likewise, coffee became essential to the trappers who followed in the wake of the Lewis and Clark expedition. On February 13, 1822, William Henry Ashley advertised in the *St. Louis Missouri Gazette & Public Advertiser* for a hundred "Enterprising Young Men to ascend the river Missouri to its source, there to be employed for one, two or three years." This was the beginning of the brigade-rendezvous system which fostered the rise of the free trapper or "mountain man." Trappers remained in the Rockies and met Ashley or a representative of the Rocky Mountain Fur Company at an annual rendezvous, where they sold their season's catch of pelts and bought supplies for the coming season.

In 1825, the rendezvous was held at Henry's Fork on the Green River. Records show that trappers purchased more than two hundred pounds of coffee at $1.50 a pound. Ashley had paid $1.25. By 1827, the retail price of coffee in the Rockies had climbed to $2 a pound and a trapper named Daniel T. Potts wrote his brother: "There is a poor prospect of making much here, owing to the evil disposition of the Indians, and the exorbitant price of goods."[23]

In 1849, while surveying for a military and commercial route across the Southwest, Lt. William H. C. Whiting called coffee "the great essential in a prairie bill of fare." He noted in his journal:

> It [tobacco] is an article indispensable to the frontiersman. Give him coffee and tobacco, and he will endure any privation, suffer any hardship, but let him be without these two necessaries of the woods, and he becomes irresolute and murmuring.[24]

For the trappers, brewing a pot of coffee was not always easy. Coffee was available at rendezvous only in bulk quantities of green beans. Before going out to tend their beaver traps, the mountain men would "parch" or roast enough to last them through the trek. As a young man, Lewis H. Garrard read of trapping expeditions to the Rockies and set out to spend ten months among the mountain men. He returned to relate his experiences in *Wah- to-yah and the Taos Trail*. He wrote of "Partaking of the nectar- like Java—every drop worth its weight in `beaver.'":

> That night parched coffee gave out. We had nothing in which to burn more; but, as necessity is, ever, the mother of invention,

we selected two flat stones from the channel [of the stream] at hand, twenty-five to thirty inches in diameter, which we placed on the fire until heated; then one was taken off, the coffee poured on, and stirred with a stick. When the coffee was sufficiently burned, a piece of skin was laid on the ground, and a clean stone, a foot in diameter, rested on the knees of the grinder, with one edge on the skin. A smaller stone, held in the hand, reduced the grains between it and the larger one, to powder, by a rotary motion.[25]

For travelers on the plains, coffee helped make a meager breakfast endurable. During his first trip to Santa Fe in 1845, Santa Fe trader James Josiah Webb's party ran short of rations:

We had corn which was laid in for the mules, but we [were] compelled to deny the mules their rations and use it ourselves. The night guards would boil it. And we had boiled corn without grease, salt, or other seasoning, and coffee without sugar for breakfast.[26]

Most guidebooks for the Colorado gold rush included a coffee mill among recommended supplies. A book by William N. Byers and John H. Kellom, published in Chicago in 1859, retailed for fifty cents. It specified seventy-five pounds of coffee, a Dutch oven, and three camp kettles; however, "to save carrying a coffee mill, coffee may be pounded in a piece of buckskin or cotton cloth; pepper, the same."[27]

Indians took to coffee immediately. The Sioux called it *kazuta sapa*—"black medicine."[28] It was a common occurrence for painted braves to charge a wagon train as a prelude to begging for coffee, tobacco, sugar, and firewater. Not infrequently, these commodities were the sole motive for an attack upon settlers' wagon trains. Garrard described the Cheyennes as "extravagantly fond" of coffee.[29] In 1858, during the Colorado gold rush, William B. Parsons wrote for the *Lawrence* (Kansas) *Republican*:

We began to meet large numbers of Indians—Arapahoes, Cheyennes, Kiowas, and Camanches [*sic*]. They all have papers from which you can learn that "the bearer is a Cheyenne chief, well-disposed, intelligent, and brave, and earnestly desires a little sugar, coffee, and tobacco"—the last part of which is undoubtedly true, generally. . . . They wear nothing but a cloth about their loins, and are generally armed with bows and arrows, though some have rifles, and a very few have revolvers. They crowd about our wagons in large numbers, importuning us constantly for sugar, coffee, and tobacco, and wanting to "swappee" (trade).

In May 1871, near Fort Richardson, Texas, Satanta, a Kiowa chief, led a raid against a wagon train. The Indians killed seven teamsters, captured forty mules, and took guns, pistols, ammunition, sugar, and coffee. At Fort Sill, Satanta boasted, "If any other Indian said he did it, he was a liar."[30]

Along the Missouri River near White Cloud, Nebraska, military posts, Indian agents, and traders were supplied by an annual trip of the American Fur Company steamboat. Dressed buffalo robes served as currency for the Indians. From 1833 until 1859, the fur company's rate of exchange at Fort Berthold was:

> 1 cup sugar = 1 buffalo robe
> 1 cup coffee = 1 buffalo robe
> 1 lb. tobacco = 1 buffalo robe

In St. Louis, the wholesale value of a buffalo robe was four dollars. After 1859, the company boosted the price: three cups of coffee and one of sugar for a good robe already dressed and ready for market. Thus, the cost to the American Fur Company was about thirty-eight cents per robe.[31]

Sometimes Indians exacted better payment in their own way. In 1862, a band of Dakotas raided a small post called Moro, near Fort Berthold, robbing it of its provisions and 400 packs of robes worth about $12,000 in St. Louis. They gave the three men in charge of the post warning to leave if they wanted to save their lives and wounded one as he ran. The Indians then proceeded to Fort Berthold to resell the robes to the American Fur Company. An unsympathetic traveler hazarded the company would not lose much with sugar and coffee at a dollar a pound.[32]

In his annual report, Samuel N. Latta, United States agent for the upper Missouri, castigated the fur company:

> This old American Fur Company (so-called) is the most corrupt institution ever tolerated in our country. They have involved the government in their speculations and schemes; they have enslaved the Indians, kept them in ignorance; taken from them year after year their pitiful earnings, in robes and furs, without giving them equivalent; discouraged them in agriculture by telling them that should the white man find that their country would produce they would come in and take their lands from them. They break up and destroy every opposition to their trade that

ventures into their country, and then make up their losses by extorting from the Indians.[33]

During the California gold rush, coffee was deemed a necessity for gold seekers taking the various trails westward. A minimum of four or five pounds was recommended for a person leaving Fort Smith, Arkansas, for California. Later, during the Pike's Peak gold rush, guidebooks recommended from fifty to eighty pounds of coffee to last a party of four for six months. Most outfitters along the frontier were charging about fifteen cents per pound. Prospectors headed for the Platte River diggings were advised to bring supplies with them because flour was selling at fifteen dollars a hundred weight and sugar and coffee at fifty cents a pound.[34]

In 1859, on a cold February morning, Horace Tabor loaded his sick wife into a wagon and headed out of Denver toward a rumored gold strike in the Pike's Peak area. Augusta kept a diary, but only one page has survived. Entries on four out of the five days on that page are concerned with coffee:

> . . . pitched tent, made a fire. Soon had a dish of hot coffee for supper. . . .March 1st. . . . Breakfast of venison ham and sasphras tea. this I call a poor appology for coffee. . . .
>
> March 2. Morning is very windy. Nat [her baby] has a bad cold and is very cross, breakfast of venison ham and coffee. . . .
>
> 4 Sunday. . . . We drove into a beautiful valley and halted for noon. There a man overtook us with some cows, and kindly offered us some milk which we thankfully received as we had had no milk for coffee since we had left civilization.[35]

The Tabors' schedule was strenuous. Before seven each morning they breakfasted, struck their tent, repacked the wagon, and captured and yoked the oxen to the wagon. They drove for five hours before stopping for the midday meal. If there was no wood where they stopped in the evening, it was Augusta's task to spend an hour or two gathering sufficient dried buffalo dung to cook beans, bacon, and coffee.[36]

When coffee was in short supply or too expensive for Western settlers, various substitutes were tried—parched corn, rye, wheat, and okra seed to name only a few. In many cases a substitute was the only choice. Howard Reude told about such a meal in a dugout at Kill Creek, Kansas:

> Yesterday I tasted a new kind of coffee. Mrs. Greenfield ran out of coffee—either the real article or the rye substitute—and

she had a gang of men to be fed, and it wouldn't be supper without coffee, so she set her wits to work, with the result that when we gathered at the table a hot amber-colored drink was poured into the cups and set before us. One after another took a sip, set the cup down and demanded what under the sun it was. The lady smiled, but refused to name it. "It ain't coffee," said Charlie, "of that I am sure, for I know the last was used at noon." "If you guess right I'll tell you," teasingly retorted his wife. Everybody took a turn, and as is often the case, the last was the lucky winner. He noticed several sacks of millet seed leaning against the side of the room and hazarded "Millet." "Right," said Lida. "I thought I'd try it, just to see what it tasted like." It was the queerest tasting coffee any of us had ever put in his mouth, but it "went," or the crowd didn't get any hot drink.[37]

During the Mexican War, members of the army in the West protested loudly if they did not get their coffee ration. A sergeant in Col. Alexander W. Doniphan's Missouri volunteers wrote a letter which was published on September 9, 1846, in the Fayette *Missouri Democrat*: "Another cause of complaint is that our coffee gave out a week since, and we have no chance to procure a supply until we reach Bent's Fort, two days' march from this place."

Weak coffee incited sarcastic protest, as reflected in the journal of Marcellus Ball Edwards, also with Doniphan's expedition: The meal was "washed down by coffee made by cooks who had so far learned economy as to know exactly how many grains it took to color a pint of water."[38] Earlier, at Fort Gibson, James Hildreth remarked concerning a meal: "Coffee . . . might have been good, had the quantity been sufficient to allow a decision on the subject."[39]

Several decades ago, an imaginative professor of business at Massachusetts Institute of Technology propounded the question: If all coffee production in the world were to cease, what would happen to the last coffee bean? After due deliberation, his class came to the conclusion that the very last coffee bean in the world would end up in a setting of precious metal on the finger of some dowager.

Although members of the class were probably not aware of it, this had already happened—about a century earlier. During the Civil War, Union naval blockade of shipping was successful in virtually stopping the supply of coffee to the southern states. The little coffee that was available became astronomically expensive in inflated Confederate currency. Then, on January 4, 1863, *The Southern Confederacy*, an Atlanta newspaper, reported that the jewelers of the city had bought up all available coffee "for sets in breast pins instead of diamonds." Civil War substitutes included acorns, dandelion roots, sugarcane, parched rice, cotton seed, sorghum molasses, English peas, peanuts, wheat, beans, sweet potatoes, corn, rye, okra, and chicory.[40]

Coffee substitutes were nothing new. In 1719, when coffee was seven shillings a pound in London, a decoction known as "saloop," sassafras and sugar, came on the market. It became popular among those who could not afford tea or coffee.[41] Reide's Coffee House, in Fleet Street, was cited as "the first respectable house" where saloop was sold.[42]

On June 16, 1853, Peter Armand le Comte de Fontainemoreau obtained a patent from the London patent office for "extracting and concentrating the juices of chicory, carrot, the soft acorn of Spain or any other country, beetroot, barley, oatmeal, and other similar substances" and employing the juices "for the improvement and cheapening of coffee infusions."[43]

West of the Atlantic, entrepreneurs were borrowing ideas from Europe. Bohler & Weikel, of Philadelphia, came forward with Dandelion Coffee: "It is delicious. It takes but half the quantity of other coffee." It was "Entered according to Act of Congress" in the year 1861:

> Dandelion Root, which enters largely into the composition of this preparation, is extensively used in Europe, being recommended as a superior beverage for persons inclined to general Debility, Dyspepsia, Disease of the Liver, Billious Affections, and irritable condition of the stomach.[44]

In spite of European acclaim, the Dandelion Coffee brew did not catch on.

In the United States, the housewife was recognized as a victim of skulduggery before the turn of the century, long before the supermarket and super advertising brought on consumer legislation and watchdog governmental agencies. One P. H. Felker, of Grand Rapids, Michigan, predated Ralph Nader by almost a century. In 1878, Felker complained, "In England and other European countries, severe laws are in force against adulterating. Many of the states of the Union have similar laws but they are generally a dead letter."[45]

He wrote a book detailing hanky-panky across the grocer's counter, a book with a title much like a politician's speech, including something for everyone: *What the Grocers Sell Us. A Manual for Buyers, Containing the Natural History and Process of Manufacture of All Grocer's Goods. Also Their Adulterations, and How to Detect Them; Rates of Tare, as Allowed by Custom and Law; Tables of Weights, Measures, Moneys, etc. The Whole Being Designed as a Guide to Aid in the Purchasing of Goods.*

Coffee headed Felker's list of warnings, and his indictment was enough to raise the hackles of even a casual drinker: Coffee "is adulterated largely with chicory." However, that wasn't enough. Chicory was in turn debased "with roasted corn, beans, lupine seeds, peas, pulse, horse chestnuts, spent coffee, and various roots, such as carrots, parsnips, mangel-wurzel, dandelion, etc." Mangel-wurzel was a red-white hybrid beet, larger than the common garden beet, ostensibly cultivated as cattle feed but frequently ground up and smuggled into the coffee-pot. But the situation could get even worse. According to Felker, if the processor of coffee could not get ersatz chicory at a reasonable price, he was likely to resort to using spent tanbark or dried bullock's liver.[46]

It is small wonder that a diner in a California gold rush town had occasion to comment bitterly on the quality of the coffee which accompanied his meal: "Pea tea, which the landlord calls coffee with a bold emphasis, is handed to us."[47]

One of the most fascinating proposals for a coffee substitute came out of Laredo, Texas, enthusiastically reported by the *Laredo News* in the early 1890s under the headline "A GREAT PROSPECTIVE INDUSTRY." Roasted mesquite tree beans were touted to smell "very much like" roasting coffee, "and the beverage made from the roasted mesquite beans has the astringent quality of coffee." A note of doubt crept in: "But it is not known that the effect upon the nerves has been fairly tested."

A San Antonio firm had been organized with "abundant capital." This new Texas product would compete "not with cheap coffee, but with the best Mocha." The Laredo area would be able to furnish "several train loads of pods every year." Abundant capital not withstanding, the "great prospective industry" died aborning. Maybe the nerve tests did not pan out, or perhaps it was noticed that Indians who had long eaten a pudding concocted from pulverized mesquite beans did so only under the most stringent economic conditions.[48]

Prior to 1865, when John Arbuckle introduced preroasted coffee to the market, the detection of adulterants paled in comparison with the problem of roasting coffee. Once roasted, the beans quickly lost the volatile oils that give the drink its taste and aroma. Consequently, roasted coffee was available only in large cities where demand was great enough to keep it from going stale in the grocer's bin.

In the West, coffee was sold as green beans in bulk. Housewives and cooks then wrestled with the task of roasting coffee in a variety of skillets, cookie tins, or patent roasters that were similar to bed-warming pans or today's stove-top popcorn poppers. An early cookbook warned: "Stir often, giving constant attention. It must be toasted the darkest brown, yet not one grain must be burned."[49] From Mexico where green coffee could be bought cheaply, came a ritual that was repeated daily or weekly in thousands of western households before the turn of the century:

Mother and sister clean-picked these green coffee beans and rotated a single layer of the beans in a shallow cookie tin, constantly shaking and stirring them to prevent any of the beans from burning, since this would have spoiled the entire batch in that tray.

Mother spoiled lots of batches, as she was never satisfied with the results of her roasting. She was forever experimenting, trying to get a more favorable flavor. Sometimes she added seasoning, spices, sauces, or oils to see if the roast could be improved. This often forced us to fall back on the good old faithful Arbuckle's brand, which was just coming on the market.[50]

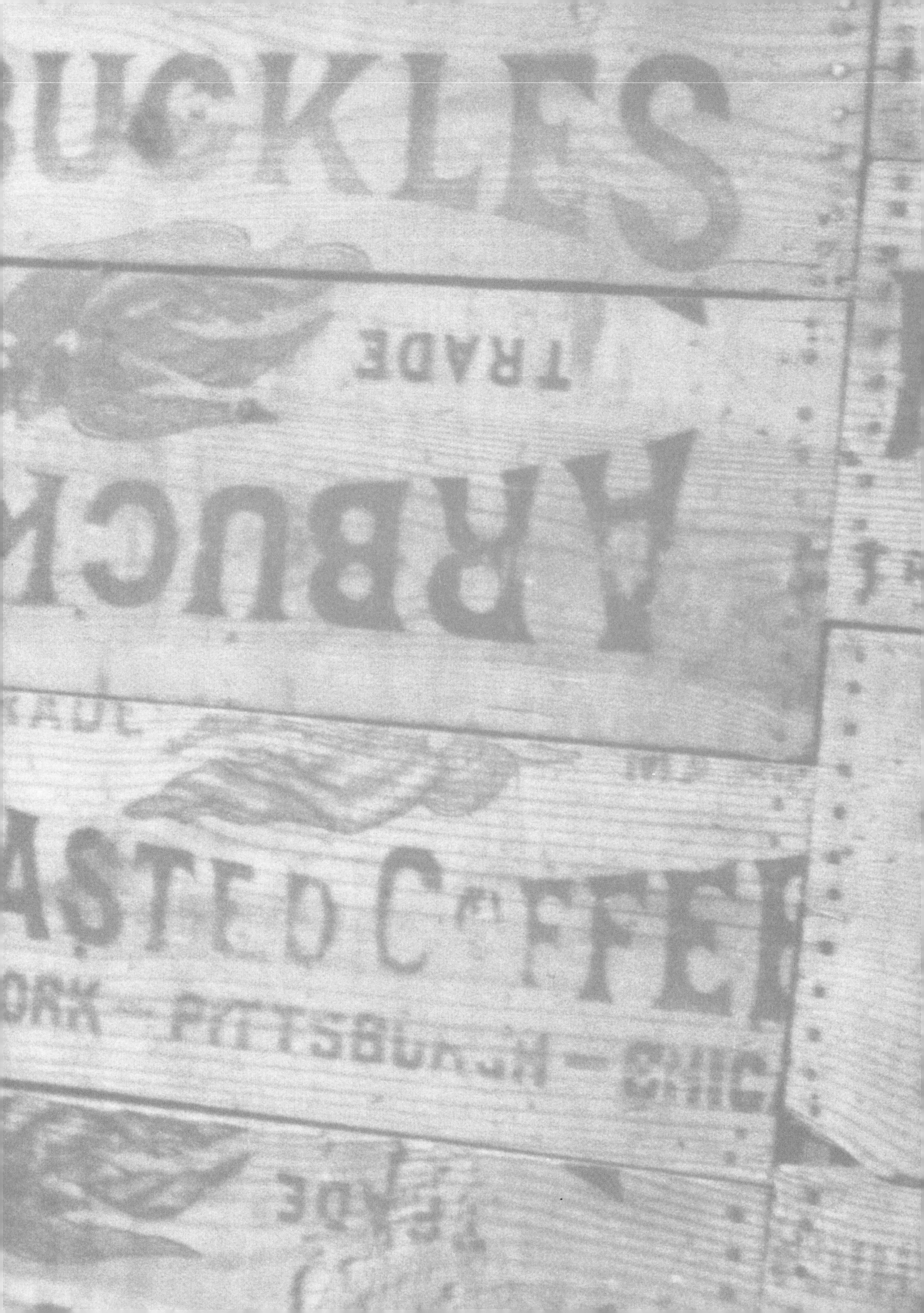
TRADE

3
JOHN ARBUCKLE:
THE COFFEE KING

Multimillionaire John Arbuckle often maintained he was raised on skim milk and once said the only important dates in his career were when he was born, when he was married, when he began business, and when he died.[1]

For the record: John Arbuckle was born on July 11, 1839, in Allegheny City, Pennsylvania, the son of a well-to-do Scottish cotton mill owner.[2] He was married in 1868, in Pittsburgh, Pennsylvania, to Mary Alice Kerr. He "began business" in 1860. He died on March 11, 1912, without children to carry on his name. He attended public schools in Allegheny City and Pittsburgh, sitting at a desk adjoining that of Henry Phipps, future steel magnate and banker. Andrew Carnegie was in another class at the same school. John Arbuckle was more interested in science and machinery than in steel and banking; inventive talent would form the cornerstone of his success.

In 1856, he became a student at Washington and Jefferson College, at Washington, Pennsylvania. He left college in 1860 to join his older brother Charles; Duncan McDonald, an uncle; and a friend named William Roseburg in a wholesale grocery business in Pittsburgh: McDonald & Arbuckle. The first two entries in the daybook of the new firm recorded the purchases of coffee, foreshadowing the company's future.

After John Arbuckle joined the burgeoning company, the name was changed to McDonald & Arbuckles to reflect the brothers. McDonald and Roseburg retired a few years later, and Charles and John again changed the name, to Arbuckles & Co.

John Arbuckle's inventive proclivity led him to investigate the question of how to roast coffee in such a way as to preserve its freshness during the interval between the roaster and the coffeepot. His first patent was for a process of glazing coffee beans to seal the pores against deterioration of flavor and aroma (Appendix B-1). His last patent was for a mammoth coffee roaster which suspended coffee beans in superheated air during the roasting process (Appendix B-22). In the thirty-five years between those two inventions, John Arbuckle revolutionized the coffee industry and became a multimillionaire.[3]

In addition to developing innovations in equipment used in the coffee industry, Arbuckle demonstrated his inventive genius by patenting such diverse items as a fireproof building (Appendix B-5) and in 1882 a safety-signal to prevent train wrecks (Appendix B-6). He patented devices for rescuing stranded ships (Appendix B-23) and for raising sunken ships (Appendix B-25) in 1903 and 1910.

John Arbuckle began his assault upon the coffee industry by packing roasted coffee in one-pound packages, undaunted by the ridicule of others in the coffee trade who derided him for selling roasted coffee "in little paper bags like peanuts." The Arbuckle firm required fifty girls to pack and label the packages until Arbuckle acquired rights to assembly-line machinery which took coffee directly from the roasting hopper—filled, weighed, sealed, and labeled the packages—performing the work of five hundred girls.[4]

The machinery for automating Arbuckle Brothers' coffee processing operation became possible because of the inventive ability of Henry E. Smyser, of Philadelphia. Over a period of six years, Arbuckle Brothers acquired rights to thirteen patents on packaging equipment invented by Smyser (Appendix B-8 through Appendix B-20). This equipment was largely responsible for the company's attaining dominance in the coffee industry and, later, being able to bring the sugar trust to its knees. William H. Ukers, a leading chronicler of the coffee industry from its beginning until 1935, noted:

> It is generally conceded that John Arbuckle's shrewdness and business sagacity in having previously acquired the Smyser patents on a weighing and packaging machine, and his control of it, really led to the coffee-sugar war. "This packing machine," said Jabez Burns's Spice Mill, when Henry E. Smyser died in 1899, "puts him [Smyser] with the greatest inventors of our day."[5]

The sale of roasted coffee in one-pound packages was so successful that John Arbuckle left the Pittsburgh business under his brother's direction and went to New York to establish a branch in the heart of the coffee industry. During his life, John Arbuckle divided his time between managing a vast coffee empire, pursuing his inventive bent, jousting against monopolistic business practices, and engaging in various philanthropic activities.

John Arbuckle did not fit the pattern established by millionaires of his day. In 1902, in a series of articles on "Captains of Industry," Samuel

JOHN ARBUCKLE.

John Arbuckle about 1902.

E. Moffett, a writer for *Cosmopolitan*, told about Arbuckle:

> You might think that a man accustomed to tossing millions
> about with the airy nonchalance of the coffee king would be per-
> ceptibly gilded in appearance and habits. Not so Mr. Arbuckle.
> The Newport set would call him hopelessly "middle class." He
> likes pie, and there are awful indications that he has not entirely
> outgrown the fried steak habit. He frequents the delirious routs
> of the Congregational Club. On a recent occasion he protested
> against the quality of the dinners served at the reunion of that
> select circle. When his criticisms were resented he generously
> offered to take the members of the executive committee to a cer-
> tain hotel he knew of and there feast them upon a better dinner
> at a total cost of fifty cents apiece. And growing reckless in the
> exuberation of controversy he offered to settle the entire bill him-
> self. This intimate knowledge of the haunts of fifty-cent dinners
> is characteristic of a man who has never outgrown the plain tastes
> of his boyhood.[6]

In appearance, Arbuckle was a powerful man with a long patriarchal
beard which turned gray and somewhat scraggly with age. He had a
massive, ruddy forehead and square jaws. He habitually wore a black,
well-worn cut-away suit and a black string tie. He became a force in the
business world as a director of the Importers and Traders Bank, the Kings
County Trust Company of Brooklyn, the Lawyers Title Insurance and
Trust Company, and the Mortgage Bond Company of New York. However, the far-reaching interests of the Arbuckles coffee domain were not
administered by a board of directors.

Six days a week, when John Arbuckle was not off on an inspection
tour, he left his home at 315 Clinton Avenue in Brooklyn to cross the East
River in one of the old ferryboats patronized for the most part by clerks
and office workers. He threaded his way among roustabouts and long-
shoremen on the riverfront and stepped into the counting room of
Arbuckle Brothers at Old Slip and Water Street, where his word was
supreme. He sat down to a desk in a small room off the main office.
There anybody who wanted to see him had no difficulty; he was not
guarded by uniformed flunkies or buffer secretaries. In his office he
talked to department heads, to subordinates with grievances or pleas
for assistance, and to an increasing number of outsiders who came to
gain his ear on behalf of charitable causes.[7]

John Arbuckle kept a notebook in which he recorded stories and comments for future use. If he did not have a notebook with him, he was
likely to make a memorandum on his shirt cuff.[8] One of his hobbies was

distributing to his friends and associates cards printed with homely mottos or advice, such as: *"Politeness is the cheapest commodity on God's earth. It costs nothing, and will carry you farther and pleasanter through life than any other ticket you can travel on."* During a bitter corporate struggle with Henry O. Havemeyer, who controlled the American sugar trust, Arbuckle would chuckle when discussing his cards and explain that the sugar trust people were on his mailing list.[9]

John Arbuckle's charitable enterprises were innovative and expensive. About the turn of the century, generally unsanitary conditions in New York sparked public concern about people, particularly women and children, remaining in the city during the deadly summer months. In 1901, Arbuckle conceived the idea of equipping a fleet of ships and yachts with all the comforts of home. Every evening, workers and their families would be loaded aboard and towed out beyond Sandy Hook. The next morning they would be brought back, refreshed by a night in fresh salt air.

At a cost of $300,000 John Arbuckle outfitted the *Jacob A. Stamler*, an old square-rigged clipper ship, and two yachts, the *Sitana* and the *Hermit*. They had suites of staterooms, bathrooms, recreation rooms, and dining rooms where passengers sat at long tables to eat hearty meals. He called his fleet "poor man's yachts."

As tugboats hauled the procession out to sea on their maiden voyage, Arbuckle said, "At last I am realizing the dream of my life." He explained that some years previously his own life had been saved by a sea voyage. "I realized what a boon the cool, salt air of the ocean is to the sweltering, overworked people of the crowded cities. Then and there I conceived the floating hotel idea." The idea was good, but patronage quickly fell off, and after a month's trial the fleet was decommissioned.[10]

He converted another boat into the Riverside Home for Crippled Children, fitted with conveniences for their comfort. Simple employment was provided for the occupants, enabling them to get board and lodging aboard at actual cost. At New Paltz, New York, he established an 800-acre farm on the shore of Lake Mohonk to provide a fresh-air home for children from the crowded city as well as a home for the aged.[11]

John Arbuckle apparently remembered his feelings upon arrival in New York City. He noted that young men and women coming to the city to seek their fortunes were "leaving behind them the safeguards of civilization to only a less degree than did the gold-seekers of Cripple Creek or the Klondike." He was ahead of his time in advocating equal rights for the sexes. When solicited for a donation to the Young Women's Christian Association, he responded that he did not believe in keeping young men and women apart. He had a plan of his own:

He wanted a great room in which young men and women who were working their own way, and were strangers in the city, could have their own club-room, library, and writing-room on one floor; their own assembly-room, with a good gymnasium, swimming-pool, and lockers, to be used on alternate days; with certain class-rooms, where young women and men could be trained in the art of self-support, through evening classes in typewriting, short-hand, bookkeeping, dressmaking, millinery, kindergartening, civil government and allied plans.[12]

John Arbuckle's admiration for the Rev. Henry Ward Beecher was built upon a forty-year membership in the congregation of the Plymouth Church in Brooklyn. At the time of his death, Arbuckle was in the process of planning the facility to house the "homeless" who came to New York to seek their fortunes: "A club for young men and women who mainly know the cheerless comfort of hall-bedrooms." He wanted to dedicate the establishment as a memorial to Reverend Beecher. After Arbuckle's death, the plan for the memorial was implemented by his sisters.[13]

Empathy for the underprivileged aroused John Arbuckle to argue vehemently against duties on sugar, claiming they were imposed solely for the benefit of the sugar beet interests. Sugar was used by the rich and poor alike, Arbuckle maintained, and the government was literally taking candy away from babies. In 1911, while suffering from a recurring attack of malaria, he declared his intention to fight the tariff, characterized as a "tax on hunger," as soon as his health improved. He left for Europe to recuperate. This time a sea voyage did little to help him recover from the effects of malaria he had contracted while inspecting his far-flung coffee interests. After his return he died at his home in Brooklyn on March 11, 1912.[14]

After his death the guiding maxim of John Arbuckle's life was found inscribed in the front of one of his notebooks: "Only workers with hand and brain are worthy of respect; all else is chaff and rubbish," a quotation from Thomas Carlyle.[15]

Arbuckle believed the best form of advertising was word-of-mouth publicity for his goods. He achieved that goal as *Arbuckles* became a synonym for coffee in the West and enjoyed word-of-mouth praise wherever cattlemen gathered.

Perhaps the greatest tribute to John Arbuckle was paid by a group of cowboys hunkered around a cookfire on the Texas high plains. They worried about what they would do for coffee if John Arbuckle died.[16]

UCKLES
TRADE
ASTED C FFE
ORK – PITTSBURGH – CHIC

4
BUILDING THE
ARBUCKLE EMPIRE

Roasting is the key to the enjoyment of coffee as a beverage. Green coffee has little or no flavor. During roasting the green beans shrink from 16 to 20 percent in weight, and complex physical and chemical changes take place. Various elements of the green coffee are decomposed: water, oil, caffeine, chlorogenic acid, trigonelline, tannin, caffetannin, caffeic acid, starch, sugars, and more. The ultimate flavor of coffee in the cup depends not only upon the quality and variety of the coffee but the manner in which it is roasted.

Roasted coffee was perishable when John Arbuckle entered the coffee business. Vacuumized packing had not yet been developed to preserve freshness. Roasted coffee could not survive a lengthy journey to market or long storage in the grocer's bin without deterioration of flavor. Roasting did not move from the kitchen to the factory until the middle of the nineteenth century, when demand for coffee became sufficiently concentrated in urban centers to guarantee a steady sale.[1]

The first reasonably successful commercial roaster was patented in 1846 by James W. Carter, of Boston—the Carter pull-out roaster. The device consisted of a cylindrical sheet-iron chamber supported on a shaft within a coal-burning furnace. The cylinder had to be pulled out of the furnace to be filled, to sample the progress of roasting, and to be emptied. After completion of roasting, a batch of coffee—a full sack as it came from South America, 160 to 175 pounds—was dumped on the floor or into a cooling box and spread with iron rakes or shovels and hoes. It was cooled by a sprinkling of water which filled the roasting room with a dense cloud of steam. The coffee then had to be hand picked to remove sticks and stones before it was bagged for delivery to grocers.

Initially consumer resistance developed to roasted coffee. People were accustomed to roasting green coffee at home. Why should they pay a nickel more a pound for roasted coffee? Consequently, job roasters sold primarily to small grocers in five-and ten-pound lots. Most larger stores bought their coffee green and would occasionally send a half sack or even a whole sack to a job roaster for processing at a cent a pound. Wholesale grocers controlled 90 percent of the grocery trade and, in the beginning, it did not pay a roaster to put salesmen on the road. Most roasters gained their livelihoods from job roasting.

In 1864, Jabez Burns, of New York, patented a roaster containing a roasting chamber which did not have to be removed from the fire to discharge the coffee. A helical screw within its cylinder agitated and mixed the beans so that they were uniformly heated.[2] This was what John Arbuckle had been looking for.

Since joining the Pittsburgh wholesale grocery firm, he had been impressed with the wasteful methods and unsatisfactory results of kitchen roasting. He was convinced that carefully roasted coffee could be packaged while still warm and sold to consumers in small individual containers. He pursued the idea in spite of misgivings on the part of his older brother Charles and the subsequent ridicule of old hands in the coffee industry.

John Arbuckle developed a process of glazing: "Coating roasted coffee with any glutinous or gelatinous matter for the purpose of retaining the aroma of the coffee, and also act as a clarifying agent." The patent was granted on January 21, 1868. Initially the glazing was a mixture of "Irish moss [a seaweed with highly gelatinous properties], 1/2 ounce; gelatine, 1/2 ounce; isinglass, 1/2 ounce; white sugar, 1 ounce; eggs, 24. The first three are boiled in water, and the moss strained." (Appendix B-1) Eventually, the glaze was simplified to use only sugar and eggs. The egg was supposed to cause quick settling of coffee grounds, and the sugar ameliorated the inherent bitterness of coffee.

Introduction of Arbuckle's new coating process did not come off without controversy. Dilworth Bros., a rival Pittsburgh firm, had patented a steam polisher for treating their coffee berries during the roasting process. A fight broke out between the two companies.

Dilworth Bros. claimed Arbuckle & Co., as the firm was then known, started the battle by publishing a handbill which vilified the Dilworth firm. The Arbuckle handbill had a woodcut depicting the interior of a coffee roasting establishment—supposedly Dilworth's—with all sorts of foreign matter in barrels and boxes apparently waiting to be used in the Dilworth product. The illustration portrayed a crowd at the door. A man said, "No wonder I have been sick," and a distraught woman was saying, "I see what killed my children." The bitter dispute wore itself out during an exchange of vituperative newspaper advertisements and the two firms went back to their respective businesses.[3]

The early brand names were ARBUCKLES (1870), FRAGAR (1871), and COMPONO (1871). (See Appendix C-1, C-2, C-3.) On August 31,

1873, the most famous of them all appeared: ARIOSA. Origin of the word is hazy, but the most frequent explanation is that A stood for "Arbuckle"; rio for "Rio"; and sa for "Santos" or "South America." Rio and Santos coffees made up the Ariosa blend.

Coffee grown at low altitudes is called "rio" or "river" coffee. According to culinary experts, by itself Rio makes "a cup of coffee harsh in flavor and lacking in other good, essential factors."[4] On the other hand, Santos coffees, named for the Brazilian port from which they were shipped, had "the distinction of being the best grown in Brazil." Bourbon Santos "produces a drink that is smooth and palatable,"[5] and "'Old Crop' Santos are mildest in flavor and acidity."[6]

During the period when Ariosa was gaining its dominance in the marketplace, the nation's coffee drinkers were discriminating in their taste to such an extent that the success of restaurants and hotels in cities "practically rests upon their ability to hit the taste of their customers. . . . In many instances, a poor brand of coffee has turned thousands of dollars a month away from the cash drawer of a large city restaurant."[7]

Whatever the combination, hearty Rios blended with milder Santos to produce a robust brew that captured the taste of eighteenth-century coffee drinkers. Its fame spread across the nation.

For the Ariosa package, Arbuckle registered a trademark that would become equally famous: "a representation of an angel floating in the air, assuming a benedictory attitude and clothed in a star-spangled robe, with a dark red flowing mantle resting lightly upon her shoulders," as the trademark registration described it.

Provision for registration of trademarks in the United States was first enacted by Congress in 1870, but was subsequently declared invalid by the Supreme Court on the ground that the Constitution did not authorize congressional legislation on the subject of trademarks, except such as had been actually used in commerce with foreign nations or with the Indian tribes. Congress again legislated to give protection to trademarks in 1881, 1905, and 1906.

The registered trademark for Ariosa included the phrase "NO SETTLING REQUIRED" with a translation in German "Sieh die Andre Seite" obviously addressed to the German-speaking Pennsylvania Dutch. (See Appendix C-5 for the complete text of the application for the Ariosa trademark.)

By 1871, roasted coffee "in little paper bags like peanuts" had proven itself in the Pittsburgh area.[8] John Arbuckle left the Pittsburgh business in charge of his elder brother and moved to New York, the seat of the coffee trade, and Arbuckle Brothers was born.

In 1872, John Arbuckle launched an attack against consumer resistance to preroasted coffee with a three-color handbill, the first use of

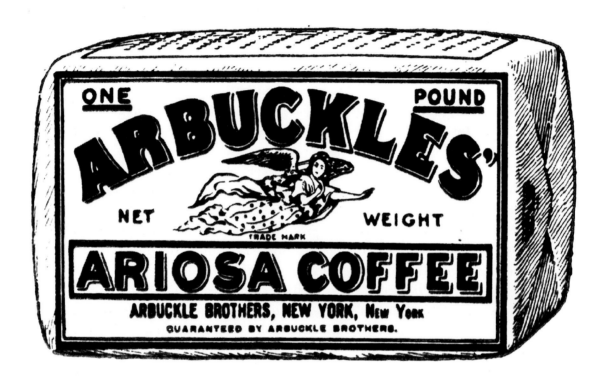

Roasted coffee "in little paper bags like peanuts" quickly began to capture the nation's coffee trade.

color in advertising a packaged coffee:

> It is cheaper to buy Arbuckles' Roasted Coffee in one pound air-tight packages, than to buy green coffee and roast it yourself. Why? Because four pounds of Arbuckles' Roasted Coffee will go as far as five pounds of green Coffee, as Coffee loses one-fifth in roasting by hand. Arbuckles' Roasted Coffee is much better, as every grain is evenly roasted, thus bringing out the full strength and aroma of the Coffee. You cannot roast Coffee properly yourself.

By 1881, the company had eighty-five roasters operating in New York and Pittsburgh, and the name was rapidly fanning out through the South and the West. The business grew apace. The firm opened a branch in Chicago equipped not only with coffee roasting and packaging equipment but with spice grinding and extract manufacturing facilities. Apart from its coffee business, over the years Arbuckle Brothers developed a brisk wholesale trade in teas, chocolate, cocoa, spices, canned fruits and vegetables, sugar, and dried fruit. Brand names such as "Nedra," "Caboola," "Drinksome," "Anona Chop Japan Tea," "Pond Lily," and "Court House" sprinkled grocery shelves. (See Appendix C for Arbuckle Brothers' trademarks and labels.)

A Kansas City branch distributed products manufactured in New York and Chicago, and there were eventually more than a hundred stock depots in as many different communities to fill coffee orders as they came in from across the country.

In Brazil, Arbuckle Brothers' offices were maintained in Rio de Janeiro, Santos, and Victoria, the three principal coffee ports. In Mexico, the company established a facility at Jalapa with branches at Cordoba and Coatepec. In season, the warehouses and hulling plants at those points employed as many as 650 hands preparing Mexican coffee for shipment to New York.

The magnitude and complexity of Arbuckle Brothers' operations are indicated by the varieties of coffee on the price list issued by the firm's "Green Coffee Department" on January 19, 1905:[9]

Polished Types	Pamanoekans	Timor Java Pluma Oaxaca
Milled & Separated Santos	African	Fancy Old Crop Mocha
Milled & Separated Rio	Guatemala	Milled Maricaibo
Santos Peaberry	Fancy Liberians	Coro
Rio Peaberry	Roasted Screenings	Bogata
Natural Santos	Hand Picked San Domingo Old Crop	Mexican Peaberry
Washed Santos	Washed Haytian	Milled Natural Mexican

Natural Bourbons	Palembang Java	Old Crop Bleached Washed Mexican
Washed Bourbons	Kroe Java	Milled Washed Mexican
Fancy Old Crop Bourbons	Private Growth Java	Milled & Separated Mexican
Fancy Yellow Santos	Private Estate Java	Natural Mexican
Natural Rio	Private Free Sumatra Java	New Crop Washed Mexican
Washed Rio	Coatepec Mexican	Bleached Washed Mexican
Maragojipe Rio	Interior Padang Java	Milled Old Crop
Bahia	Corintjie Java	Bleached Mexican Liberians

A writer for the *New York Evening Post* described John Arbuckle as "half farmer, half seaman." Gradually he expanded his merchant vessel holdings until practically every merchant ship engaged in the South American coffee trade either belonged to John Arbuckle or was controlled by his firm. At the time of his death, he was reputed to be the largest individual owner of seagoing vessels under American registry.

To bring their products into the New York harbor, Arbuckle Brothers required a fleet of barges and towboats. When his tugs were idle, John Arbuckle went looking for business. During every summer, a "towboat war" broke out between the skippers of boats and towboat operators on the Hudson River between New York and Albany. Members of the Towboat Trust had the upper hand. They regarded the Hudson as their backyard. They charged $50 a boat, a tidy fee considering that they usually picked up six or eight boats in each haul. Arbuckle entered the fray:

> The little canalers swung their caps in the air when they heard that John Arbuckle was after their patronage, and it is related that one wife of an Erie skipper, smoking her pipe among her flower-pots on the edge of the 12 x 14 cabinroof, almost went into hysterics when her man came aboard and told her the news.
>
> "Wall, I swan," she is reported to have declared, and this is the tale that Arbuckle himself liked to hear, "they'll be giving us trading-stamps next."[10]

Arbuckle cut prices under the lowest the river had known for years. At one time the cost of a tow dropped as low as five dollars. It was said that in an effort to get their ebbing business back, trust members were offering money to skippers for the privilege of towing them the length of the river.

Arbuckle's next venture was into the ocean towing and wrecking business. Here again, he encountered a monopoly. One corporation virtually controlled the wrecking business from Galveston to Halifax. John Arbuckle teamed up with two Canadian engineers who had raised sunken ships by the use of compressed air, and formed the Arbuckle Wrecking Company.

In 1908, when the United States cruiser *Yankee* went aground on Spindle Rock, more than $100,000 was spent in vain efforts to raise her. Then Arbuckle bid for the job. Other salvage companies laughed at him, but the government took his offer seriously. Within forty-five days after Arbuckle's sandhogs and air compressors came on the scene, the *Yankee* was afloat. Most of the time had been spent removing concrete which previous wreckers had used to patch up a hole in the vessel's bow.

"Why do I go in for this wrecking business?" said Arbuckle. "Well, I like the sea, for one thing. It helped me to bring back my health once, and then, of course, there is a possible chance of making an honest penny at it. There is a stimulus about the ocean that you can't get anywhere else. It helps your strength, and it softens your disposition. You're picking up some of the milk of human kindness every day you are afloat, and the men you meet there are big and strong—and, most of them, honest."[11]

The following year, in 1909, the Arbuckle crew successfully raised the United States collier *Nero*, which went aground on a reef near Newport, even though the work was hampered by severe storms. Arbuckle proposed a plan to Congress to meet the needs of passenger vessels in danger from shipwreck, fire, or other hazards. Telegraphic communication, he suggested, should be maintained with harbors containing wrecking apparatus. Arbuckle maintained that rescues should be accomplished from the sea side of a troubled vessel, using oil to calm the water and breeches buoys to remove passengers, rather than the customary procedure of launching lifeboats through the breakers.[12]

The Arbuckle Brothers plant along the Brooklyn waterfront occupied an area of a dozen city blocks. Shipment of more than a hundred cars of coffee and sugar a day required development of a New York railroad and waterfront terminal known as the Jay Street Terminal, equipped with a freight station, locomotives, tug boats, steam lighters, car floats, and barges.

Until motor trucks took over, New York city delivery required a blacksmith shop, harness shop, wagon shop, and a stable of almost two hundred draft horses. This was replaced by a fleet of thirty-five trucks with accompanying garage and repair facilities, but "some fifty or sixty of the faithful" horses were kept on.

In 1872, a three-color printing press was designed expressly for Arbuckle Brothers and installed in the company printing shop to turn out coffee wrappers and circulars. A hospital and dining room took care of employee needs. During winter months, twenty- six steam boilers consumed as much as four hundred tons of coal a day.

After Arbuckle Brothers got into the sugar business, a barrel factory was located about a mile away with a daily capacity of 6,800 sugar barrels a day. Barrel staves and heads were received from the company's stave mill in Virginia, made from logs cut from Arbuckle timber lands in Virginia and North Carolina. During the sugar season, eight to ten thousand bags of raw sugar were emptied every day. These were washed and dried in a rotary drier of Arbuckle design which did the work of about three miles of clothes lines.

In addition to technicians in the coffee and sugar fields and office personnel, Arbuckle Brothers' payroll included a physician; a chemist; civil, mechanical, and electrical engineers; railroad engineers and brakemen; steamboat captains and engineers; chauffeurs; teamsters; wagon makers; harness makers; machinists; draughtsmen; blacksmiths; tinsmiths; coppersmiths; coopers; carpenters; masons; painters; plumbers; riggers; typesetters and pressmen; a chef; and tablewaiters.

By the 1890s, Arbuckles' Coffee occupied a near-dominant position in the national coffee trade. Agents across the country were pushing the product with wholesalers. Arbuckles' Ariosa shared equal billing and equal pricing with McLaughlin's XXXX in the 1897 Sears, Roebuck & Co. catalogue. Both were listed at 19 $1/4$ cents per pound in 100-pound cases or 20 cents per pound in lesser quantities. Sears advertised bulk green and roasted coffee in the bean. The catalogue featured ground "special blends" as well as Arbuckles' and McLaughlin's in one-pound packages:

> BUY YOUR COFFEE DIRECT; you can just as well save the profit of the retailer; it will amount to a great deal in a year. . . .
>
> Our coffees we import direct. Everybody praises their delicious aroma and flavor. It is very important to get fresh roasted coffee. Once the bean becomes stale and absorbs moisture, the flavor and good drinking qualities leave the bean, and render it unfit for use. Often the merchant has coffee on hand for months; in such cases it loses both strength and flavor. If you want strictly fresh roasted coffee, place your order with us.[13]

In 1897 John Arbuckle filed application for a coffee roaster of his own design, one which would suspend coffee beans individually in hot gases while they were being roasted (Appendix B-22). In his book *The Saga of Coffee*, Heinrich Eduard Jacob described his reaction to this behemoth device upon encountering it at the Berlin Industrial Exhibit of 1896:

> There a cylindrical machine, invented by John Arbuckle, was on show. Wonderful to me, was this roasting-drum, in which by

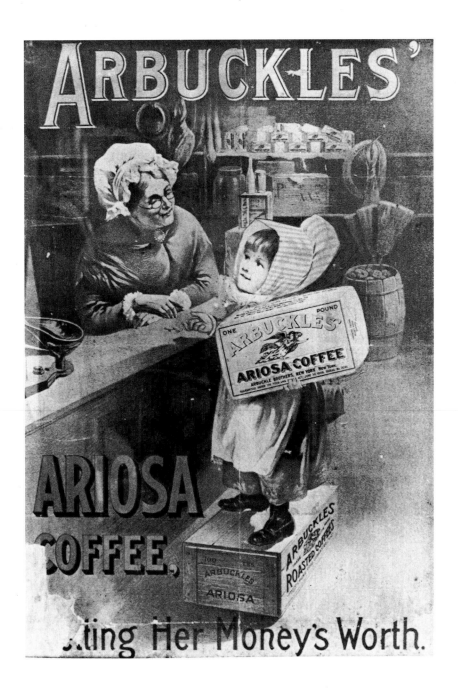

From the beginning Arbuckle Brothers emphasized the value and quality of Arbuckles Ariosa over competing brands. This early folksy advertisement was supplied to retailers in large handbill format to hang in their stores.

opening a flap, one could watch how far the process had advanced. Some of the coffees that were being roasted were of very light colour, others were medium-brown, and others dark-brown. I envied the employees who were demonstrating the use of the machine, and who lived in the hot vapours that rose from the roasting beans.[14]

During the 1890s, John Arbuckle seized upon the idea of giving premiums to loyal purchasers of Arbuckles' coffee. He started printing a coupon bearing the signature "Arbuckle Bros." on each package. These coupons or vouchers had a cash value of one cent. A given number of coupons and a two-cent stamp would get a premium that could be selected from a catalogue of a hundred different items. Arbuckles' signatures could be exchanged for almost anything from a pair of suspenders or a toothbrush to clocks, wringers, and jewelry.

For the ladies there were window curtains (65 signatures), aprons (25), a lady's belt (20), and twelve yards of printed organdie (100). For men there were such things as razors (28), pocket knives (40), watches (90); and a persistent coffee drinker could get an X-L, .32-calibre, centre-fire, double-action revolver of "highest grade material and workmanship" for 150 signatures.

Arbuckle Brothers established a Notion Department to handle this end of the business, and quite a business it turned out to be. In a typical year the Notion Department received more than 108 million signatures in exchange for more than 4 million premiums. These included 818,928 handkerchiefs, 216,000 pairs of lace curtains, 238,738 pairs of shears, and 185,920 Torrey razors. Finger rings were a perennial favorite, and Arbuckle Brothers became known as the largest distributor of finger rings in the world. An official of the company remarked: "One of our premiums is a wedding ring, and if all the rings of this pattern serve their intended purpose then we have been participants in eighty thousand weddings a year."[15]

Arbuckle Brothers' agents were given the responsibility of arranging for the distribution of premium catalogues to housewives in their territories. In predominantly Spanish-speaking areas, the catalogue was printed in Spanish. In Santa Fe, New Mexico, the September 30, 1899, issue of *El Nuevo Mexicano* carried a catalogue sheet headlined: "DOS HECHOS SOBRE EL CAFÉ DE LOS ARBUCKLES."

Records have not surfaced as to who in Arbuckle Brothers initiated the plan or exactly when it happened. However, somebody got the idea of sweetening the deal. A stick of sugar candy—later striped peppermint—was inserted into every package of Arbuckles' Ariosa, a powerful inducement to children and to cowboys on the western ranges where

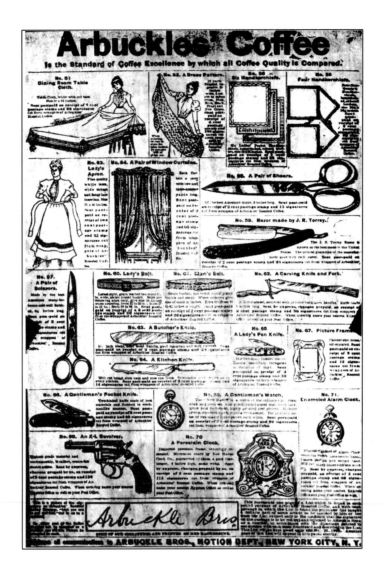

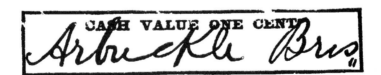

Top: The Arbuckles' premium catalogue was the "wish book" of its day. This early specimen had been mounted on a board for preservation. It was found hanging on the wall of an abandoned cabin in Chloride, New Mexico.

Bottom: Arbuckle Brothers' signatures to be cut out of coffee packages and exchanged for premiums were a forerunner of trading stamps.

sugar was a rarity.

Charles Arbuckle died in 1891, and John Arbuckle admitted as partners his nephew, William Arbuckle Jamison, and two employees, William V. R. Smith and James N. Jarvie. Business continued under the name Arbuckle Brothers. Smith and Jarvie retired from the firm in 1906, and John Arbuckle and W. A. Jamison continued as sole owners and partners until John Arbuckle's death in 1912.

Mrs. Arbuckle had died in 1907. John Arbuckle's only heirs were two sisters, Mrs. Catherine Arbuckle Jamison and Miss Christina Arbuckle. Mrs. Jamison was the widow of Robert Jamison, a Pittsburgh drygoods merchant. William A. Jamison was her eldest son. Christina Arbuckle was named administrator of the Arbuckle estate, valued at $37,500,000. The new partnership for the management of Arbuckle Brothers consisted of Mrs. Jamison, Miss Arbuckle, and W. A. Jamison.[16]

In 1913, Arbuckle Brothers introduced YUBAN, "The Arbuckle Guest Coffee." (See Appendix C-33 for trademark information.) This was John Arbuckle's private blend. During the Christmas season he served it at an annual holiday dinner which he referred to as his Yuletide Banquet. This blend was available only at dinner parties for his friends or as a gift from John Arbuckle.

For years it was thought the name had been coined from "Yultide Banquet" in sentimental memory of John Arbuckle's dinner parties. Then a former employee of Arbuckle Brothers came forward with a different version. When green coffee shipments of Arbuckle's special blend arrived from South America, they were marked

A B

N Y

for Arbuckle Brothers, New York. An attempt was made to coin a brand name from the letters on the bags. Neither "Bany" nor "Naby" sounded good. "Yban" looked odd until someone inserted the letter "u."[17] YUBAN was introduced on November 1, 1913, according to the application for the trademark.

The introduction of Yuban was a high point in the history of Arbuckle Brothers. In 1921, M. E. Goetzinger waxed ecstatic in his history of the firm for publication in a house organ:

> The present partnership has seen a wonderful expansion of its business, necessitating several enlargements of our manufacturing plant; it has seen the great swing of public favor from coffee in the whole bean to ground coffee, and has seen us prepare ourselves for and become equal to that demand; but more notable than all, the present firm has seen the wonderfully successful

This advertisement from a 1915 issue of Needlecraft *was directed toward the feminine audience. It featured finger rings, the premium department's number one attraction.*

launching of YUBAN, the last word in packaged roasted coffee. Where formerly almost our entire attention was devoted to supplying the demand for popular priced packaged coffees, YUBAN at one bound has so firmly taken its place as the foremost high grade packaged coffee wherever it has been introduced, that a large force in New York and another in Chicago are employed in meeting the new demand.[18]

In 1937, General Foods Corporation purchased a number of Arbuckle Brothers' brand names, including Arbuckles' Ariosa. Their new paper packages—bright yellow, red, and black—displayed the familiar flying angel and proclaimed "prepared and packed according to the formula of Arbuckle Brothers, New York, N. Y. General Foods Corporation—Successor—Manufacturer." It was, the package reminded, "a satisfying economical coffee. A favorite for over 60 years."

Arbuckle's Ariosa faded from the marketplace, but in 1944, General Foods Corporation acquired Yuban, John Arbuckle's "Guest Coffee." It has stood the test of time. Eventually, General Foods was able to boast it had "succeeded in making it the largest selling premium coffee on the market." At this writing, Yuban is still available on grocers' shelves. Only General Foods knows if the makeup remains true to the blend John Arbuckle took pride in serving to his friends.

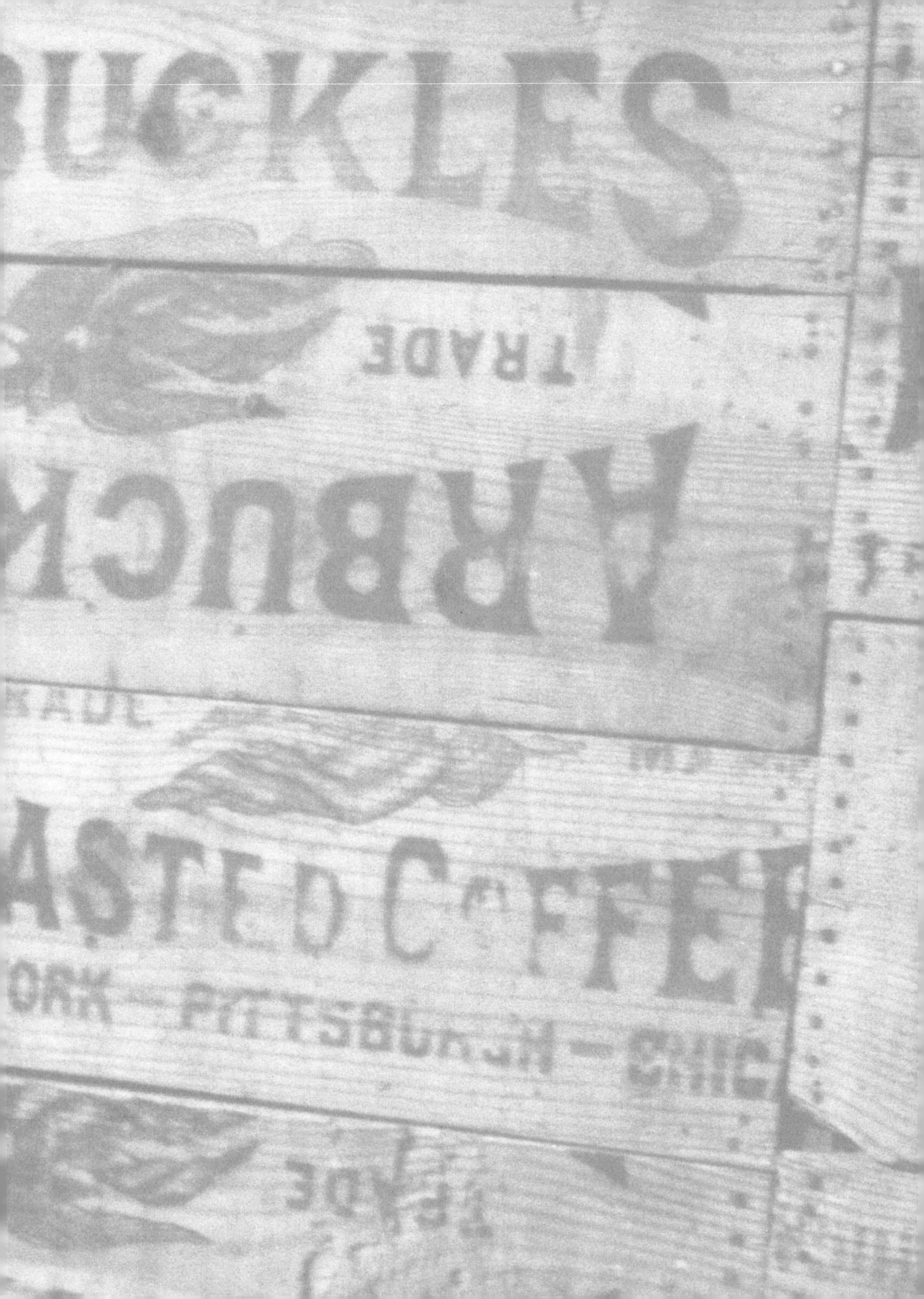
UCKLES
TRADE
ARBUCK
ASTED COFFE
ORK - PITTSBURGH - CHIC

5
JOHN ARBUCKLE
V. THE SUGAR TRUST

From colonial times until about the 1840s, the United States was supplied with both the necessities and the luxuries of life either by import from abroad or by local artisans such as Paul Revere and his father. Production was primarily by cottage industry or by small business partnerships owned by two or three individuals. Marketing was regional, limited by the transportation networks and facilities of the day. Quality of products and prices determined the success of competitors within a region.

As the nation was recovering from an economic decline about 1843, entrepreneurs began implementing technological developments for large-scale, low-cost production of manufactured goods. The factory system expanded during the period of prosperity which lasted through the Civil War until the Panic of 1873. During dull times when supply exceeded demand, competition forced manufacturers to cut prices, and as new technologies developed to lower manufacturing costs they were forced to modernize equipment or go out of business.

As the nation's transportation system improved, markets expanded and competition became more fierce. Businessmen attempted to nullify the effect of competition by agreeing among themselves to limit production and/or not to sell below a given price, but inevitably someone would cheat. Others would follow suit and the pricing pool would dissolve.[1]

Then, in 1881, Samuel C. T. Dodd, a Standard Oil Company attorney, found a solution to the bothersome problem of competition—the trust. By a secret agreement in 1882, the stockholders of some forty petroleum companies controlled by John D. Rockefeller and his associates turned over their shares of stock "in trust" to nine trustees. In return the original stockholders received "trust certificates" and the trustees became the direct stockholders of all the companies in the system, empowered to serve as directors thereof, holding in their hands final control of all the properties. The trustees could dissolve any corporation within the system and organize new ones in each state, such as the Standard Oil of New Jersey or Standard Oil of New York.

Low-cost production methods and railroad rebates gave the Standard Oil Company an unapproachable advantage. Rival refiners had the choice of selling out to the trust or facing competitive ruin. The trust perfected monopoly and pointed the way to future industrial organization in the United States.[2]

It also pointed the way to a historic battle between John Arbuckle and the American Sugar Refining Company.

Early unfair domination of the sugar refining industry was brought to public attention by the *New York Tribune* in 1878, in a report that certain importers and refiners of sugar were defrauding the government of import duties: "Many refiners and importers, who refused to go into this combination, have been driven out of business and no honest man can successfully compete with the combination."[3]

As Congress moved to correct the situation, major sugar refiners located at private wharves along the water's edge, led by the brothers Henry O. and Theodore A. Havemeyer, began to buy raw sugar directly from overseas agents, thus eliminating the charges imposed by raw sugar brokers. This put small inland refiners at a competitive disadvantage.

The next step was the formation by sugar refiners of a pooling arrangement, organized at a meeting on June 1, 1880, under administration of an executive committee which included Henry and William Havemeyer. Such arrangements were legally unenforceable under an 1839 New York court decision regarding "contracts in restraint of trade." The success of the pool can be measured by a report in *Bradstreet's Journal* on July 16, 1881: "The refiners of Boston and Philadelphia have refused to join these monopolists in their efforts to advance price."[4]

Taking a page from Rockefeller, in August 1887, the Havemeyer family began to enlist independent refineries into the Sugar Refineries Company. Despite denial by members of the combination, the *New York Times* leaked the story on September 23, 1887: "The talk now is that the principal refiners of the country are contemplating the formation of a sugar trust, as that sort of business combination seems to be in fashion just now." On October 13, the sugar industry's most authoritative publication confirmed the merger: "It may be considered a settled fact that a combination has been completed, . . . thus bringing under the management and control of a Committee of Eleven Refiners almost the entire consumption of raw sugar and production of refined sugar in the United States."[5]

Ownership of the participating companies was transferred to the Sugar Refineries Company in exchange for trust certificates. As in the case of the Standard Oil trust, the management committee exercised absolute control to close down inefficient plants or suspend operations during periods of oversupply. Later a former superintendent of the Havemeyer Sugar Refinery in Brooklyn told of the sugar trust's operation in taking over refineries. When the American Sugar Refining Company absorbed a rival plant it would be closed down as if it were not important and used as a storehouse.[6]

As refineries were closed during the consolidation, employees lost their jobs and were willing to work at other refineries for lower wages. Initially, when a number of Boston refineries were shut down, officials of the trust enforced a 10 percent wage cut among employees still holding jobs. However, the trust later reversed this policy because it repudiated the trust's claim that it needed tariff protection because labor costs were higher in the United States than in Europe.

The sugar trust allowed a rebate of 40 cents per barrel to wholesalers who maintained the retail price. Wholesalers who handled the products of rival refineries were warned their price maintenance agreements with the Sugar Refineries Company were in jeopardy.[7] In 1892, a *New York Times* editorial charged the trust had "absolute" control of the refining industry. The advantage allowed by the tariff on imported sugar and the suppression of competition was netting the trust an annual profit of about $29 million.[8]

During subsequent Congressional investigations, Henry Havemeyer insisted the trust's activities did not increase the cost of refined sugar to the consumer. Neither did they result in lower prices. Havemeyer told the U.S. Industrial Commission: "We maintain that when we reduced the cost we were entitled to the profit, and that it was none of the public's business; we took it and paid it out to our stockholders; it may be business policy to share that with the public sometimes; we did not do that then; we have done it since."[9]

The reign of Havemeyer and the Sugar Refineries Company was short. As the organization moved to take over a New York refinery, the attorney general of the state challenged its right on the basis of a common-law prohibition against partnership of corporations. On January 9, 1889, Judge George C. Barrett of the New York Supreme Court directed the jury to bring in a verdict for the plaintiff in the case of *People v. North River Sugar Refining Company*: "It is the case of great capitalists uniting their enormous wealth in mighty corporations, and utilizing the franchises granted to them by the people to oppress the people."[10]

As soon at the litigation was completed, Havemeyer's sugar trust reorganized as the American Sugar Refining Company under New Jersey's lenient corporate statutes which had been promulgated for the purpose of attracting incorporated capital to the state. After the issuance of the new charter on January 10, 1891, it was back to business as usual for the sugar trust.

The money-laden tentacles of the American Sugar Refining Company reached out across the nation to the west coast; even Claus Spreckles, Sr., the "Hawaiian sugar king," fell prey to the trust. Havemeyer was ruthless in the elimination of potential rivals. When he learned Henry Doscher was building a refinery, Havemeyer issued an order to one of his underlings: "Doscher is building a refinery. Tell him he has to get out. Then it will be up to you to crush him."[11]

In 1895, the trust escaped prosecution under the Sherman Antitrust Act by a U.S. Supreme Court decision which conceded that a monopoly in sugar refining might exist, but that it bore no relationship to commerce between the states: "Commerce succeeds to manufacture, and is not a part of it."[12] The federal government could regulate interstate commerce but not manufacturing. In effect, the trusts were home free.

By the following year, Henry Havemeyer and the American Sugar Refining Company were in the catbird seat. They had cornered 80 percent of the market. Three independent refineries were allowed to continue operation because they agreed to follow American's lead in pricing for a small share of the market. Their existence provided an answer to critics who charged that the trust had a monopoly on sugar refining.

Other potential refiners were discouraged by arrangements with wholesale grocers to refuse to handle brands other than those named by the trust and by rebates and concessions by railroads which gave the trust an advantage in shipping costs. It looked like smooth sailing ahead for Henry Havemeyer and the American Sugar Refining Company, but a meeting with John Arbuckle was in the offing.

With acquisition of the patent on a machine to package roasted coffee in one-pound bags, the sale of Arbuckles' Ariosa boomed. By 1892, Arbuckle Brothers' share of the coffee market was greater than its two largest competitors combined. John Arbuckle decided that the sale of sugar in small paper packages would go just as well. The company was already buying sugar in large quantities to use in the sugar and egg glaze which kept roasted coffee from going stale on the shelf. The packaging machine was adapted to put up sugar in two-pound bags, and Arbuckle Brothers increased their order from the American Sugar Refining Company.

Within four years, their business increased from packaging 100 barrels a week to 250 barrels a week; however, profits were disappointing. Following the death of Charles Arbuckle, James N. Jarvie became a member of the Arbuckle Brothers partnership. He later testified before a Congressional investigation, "We could not make any money buying sugar from refineries [at wholesale prices] and putting it up in that way and then selling again to the wholesale grocers."[13]

The result precipitated a monumental battle between Arbuckle and Havemeyer. The exact beginning and cause of the conflict are difficult to pinpoint. On October 7, 1896, a rumor circulated along Wall Street that Arbuckle Brothers might build a sugar refinery in Brooklyn in competition with the sugar trust. The following day the *New York Times* noted that there had been a drop of almost two points in the market price of American Sugar Refining Company certificates.[14]

The next day's report changed the location of the proposed Arbuckle refinery to New Jersey, and the *Times* article said Arbuckle Brothers was planning a "vast opposition" to the American Sugar Refining Company, but the reporter could not get confirmation of the story: "The Arbuckles maintained their usual policy of silence when questioned about the matter, and the American sugar people simply smiled."[15]

The following day a new rumor circulated up and down Wall Street:

> Sometime ago there was a patented scheme for making a block of granulated sugar about the size of the ordinary sugar loaf, having in its centre some coffee essence. The loaf was to be dropped into a cup of hot water, and the result would be a cup of coffee. It is stated that Arbuckle Brothers bought this patent and made a contract with the Sugar Company to turn out the sugar.
>
> As the story goes, the company turned out some of these goods and then notified Arbuckle Brothers of an increase in price. That firm very promptly refused to meet the advance and told Sugar Trust officials that if they insisted on it the contract would be taken away from them and Arbuckle Brothers would erect their own plant and make the goods themselves.[16]

The *Times* reporter interviewed a Wall Street guru for an opinion regarding this story: "They are too old and too conservative a house to go into anything of this kind. Their line is coffee, and I do not believe they are going to turn sugar manufacturers."

Next the reporter confronted Arbuckle Brothers with the statement: "It is an interesting story, but the policy of Arbuckle Brothers is to say nothing about any rumors concerning their business affairs or plans. I regret that we can not give you any information on this point."[17]

The rumor factory continued to churn. On October 16, the *Times* reported Arbuckle Brothers was considering forming a $50 million consortium of independent sugar refiners to fight the trust. Neither John Arbuckle nor his partner James Jarvie would comment on the story. A neighboring merchant on Front Street near the Arbuckles' plant hazarded they might build a small plant to satisfy their own needs.[18]

Much later, the true story of the beginning of the breach between John

Arbuckle and the sugar trust was aired in court. Arbuckle had insisted that the sugar trust take its barrels back at a rate of 20 cents a barrel. F. O. Matthiessen, an official of the sugar trust, thought this was extravagent. He cut off the allowance, and shortly thereafter met an irate Arbuckle, who informed Matthiessen that he would build his own sugar refinery. Ernst W. Gebracht, a former superintendent of the Havemeyer Sugar Refinery in Brooklyn, told about it on the witness stand. Gebracht had been convicted in connection with a sugar-weighing fraud to escape tariff. The Supreme Court sentenced him to two years in prison and a five-thousand-dollar fine. He testified while awaiting transportation to the federal prison in Atlanta. It may be that Gerbracht's frank testimony was motivated by a belief that the sugar trust had floundered in his defense:[19]

"Did J. O. Donner, consulting refiner of the Sugar Trust, talk with you about Arbuckle?" asked Assistant District Attorney Dorr.

"Yes, when it was a fact that the refinery was to be built, Mr. Donner said to me, `If it hadn't been for Matthiessen's bullheadedness, the refinery would never have been built.' There was no need for it."

"Did Mr. Matthiessen threaten Mr. Arbuckle he would put him out of business?"

"He did, but he found it was no use to threaten a man with $25,000,000 behind him."

Gerbracht went on to give Henry Havemeyer's reaction to the news: "Let them start it. They can't get any sugar talent, and if they did, I would put them out of business."[20]

In September 1896, Matthiessen visited Arbuckle in an attempt to buy patent rights to the Arbuckle Brothers' sugar packaging machine. Arbuckle refused and repeated his determination to build a sugar refinery. On December 4, speculation came to a halt. Arbuckle Brothers advertised for a sugar refining superintendent and announced plans to build a two-thousand-barrel-a-day refinery on John Street between Pearl and Jay streets, near their coffee facility. A *New York Times* reporter sampled the discussion running through the sugar district and "pro-trust men" responded:

"If the Arbuckles are going into sugar, what's the matter with the American Refining Company going into coffee? Turn and turn about's fair play."[21]

On December 17, John Arbuckle learned that Arbuckle Brothers had competition in the coffee business. The Woolson Spice Company of Toledo, Ohio, announced a price reduction of their Lion brand coffee.

As soon as the Arbuckles sugar refinery was constructed, the firm revised and enlarged its letterhead illustration to show the Arbuckle facility with the refinery in its midst.

Arbuckles immediately matched the reduction and, as the *New York Times* put it, "the fight was on":

> "I have," said a member of this firm [Arbuckle Brothers], "little to say on the subject, but the information comes from a trustworthy source. It may be that 'the sugar and coffee war' is on. We are attending to business, and with a measure of success that suits us. There is nothing to be said now about our Brooklyn sugar refining venture, except what has been told. As to our attitude toward the American Sugar Refining Company, it's just this: We are a private concern, playing with our own money; they are a corporation, playing with that of several thousand stockholders."[22]

In rebuttal, the sugar trust seemed to be most interested in maintaining Wall Street confidence in the position of their securities:

> "I do not care to make any statement officially. This property is all right. We are earning money. The dividends we pay are dividends which we earn. We have just paid 3 per cent.—a rate of 1 per cent. per month; and this payment, like every preceding payment, has come out of surplus earnings legitimately available. . . .
>
> "What Sugar Trust shares may do in the stock market isn't of any particular consequence. Our stockholders, sure of their 12 percent a year, can see quotations hammered down by the stock jobbers and not be much concerned. . . .
>
> "As to the talk about our being embroiled by new competition, there's nothing to be said. We are sure of our position, and whether in trade circles there is peace or war, we are able to take care of ourselves."[23]

The fight had started on November 25, when directors of the American Sugar Refining Company voted to build a roasting plant and go into the coffee business, but that would not be soon enough for Havemeyer. With his own funds, he bought controlling interest in Arbuckle Brothers' leading competitor, the Woolson Spice Company. The initial purchase was 1,100 shares, the majority of the company's stock, at $1,150 per share. Havemeyer beat down the price of the stock from $1,500 a share by threatening to build his own roasting plant.[24] Later, when the minority stockholders threatened to sue, he arranged to have them bought out.

John Arbuckle did find "sugar talent." In 1897, Joseph F. Stillman, manager of the Continental and Standard refineries of the American sugar trust, resigned and went with Arbuckle Brothers. He built Arbuckle a model sugar refinery in Booklyn, the first to be equipped with electrical power and the first to use the direct motor-driven centrifugal machine in refining sugar.[25] As soon as the refinery was completed, Arbuckle Brothers revised its letterhead with a new drawing showing the Arbuckle Brothers Sugar Refinery in the center of the firm's sprawling complex.

It was be two years before the Arbuckles' facility could go into production. In the meantime, observers of the coffee and sugar trade were certain the two contenders would come to a compromise to avoid the expense of a long, bitter competitive battle. The *New York Times* estimated the assets of the sugar trust at $120 million, including $15 million in cash reserves and Arbuckle Brothers at $20 million. But both Arbuckle and Havemeyer were stubborn men; each felt a need to protect his position in the marketplace.[26]

At first Arbuckle took a beating as he lowered the price of Arbuckles Ariosa to match the price of Lion Coffee. Both companies were losing money, but Havemeyer could recoup the loss on coffee by profits in the sugar refining industry. Late in 1898, the Arbuckle sugar refinery went into operation, and drove the price of sugar down to an unprecedented low, a margin of only 0.41 cent a pound between raw and refined sugar. Now, because of the American Sugar Refining Company's tremendous volume of sales, it was losing more than Arbuckle Brothers.

When Havemeyer brought pressure on wholesalers to refuse to carry the Arbuckle Brothers' brand of sugar, Arbuckle went over their heads to sell directly to retailers. Havemeyer countered by threatening to open retail outlets. As price cutting continued, roasted coffee got down to 8 $^{1}/_{2}$ cents a pound and both sides were losing money. Arbuckle managed to acquire a few shares of Woolson stock and through a stockholders' suit forced the company to stop selling at a loss.[27]

Havemeyer began selling sugar in small cotton bags, first five-pound and then two-pound, but they were not as popular as Arbuckles' paper sacks. Next, Havemeyer's Franklin Sugar Refining Company put up sugar in rather bulky pasteboard containers. The firm teamed up with the Woolson company to advertise. They issued trade cards. One side extolled the qualities of Lion Coffee; the other side pictured a hapless boy on his way home from the store. He had dropped a paper sack of sugar. The sack burst, spilling sugar on the sidewalk:

> THIS BOY has dropped his paper bag of sugar, and now it is half wasted. If he had bought THE FRANKLIN SUGAR REFINING CO.'S SUGAR it would have been given to him in a tightly-sealed packet, accident-proof.

Unable to acquire patent rights to paper bags, the Franklin Sugar Refining Co. countered Arbuckle Brothers' bags with a trade card showing the danger of dropping a paper bag on the way home from the grocery store.

The Woolson company countered Arbuckle premiums by issuing a premium catalogue, offering various items in exchange for Lion's Heads cut from the fronts of Lion Coffee packages. Copy in the Woolson catalogue was virtually identical to verbiage in the Arbuckles' catalogue. Neither of these campaigns appreciably dented Arbuckle Brothers' sales.

The capacity of the Arbuckle Brothers Sugar Refinery increased to three thousand barrels a day. When Havemeyer negotiated rebates on international shipping, Arbuckle countered by buying his own ships; he qualified for railroad rebates by building his own terminal facilities.[28]

When the warfare finally ended, total losses suffered by the two contending forces were estimated at $25 million. By 1903, Havemeyer realized the sugar trust was fighting a lost cause. The Woolson company paid no dividends in 1904. In 1909, Havemeyer signaled his capitulation by selling the Woolson Spice Company stock for five hundred dollars a share.[29]

Arbuckle Brothers continued in the sugar refining business and the sugar trust retired from the coffee business. John Arbuckle had won. No written agreement between Henry Havemeyer and John Arbuckle has been found to mark the end of the costly conflict. After John Arbuckle's death, on September 30, 1912, Arbuckle Brothers filed for a trademark on the company's sugar, claiming the trademark had been in use since September 19, 1912 (Appendix C-39). Later Havemeyer's son, Henry O., Jr., suggested in a privately printed family history[30] that his father and John Arbuckle had ended the price war by an informal verbal agreement to avoid the possibility of prosecution under the Sherman Antitrust Act.[31]

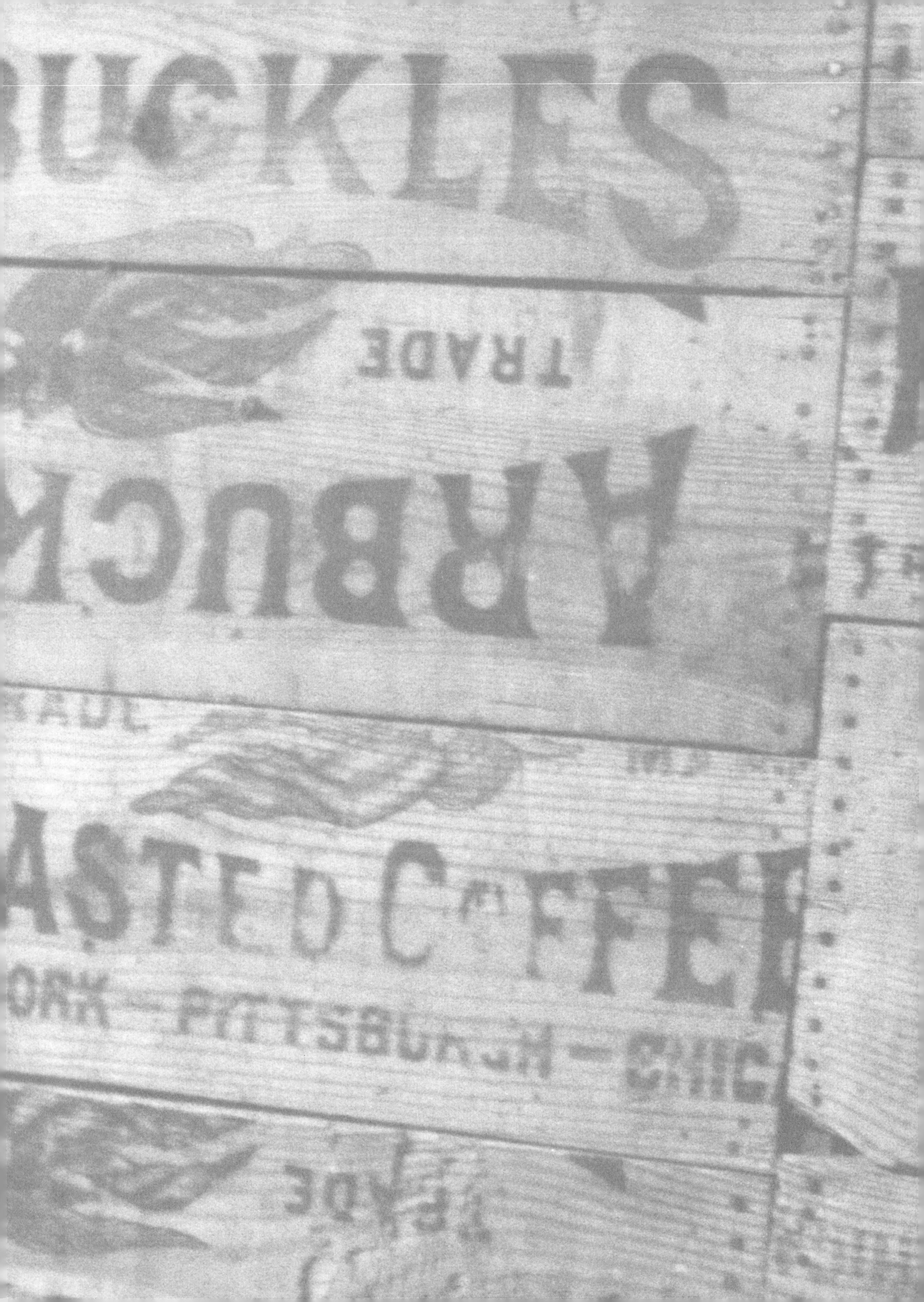

UCKLES
TRADE
ARBUCK
ASTED COFFE
ORK – PITTSBURGH – CHIC

6
COFFEE ON THE RANGE

Following the Civil War, as cattle spread across the western territories, so did Arbuckles' Ariosa. Around chuck wagons, in ranch kitchens, and on family dining tables, the use of Arbuckles was so widespread that the brand name became synonymous with the word "coffee." Ramon F. Adams, a leading lexicographer of Western vocabulary, defined the term: "The brand of coffee so common on the range that most cowmen never knew there was any other kind."[1]

During and immediately following the Civil War, coffee was out of reach of most settlers along the Western frontier, if not because of rarity because of price. A Beeville, Texas, family noted: "Coffee was then a dollar a pound and lots of people parched meal bran and sweet potato peelings for coffee."[2] Henry Fest wrote:

> . . . during the Confederate War, . . . The important matter of food was well looked after, with plenty of meat and field produce there was no need to go hungry. But the things that go with it. Coffee? Yes, we had coffee—made out of corn, acorns and sweet potatoes, while honey was used as a substitute for sugar. With an abundance of milk, cream, butter and eggs, this home-made "Postum" went all right until we renewed acquaintance with real coffee afterwards.[3]

John Arbuckle's development of a coating to preserve roasted coffee relieved housewives and cooks of the bothersome chore of roasting coffee. Railroads which probed westward in the wake of covered wagons made coffee available at affordable prices. It became an ever-ready commodity on ranches and in cow camps—indeed a necessity. During the 1880s, Oliver Nelson, cook on the T5 Ranch in the Cherokee Outlet of Oklahoma Territory, reported using thirteen 160-pound sacks of coffee during a year, roughly 175 pounds a month.[4]

As Edward Everett Dale, the cowboy historian, put it, "An enormous quantity was required, for the cook firmly believed that there is no such thing as strong coffee but only `weak people' and the men for whom he must provide were surely not of that type!"[5] And indeed they weren't:

"Cookie, pour me a cup o' that condensed panther y'u call coffee," said Joe Beal as we sat at the table of the Swinging L Ranch. "This is the way I like it, plum barefooted," he continued after gulping a quantity of the boiling liquid. "None o' that de-horned stuff y'u get in town cafes for me."[6]

In *No Life for a Lady*, Agnes Morley Cleaveland recollected that in her day "The practice was not to empty out the grounds until the pot was too full for further brewing."[7] "Plum barefooted" was the cowman's term for strong coffee, uncontaminated by sugar or cream, coffee that would "kick up in the middle and pack double."[8] The cowboy's aversion to the use of milk and cream stemmed from fear that it might lead to a milking job, a task beneath his dignity. A "cow milker" was his contemptuous name for a hired man. Even after the availability of preserved milk, he had little use for "canned cow."[9]

During the early days on the range, sugar was seldom available. If ants weren't in it, rains kept it damp. A meal might be topped off with "lick" or molasses, also called "long sweetening." There is the story of a Texas cowboy who was working in Montana. When he rode into a roundup camp at dinner, a hand passed him sugar. He said, "No thanks, I don't take salt in my coffee." He had never seen sugar, only sorghum syrup.[10]

Weak coffee was sure to be greeted by epithets such as "belly-wash" and "brown gargle."[11] Biting comments greeted an anemic brew: "The coffee tasted like water scalded to death."[12] As a cowhand named Bill Jones put it: "It seems that a lot of people never realize how little water it takes to make good coffee!"[13]

Practically every cowman who has written about western cookery has included an apocryphal recipe of vague origin and many variations: "Take two pounds of Arbuckles', put in 'nough water to wet it down, boil for two hours, and then throw in a hoss shoe. If the hoss shoe sinks, she ain't ready."[14]

The same recipe was often repeated with a six-shooter instead of a horseshoe, engendering the term "six-shooter coffee" for good strong coffee.[15] In The Old West Quiz and Fact Book, Rod Gragg gave a succinct recipe for "cowboy coffee": "A handful of coffee and a cup of water."[16]

Bryan W. Brown told of his father's recipe:

Pa claimed that in camp he would put a few cups of coffee in a sock, tie the end, and throw it into a pot. By adding water and another sock of coffee once in a while, he always had what he called "steamboat coffee."[17]

During early days on the range when the cook was frequently pestered by Indians begging for coffee, he served what became known as "Indian coffee." He poured water on old coffee grounds and brought it to a boil.[18]

During roundup, a three- to five-gallon pot, usually wide-bottomed and smoke-blackened, was considered standard for an outfit of ten or twelve men. The pot was filled two-thirds full of cold water and set on coals to boil. Then, after Arbuckle Brothers began inserting a stick of sugar candy or peppermint in each pound-bag of Ariosa, the cook would call out "Who wants the candy tonight?" and there would be a rush of volunteers to the coffee grinder which was inevitably attached to the side of the chuck wagon. If there was a scuffle between first arrivals, another would slip past and earn the candy for grinding the coffee.[19] When the water reached the boiling point, the cook would dump in the coffee. After it had boiled three or four minutes, he would give it a dash of cold water to settle the grounds and set the pot to the side of the fire to keep hot. Woe unto the hapless cowboy who was so awkward as to kick over the coffeepot!

The cook was the undisputed master of his domain, on the ranch and on the range. Even the most reckless cowboy in the outfit would think twice before "fooling with him":

> Not that the cook was really a better man, but he had resources for "getting even," that were not available to the "cow-puncher." A "feller's" coffee suddenly might betray remarkable weakness, an "accident" might work a shortage in grub or a deterioration in its quality, and so on.[20]

A code of etiquette developed on the range. Sometimes a camp kettle or a bucket was used for coffee. Then the cowboy dipped his cup into the container. When helping himself to a second serving, he had to be careful to wipe the bottom of his cup on his pants or chaps so no dirt his cup had gathered on the ground would be deposited in the pot.[21] During a meal, if a hand got up to fill his cup, somebody would yell "Man at the pot!" and the waddy was obliged to carry the pot around and fill all of the cups held out to him.[22]

A traveling anecdote illustrating western hospitality and the cowboy's inherent consideration for the opposite sex revolves around a cup of hot coffee. Over the past century, this story has been attributed to virtually every stage and bus stop, railroad station, and airline terminal in Oklahoma, Texas, New Mexico, Colorado, Wyoming, Montana, Utah, Idaho, Nevada, and Arizona—always narrated by an eyewitness.

During a brief stop, a woman passenger, always an easterner, ordered a cup of coffee, only to have the departure of her stage, train, bus, or plane announced before the steaming cup had cooled enough to drink. A cowboy seated nearby noted her plight. Removing his hat, he proferred his own cup with a sweeping bow: "Take mine, ma'am. It's already been saucered and blowed." Undoubtedly, it happened at some time in some place in the West— and if it didn't it should have.

The cowboy's regard for coffee can be measured by the fact that he had almost as many terms and epithets for coffee as he used in reference to his horse. In addition to those mentioned above, "jamoka" was a combination of "java" and "mocha." "Black water" was borrowed from the freighters. "Blackjack" and "blackstrap" were more common to lumber camps than cow camps. "Coffee cooler" expressed contempt for a perennial loafer or a prospector.

Coffee was related to various activities and things in the cowboy's life. After catching a horse or steer with his lasso, if a cowboy wrapped his rope clockwise (the wrong way) around his saddle horn instead of counterclockwise, he was said to be "coffee grinding." During early development of the revolver, a pistol with a revolving cylinder containing a number of barrels, it was frequently referred to as a "coffee mill."

After Arbuckles' Ariosa packages began to bear signatures which could be exchanged for premiums, "Arbuckle" became a derisive term for a green hand on the assumption that his dubious services had been obtained in exchange for coupons.[23] The name of the coffee was also used in approbation to indicate a standard of excellence, as indicated by an exchange in Frances Nimmo Greene's novel *The Right of the Strongest*:

> Uncle Beck followed Mary Elizabeth to her mount, and as they went she whispered:
> "Make him go home, hear!"
> "I will, child, an' you are wuth your weight in Arbuckle's coffee."[24]

Early on, ranchers usually bought coffee in fifty-and one hundred-pound sacks for use on the ranch and in one-pound bags for the convenience of the cook during roundup. When empty, the sacks were used for dishtowels, bandages, and aprons.[25] After the advent of premiums, coffee was most frequently bought by the case in one-pound packages. During the heyday of Arbuckles' Ariosa, cases contained a hundred bags.

Arbuckles coffee crates furnished sturdy building material but many have been preserved as prized memorabilia of the American West. This specimen is in the Panhandle-Plains Museum on the campus of West Texas State University, Canyon, Texas.

Each empty wooden crate weighed about twenty-eight pounds. Joseph Schmedding, an Indian trader in Arizona, told of receiving a shipment of two hundred cases of Arbuckles' which had to be freighted from the railroad to the trading post—ten tons of coffee in addition to the weight of the crates.[26]

Shortly before 1930, Arbuckle Brothers introduced a smaller shipping crate containing twenty-five one-pound packages. These cases could be sent by parcel post rather than by freight, a boon for small, one-man trading posts which sold only fifty to a hundred pounds of coffee a month.[27]

The crates were made of sturdy Maine fir, strong enough to withstand the trip from New York or Chicago to the farthest corner of the nation. Every case was emblazoned on two sides with the Arbuckles' flying angel. The boards of the larger cases were thirty-six inches long, three-eighths of an inch thick, and from four to ten inches wide.

All cases were carefully opened and the wood was used to make furniture, shelving, storage bins, doors, chicken coops, and even additions to buildings such as the Rainbow Lodge and Trading Post in Arizona. Former owner Barry Goldwater told of the building's loss:

> Arbuckles' Coffee, heck, yes, I remember it! At one time I owned the old Rainbow Lodge and Trading Post, located on the southeast edge of Navajo Mountain. It was from this post that the trail to Rainbow Natural Bridge commenced, and I owned the post for the business of taking people down to see that bridge. The garage was almost entirely constructed of old Arbuckles' boxes. The place burned completely down around 1952 or 1953 and, naturally, the first things to go were those wonderful Arbuckles' crates. I never had the money to rebuild it.[28]

The smaller shipping crates were 22 $^1/_2$ inches by 12 $^3/_4$ inches by 12 inches; the wood was the same thickness. These smaller crates were highly servicable for tool chests, wagon and truck boxes, woodboxes, and kitchen shelves and cupboards. Two of them fastened together and covered with hide made excellent panniers for pack saddles.[29] There were few homes in the West without Arbuckles' crates serving in one way or another.

Agnes Morley Cleaveland told about visiting a ranch owned by a Britisher in Socorro County, New Mexico:

> More boxes from England had yielded their contents in the form of hangings, tapestries, silver plate that had belonged to more than one earl; but an Arbuckle's Coffee packing case served

as woodbox beside the fireplace. Equally violent contrasts were in evidence on all sides.[30]

Arbuckles' closest competitor in the West was McLaughlin's XXXX Brand, commonly called Four X. It was shipped in a similar crate, but the wood was not nearly as strong. Without a doubt, the utility of its sturdy packing case contributed to the dominance of Arbuckles' Ariosa.

As homesteaders spread across the western plains, few could afford honest-to-goodness coffee. Howard Reude, who occupied a 160-acre homestead near Osborne, Kansas, wrote a letter to a friend on June 13, 1877, telling about the situation:

> Most people out here don't drink real coffee, because it is too expensive. Green coffee berries sell at anywhere from 40 to 60 cents a pound, and such a price is beyond the means of the average person. Even Arbuckles Ariosa at 35 cents a pound takes too much out of the trade when eggs sell at three to six cents a dozen and butter at six or eight cents a pound. So rye coffee is used a great deal—parched brown or black according to whether the users like a strong or mild drink. To give the beverage a ranker flavor, what is known as "coffee essence" is used. . . . This essence is a hard, black paste put up in tins holding some two ounces. . . . The women folks use "about so much" for a pot of coffee, and often they have to use the stove-lid lifter, or a hammer, or anything else that is handy to pound with, to break the hard paste before they can get it out of the tin. It is probably made of bran and molasses. When rye is not used, wheat is sometimes used for coffee, but it is considered inferior.[31]

Stores were often primitive on the western frontier. Sometimes storekeepers kept books by making notations on the walls of their stores. William MacLeod Raine and Will Barnes told the story of a proprietor who could neither read nor write. A rancher came in to pay his bill and found himself charged with a cheese which he had not received:

> "Guess again," the cowman said, "I don't eat cheese."
> "Well, you got a cheese, an' it weighed eight pounds, an' I reckon you got to pay for it."
> The customer demurred. They argued the matter for a time. The storekeeper was obstinate about it. He took the ranchman in to see the account on the wall. This was what he saw:

"Three pounds of coffee, eight pounds of bacon, three cans of tomatoes, four horseshoes, and a cheese," the storekeeper elucidated. Light came to the customer. "Didn't I get it when I got the horseshoes? It wasn't a cheese. It was a grindstone."

"Well, I'll be doggoned. Reckon you're right. I done forgot to put the square hole in the middle. Let's go get a drink. It's sure on me."[32]

During the lean, droughty years 1890-1895, when range cattle were virtually unsalable at any price, Arbuckle Brothers conceived the idea of using their coffee labels as premiums to offer the consumer a bonus. The "coupons" were $3/4$ inches wide and $3\,3/4$ inches long with the signature "Arbuckle Bros." against a mottled background and bearing the legend "CASH VALUE ONE CENT."

When one didn't have change, the signatures served as legal tender. There were few houses in the West without numerous items from the Arbuckle Brothers Notion Department and most cowhands used Torrey razors. ("The J. R. Torrey Razor is known as the best made in the United States. The printed guarantee of the manufacturer goes with each razor. Sent post-paid on receipt of 2 cent postage stamp and 28 signatures cut from wrappers of Arbuckles' Roasted Coffee.") Merchants found it almost useless to stock competing brands such as Lion's, McLaughlin's XXXX, and Yosemite. They could not compete with Arbuckles' premiums.

It was a crime of near-capital dimension for a ranch cook to run out of coffee, and tea would not do as a substitute. When Oliver Nelson ran out of coffee on the T5 Ranch, the owner told him to use tea. The cook dumped a tomato can of green tea into a four-gallon coffeepot.

"Did you save any for dishwater?" asked the first to get a cup.[33]

The cowboy had no use for tea and low regard for those who drank it. Ramon Adams told of a hand who had to go to a nearby English outfit to ask about a stray. He returned to his home ranch to tell about the marvel he had witnessed:

"There they sets, at *breakfast*, mind y'u, sippin' tea like it was hot solder."[34]

During roundup there was no quicker way to arouse hands from their bedrolls than for a poetic camp cook to call out:

Bacon in the pan,
Coffee in the pot;
Get up an' get it—
Get it while it's hot.[35]

72

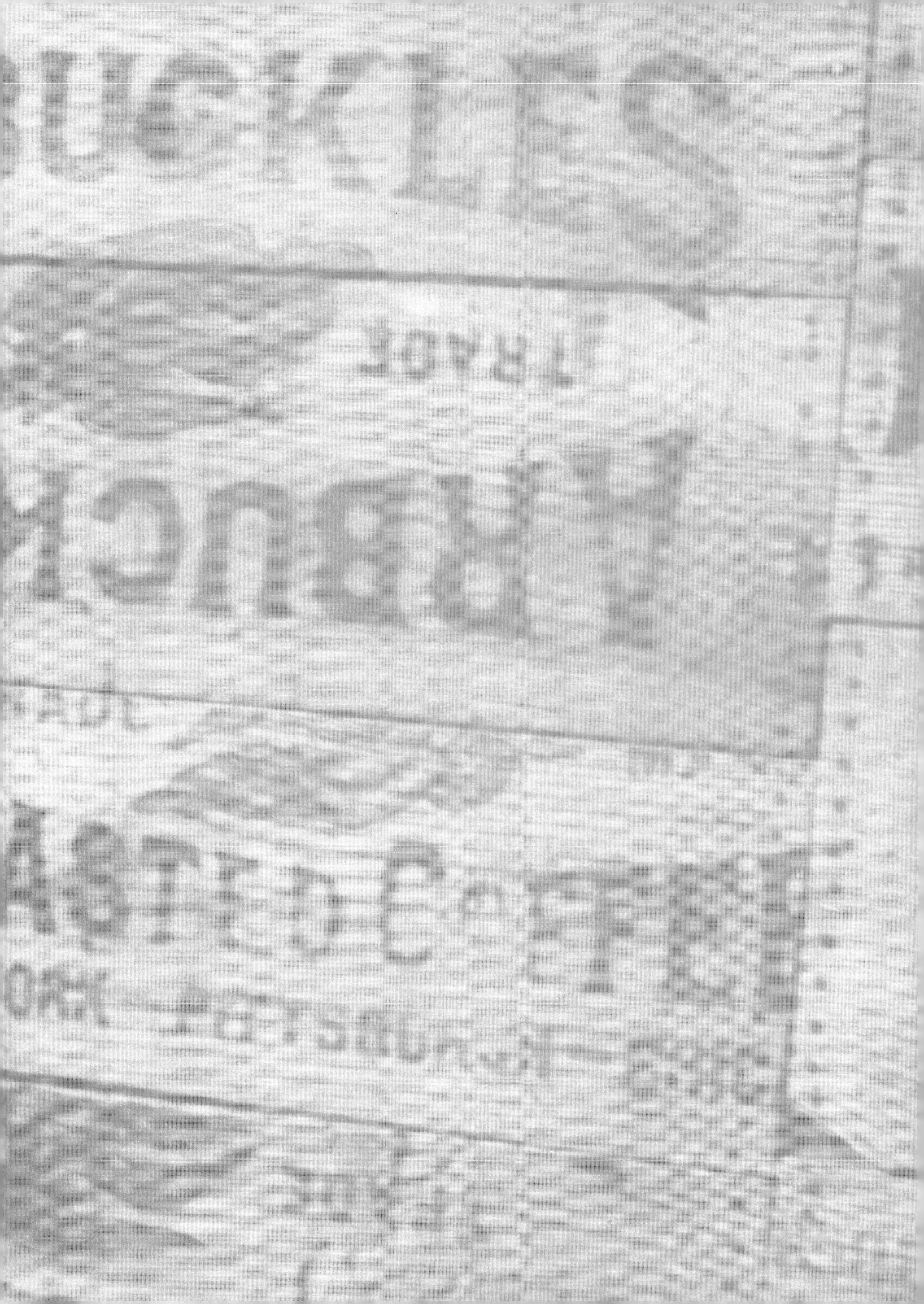
TRADE
PITTSBURGH

7
THE ARBUCKLES GO WEST

During the late 1880s, John Arbuckle "went West." We do not know whether he went specifically with the intent of buying a ranch, or whether he developed an interest during a visit. In any case, Arbuckle Brothers consummated a deal to purchase the PO Ranch, a horse ranch on Lodge Pole Creek about twenty miles north of Cheyenne, Wyoming. Later they acquired the L5, a cattle ranch on Horse Creek a few miles away.

Some observers termed the Arbuckles' ranch a "plaything." However, at that time Arbuckle Brothers had to maintain a large stable of draught horses; additionally, John Arbuckle was noted for engaging in any enterprise that he thought would "make an honest penny."

It is reasonably certain that the agreement to purchase the PO Ranch was struck early in 1888, because on July 10, 1888, the name for a post office there was officially approved: Ariosa. There is another strong indication that John Arbuckle was on the scene in 1888 or prior thereto, possibly during the bone-chilling winter of 1886-87.

On December 6, 1888, he filed application for a patent on a mitten (Appendix B-7). His idea had to have been bred of exposure to extreme cold. Arbuckle's mitten had openings at the tips of the fingers and the thumb so the wearer could warm his hands by blowing his breath into the holes. Springpressed valves allowed warm air to enter and prevented its leaking out. In part, the patent application read:

> When wearing mittens or gloves in cold weather one is often troubled with cold fingers, notwithstanding the protection of the garment, while the body of the hand feels sufficiently warm. This experience is common when one is driving in a severely cold atmosphere, as it is not convenient then to put the hands under additional covering. Much suffering results from this cause; and the object of this invention is to provide means for warming the fingers and hands when exposed to a low atmosphere without

This 1902 photograph shows the PO Ranch sprawling across the Wyoming prairie. (Courtesy Museum Division, Wyoming State Archives)

being required to remove the glove or mitten and expose the hands before a fire or radiator of heat.[1]

The patent application was submitted with a drawing but without a model. It is not known if these mittens were ever produced commercially, but it is a pretty safe bet that John Arbuckle had a pair for his next visit to the PO Ranch.

In 1872, Morton Post and a partner named Brown had established the PO Ranch with an investment of more than five hundred thousand dollars. Post said there would be a demand for horses as long as civilization lasted. Obviously, he did not foresee the advent of electric street railway systems in the East, which put a damper on large-scale horse operations as trolleys replaced horsecars.

Post imported fifteen Percheron stallions and bought prairie-bred mares from Nevada. The resulting colts were hardy.

The headquarters barn was 150 feet long and 35 feet wide. Corrals were built to handle five thousand head of horses. When a shipment of four thousand horses for the Eastern market was being rounded up, the first of the herd would reach the stockyards at Hillsdale, fifteen miles east of the ranch, before the last left the home corral. Post also owned a cattle ranch, the L5, along nearby Horse Creek.

Post's bubble burst after the winter of 1886-87. Winter started early that year with one blizzard after another. On December 12, the mercury fell to minus 27 degrees; on December 14, it registered minus 30 degrees; and on December 15 came the appalling drop to minus 47 degrees at Lander, Wyoming. Some ranchers lost more than 90 percent of their animals.

Morton Post was wiped out. Through his M. E. Post Banking Company, he had loaned heavily to ranchers who ran cattle principally on government land. Unable to foreclose on unowned land, Post lost everything. Arbuckle Brothers acquired the PO and the L5 ranches.

The ranchhouse, built about 1893, was quite modern for its day. The windmill pumped water into a tank located in the top of a building at the west end of the house. Even upstairs bedrooms had running water in the days when most ranchers carried water in and out. The house was plumbed with lead pipes. Floors were one-inch hardwood put together with wires instead of nails. Ice from the creek was stored in a building adjoining the kitchen of the main house. The center of the icehouse was a walk-in cooler. Mrs. John Jacob Astor was reputed to have been born in an upstairs bedroom.[2]

According to Harry Robb, an early-day Wyoming and Montana cowboy, the PO Ranch became a showplace, used primarily for entertainment:

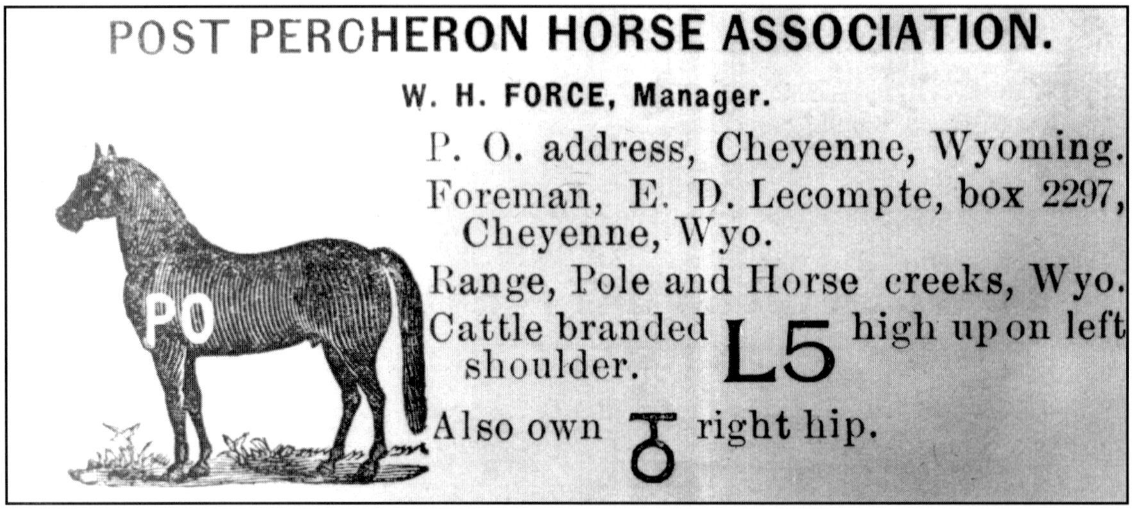

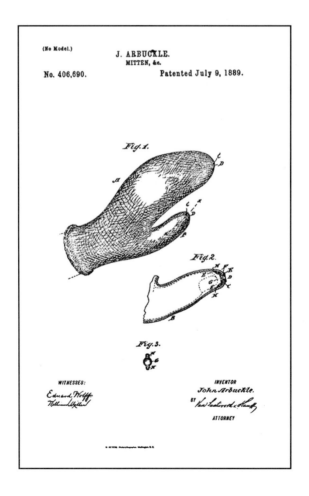

POST PERCHERON HORSE ASSOCIATION.

W. H. FORCE, Manager.

P. O. address, Cheyenne, Wyoming.
Foreman, E. D. Lecompte, box 2297,
Cheyenne, Wyo.
Range, Pole and Horse creeks, Wyo.
Cattle branded **L5** high up on left shoulder.

Also own right hip.

(No Model.)

J. ARBUCKLE.
MITTEN, &c.

No. 406,690.   Patented July 9, 1889.

Fig.1.

Fig.2.

Fig.3.

WITNESSES:
Edward Wolff
William Miller

INVENTOR
John Arbuckle
By
ATTORNEY

*Top: Wyoming Brand Book recording of the PO Ranch's brands.
(Courtesy Museum Division, Wyoming State Archives)*

*Bottom: Drawing from the patent application showing John
Arbuckle's mittens.*

What ever got the Arbuckles interested in horses so far from their New York business I never knew, so just call it a plaything. . . . A fellow didn't need to be much of a peeler to get a job there but he better be good if he wanted to stay, unless he could content himself greasing windmills and fixing fence and they had lots of both.

Big yellow barns, big yellow house and plenty of corrals and yellow buildings to match, including two pigeon houses with enough peaks and gables on them for a church, and any Arbuckle brother that I ever seen there looking after their interests was more interested in shooting pigeons as they swarmed from roof top to roof top, or else chasing coyotes and jack-rabbits with the dozens and dozens of hounds, so many in fact, that it kept old PO John busy the year around keeping them stuffed full enough so that they wouldn't kill calves.[3]

Much of the ranch was fenced with barbed wire, but a considerable part was fenced with wire interwoven with blocks of wood so wild horses could see the fence and not get cut up and scarred by running into it. The "big north" pasture was inclosed by more than a hundred miles of fencing. Spring repair took days; the crew required a cook, a grub wagon, and a wagon loaded with supplies and bedrolls.[4]

Local newspapers kept abreast of PO Ranch activities. On March 27, 1891, the *Cheyenne Daily Star* reported:

> The Royal Horse Association and Rainsford and Butler will soon make shipment of horses to the eastern market. . . .
>
> In Brooklyn lately a play in which three Wyoming horses were prominently cast, had a long run. The animals carried the PO brand, and Mr. Force and Dan Hogan took in the show every night. There was a race in the last act and the PO colors of cherry and canary won.

One year the ranch was stocked with three hundred head of longhorn cattle. Just after their arrival, an April blizzard blew in. Unaccustomed to the cold, more than two hundred of the longhorns died. By the 1920s, the ranch was stocked with Hereford cattle. The three thousand acres of meadow land furnished only part of the winter feed; the cattle had to be trailed to feed purchased on other ranches.[5]

One of the ranch buildings had a bell tower. It served as a dinner bell, but that was not its principal purpose. Melvin "Muggs" Pennington's mother was the cook on the ranch, and Muggs grew up to be a hand. He told about the bell: "Many's the time we've been out in a blizzard south

Top: The PO Ranch corrals could accommodate a herd of 5,000 horses. (Courtesy Melvin Pennington)

Bottom: Parties at the PO Ranch near Cheyenne, Wyoming, were well attended during the Arbuckle Brothers' regime. (Courtesy Museum Division, Wyoming State Archives)

of here trying to get the cattle in, and my mother would go out and ring that bell to guide us home. You couldn't see anything in a blizzard or a fog, but you could hear that bell for miles."[6]

For reasons unknown, the Ariosa post office at the PO Ranch closed November 30, 1901. Ariosa Coffee also had a namesake post office in Pennsylvania. The U.S. Post Office Guide lists a post office named Ariosa in Adams County, Pennsylvania, for the years 1893-1906 inclusive.

The Arbuckles took another flier into the ranching business. Capt. Joseph C. Lea, the "father of Roswell, New Mexico," had visions of becoming a large-scale rancher, possibly the equal of John Chisum, a legendary New Mexico cattleman. He got financing from Horace K. Thurber, a wealthy New York wholesale grocer, and the Arbuckles. Lea incorporated the Lea Cattle Company for one million dollars with Thurber and the Arbuckles providing the funds and Lea contributing nine thousand head of cattle.

The operation grew to as many as forty thousand head of cattle grazing over a forty-mile stretch of grass which reached from Roswell to Capitan Mountain. There were constant demands upon the investors for more money as Lea developed grandiose plans for ranch improvements, not the least of which was fifty thousand dollars for a six-mile flume to carry Pecos River water to an alfalfa field. Thurber and the Arbuckles cut off the flow of funds and swallowed their losses.

The financial panic of the 1890s dealt a death blow to El Capitan Ranch. The Lea Cattle Company went into receivership and was liquidated in 1898.[7]

After the death of John Arbuckle in 1912, ownership of the ranching interests passed to his sisters. In writing his history of Arbuckle Brothers, M. E. Goetzinger was understandably discreet in discussing the women's roles in the firm's operation: "Mrs. Jamison and Miss Arbuckle take the keenest interest in all our more important problems, but as we all know, they are not active in the daily management of the business."[8]

Apparently this hands-off policy did not apply to the PO Ranch. The PO hands were less than happy with eastern management, particularly after "one of the old maid managers wrote that she had read that the ranchers no longer needed to hire as many cowboys as previously since the sheep were now fenced out of the pastures. Therefore, the company would not pay so many wages."[9]

A portion of the ranch was subsequently willed to the Presbyterian Mission Board. The headquarters, including the ranchhouse, some outbuildings and corrals that were built before the turn of the century, are still intact as part of a working ranch operated by a lessee. Some of the land has been subdivided into acreage plots.

In spite of the passing of the PO Ranch, John Arbuckle, and Arbuckles'

Above: The dinner bell on the PO Ranch served a more important function that calling the hands to meals. It was used to guide those out on the range back to the ranch during Wyoming blizzards.

Top left: PO Ranch horses were well-trained using a "Breaking cart."
A well-broken horse hitched in tandem with an unbroken horse.
An arrangement of harness and hobbles called the "running W" was fitted
to the unbroken horse and when the driver pulled the reins and hollered "whoa"
the running W would pull the untrained horse to its knees. This
was continued until the horse learned to stop on command. Melvin "Muggs"
Pennington and Francis Johnson are aboard the breaking cart.
(Courtesy Melvin Pennington)

Bottom left: The round-up wagon on the PO Ranch. Left to right: Walt Leith, Wayne Scott, and Fred Boice, ranch manager. (Courtesy Melvin Pennington)

Ariosa, the memory lives on. Arbuckles' coffee has long been a subject of conversation wherever the dwindling breed of old-time cowmen gather. At a nostalgic get-together of the Chuck Wagon Trailers' Association, Jack Culley, former manager of the Bell Ranch in New Mexico, commented: "I don't know who the Arbuckles were, but they should have a monument erected in their honor somewhere on the High Plains. For many years they were the principal standby of the range cow business."[10]

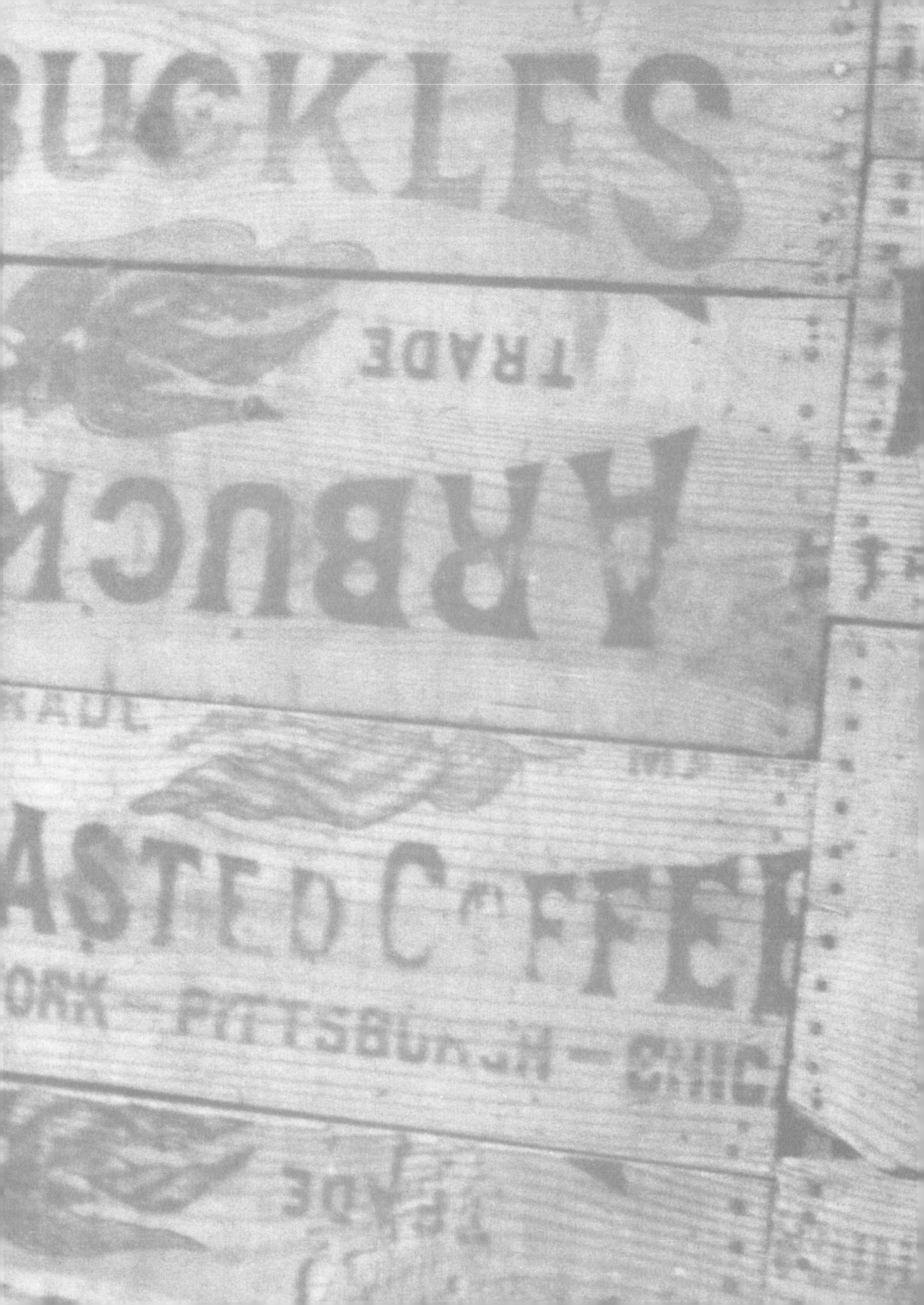
UCKLES
TRADE
ARBUCK
ASTED C FFE
ORK — PITTSBURGH — CHIC

8
MOSE DRACHMAN: ARBUCKLES' SALESMAN IN THE SOUTHWEST

Without a doubt, Mose Drachman of Tucson, Arizona, was the most colorful agent for Arbuckles' coffee in the far-flung Arbuckle Brothers' sales force.

Mose was born November 16, 1876. Family finances forced him to go to work at an early age. According to his "Reminiscences," his first job, at the age of eight, was ringing a bell up and down Tucson streets crying an auction: *"Remate! Remate! Zapatos muy barrato!"* ("Auction! Auction! Shoes very cheap!")[1] He sold newspapers and worked in a "gent's furnishing store" owned by William Florsheim for three dollars a week.

At the age of nine, Mose left school and started a five-year stint in his Uncle Samuel Drachman's cigar store in the heart of Tucson's saloon and gambling district.[2] His next job was working for Julius Leiberman and Company, a wholesale dealer in Willcox, Arizona. It was here that gambling changed his life. One evening his employer caught him playing cards in a saloon. The following morning he hailed Mose into his office: "Instead of going around saloons playing cards, get yourself something to read; if you can't find anything else to read—you see those copy books and invoice books there? Well, read them—you might learn something!"

Mose Drachman read and he learned:

I took him at his word and started in to read the letters and some of them opened my eyes as I saw the great amount of money this firm was taking out of this little town of Willcox. I ran across letters where they had placed on deposit $50,000.00, $100,000.00— it started me to thinking. Why wasn't I out doing something for myself rather than to be working for wages—so far as that was concerned, I was not saving any money for I received a certain amount plus board and sleeping quarters in the warehouse. The money I sent to my mother. It made me rather disgusted with

Mose Drachman, of Tucson, Arbuckles' coffee supersalesman.
(Courtesy Arizona Historical Library, Tucson)

myself to think that I had accomplished so little. I made up my mind right then to change my condition.[3]

At that point, Mose resolved never again to work for someone else. He quit his job, "jumped a freight train and landed in Tucson—broke." He had noticed that one of the best-selling items in the wholesale house was Arbuckles' coffee. He composed a letter:

Arbuckle Brothers
Old Slip and Water Street
New York City
Gentlemen:
I am a young man. . . .[4]

We do not have the remainder of the letter, but it may have reminded John Arbuckle of his own youthful assault upon the coffee industry in New York back during the early 1870s. For whatever reason, young Mose Drachman was appointed Arbuckle Brothers' agent for the Territory of Arizona, a post he would hold for the next twenty-one years. His first month's commission was eight dollars.

Business was slow at first, but Mose stuck it out, augmenting his Arbuckles' commission by selling other kinds of merchandise on the side. In 1895, the Santa Fe Railroad completed a line from Prescott to Phoenix, opening up the northern part of the territory. Thanks to railroad passes as a result of appointment to the Territorial Board of Equalization, Mose could tour the northern part of Arizona on behalf of Arbuckles' at no cost for railroad fare.[5] The trip was so successful that Arbuckle Brothers increased his commission and gave him a bonus. At the end of 1896, he received a check for twelve hundred dollars.

I thought I was the richest man in the world. . . . I will never forget the pride I felt when I went down to the Consolidated National Bank . . . and deposited this check with Mr. Freeman. He opened his eyes—he could not understand how a young fellow who, to his way of thinking, didn't amount to much, could have gotten such a sum of money. There was a double pleasure in putting the money with him since only a short time before I had tried to borrow $100.00 from him and met with refusal.[6]

Mose got married in 1897. Later, his daughter wrote about the good times in the coffee business:

Father certainly sold a world of coffee. The evergrowing West was gulping up the Java and most of it was Arbuckle's. Sometimes he'd come back from his trips with orders enough to make up twenty carloads, a whole train, of Arbuckle's Ariosa. He could scarcely keep up with the demands. The frantic telegrams poured in:

"Out of coffee. Start another car."

"Stock at Bowie low. Rush car."

"Only seven cases on hand. Is there anything in sight?"

"Last shipment just arrived, but we need more."

"Running short. . . ."

"Down to last case. . . ."

"Want more. . . ."

"Rush. . . ."

"Hurry. . . ."

"Rush. . . ."

Some months Father's commissions would amount to over $200, which for those days was tremendous.[7]

Mose Drachman was an entrepreneur of the first order. He was always looking to make a killing and end up on Easy Street. In addition to coffee, his sales efforts extended to mines and oil wells, lots and acreage, cattle ranches, and even a soda cracker factory. He became involved in a scheme to raise piñon nuts. And there was the ostrich farm: He missed becoming vice president of the Phoenix Ostrich Farm because a boiler burst in the laundry he owned, delaying him while a competing real estate agent found a location for the proposed ostrich farm.[8] Besides owning a laundry, Drachman was partner in a shoe business and a member of a real estate firm. He promoted streetcar lines and railroads, and invaded the political field to serve two terms on the city council and become a senator during the second state legislature in 1915-16. As a salesman, his favorite expression to lure customers was "Let's ride the rainbow to the pot of gold."[9]

Sometimes the pot at the end of his rainbow turned up empty. One such time was in 1894, just after he had become the agent for Arbuckles' coffee. The new safety bicycle had come out, taking over from the old high-wheel-in-front and little-wheel-in-the- rear. A craze was mounting. Mose Drachman and a friend decided they could make a killing in Mexico City. They secured the agency for a popular make of bicycles, borrowed five hundred dollars apiece, and set out—only to find other well-financed dealers were ahead of them. Mose pawned a six-shooter and a watch chain to get back to Tucson.[10]

Other ventures were more successful. He began eyeing attractive

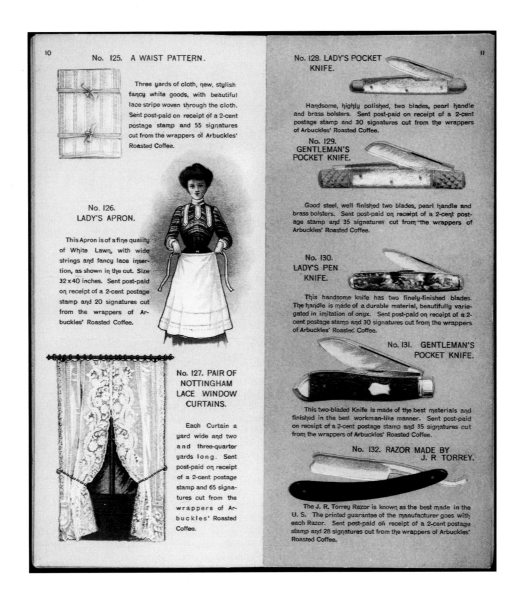

One of Mose Drachman's duties was to arrange for the distribution of premium catalogues, making sure there is "a local distributor that you know about and on whose honesty you can depend, and who will see that every book is placed in a home and not dumped into the ditches by his helpers." (Courtesy Warshaw Collection of Business Americana, Smithsonian Institution)

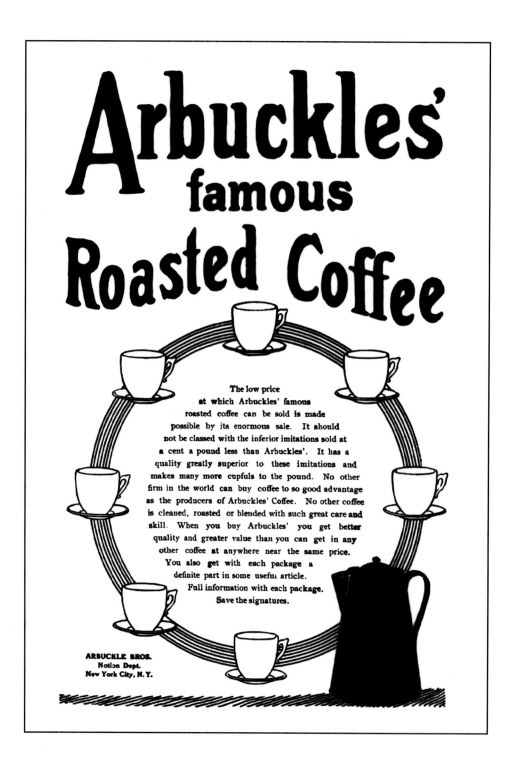

About the turn of the century Arbuckle Brothers shifted the emphasis of the advertising to magazines. This advertisement, published in 1901 in Farm and Ranch *in Texas, stressed the quality of Arbuckles' Coffee and the premium program.*

acreage out by the University of Arizona. A banker told him, "My boy, the town'll never cross the railroad tracks, never in this world." Mose wangled an advance against his Arbuckles' commissions with which to buy the land. He carved it into lots, distributed handbills, rented a brass band, gave away lemonade, and hired an auctioneer. He went home with eighteen hundred dollars profit.[11]

Mose Drachman was an eternal optimist. He was invited to participate in a political junket to New York as an honorary colonel on the governor's staff to welcome Adm. George Dewey home from his victory in Manila Bay. When his wife objected to the time and expense involved, Mose talked expansively. He might sell James N. Jarvie, an Arbuckles' vice president, a gold mine. Also, he had heard Arbuckles' California representative was leaving; he wanted that territory. Why, he might even extend his territory to Hawaii, the Philippines, and China! His wife reminded him that Chinese drank tea and Hawaiians drank coconut juice. Upon his return he had to confess to his wife that Jarvie was not in the market for a gold mine; neither did he get China, the Philippines, nor Hawaii.

"What did you get?"

"New Mexico. I got half of New Mexico."

But he had to reveal that his commission had been cut from twenty-five cents a case to twenty cents. "They said with a larger territory I'd get so much more business that twenty cents was all they could afford to allow me."[12]

Drachman made at least two more attempts to sell Arbuckle Brothers' officials on business opportunities in Arizona. On September 21, 1906, he wrote William A. Jamison:

> You no doubt have kept track of the continued high price of copper, and the shortage of this metal. Arizona will lead in the copper production this year, and there are splendid opportunities to get ahold of valuable copper mines. One in particular, I wish to call your attention to. It is a group of thirty claims situated near this city. The owners of the claims will prefer to give a controlling interest in the claims for the purpose of having them further developed and a reduction put upon the same for treating the ore.... I am informed and believe that a favorable report can be had from a competent mining engineer, who is at present the geologist of the Arizona School of Mines.
>
> If you or your friends are in any way interested, I would be pleased to send you a full report and samples of ore.
>
> Jamison wrote for additional information but was not satisfied: "It does not cover the point I had in view."[13]

Then there was the trip Mr. and Mrs. Drachman made to New York in 1907 to sell James N. Jarvie interest in a proposed Tucson hotel—four stories high with 180 rooms. Negotiations were going well when financial panic struck New York City. News leaked out that bankers were speculating in shaky real estate and copper deals. Depositors besieged banks. In one day $8 million was withdrawn from the Knickerbocker Trust Company; it closed its doors. The next day $34 million was withdrawn from another trust company. Banks halted withdrawals excepting small sums for urgent reasons. One banker committed suicide.

Jarvie decided he would stick to coffee instead of dabbling in western real estate. He advised Mose, "You'd better go west, young man, and sell some coffee. I hope you have the cash to get there."[14]

Arbuckle Brothers was a demanding taskmaster. In addition to promoting and selling Arbuckles' coffee to jobbers, Mose Drachman had other duties. He had to investigate the credit ratings of jobbers and ameliorate those who objected to being placed on a cash basis. He had to arbitrate with jobbers who wanted exclusive towns or territories, in violation of Arbuckle Brothers' policy. He had to investigate and report on the prices of competing brands. He had to negotiate favorable railroad shipping rates and obtain payment for damaged shipments. He had to introduce and promote new Arbuckle brands. He had to arrange for the distribution of advertising material. He had to keep abreast of ever-changing prices on the New York coffee market and charge jobbers accordingly, making sure that all payments to Arbuckle Brothers were in "New York exchange." He had to locate and arrange for warehouse space at depots scattered over his territory, and deal with rival salesmen who connived with warehousemen to have onions stored next to Arbuckles Ariosa.

Sometimes Mose Drachman's civic activities threatened his coffee business. There was the time Pres. William McKinley came to Phoenix. Arizona wanted to make a good impression in the interests of achieving statehood. Mose was appointed secretary of the McKinley Reception Committee. One of his best customers insisted that his daughter—"dressed up like Columbia or Pocahontas, or something"—should present McKinley with a wreath of roses during the President's hectic schedule, otherwise he would never buy another case of Arbuckles' Ariosa. After it was over Mose coined an advertising slogan: "The President has come and gone, but Arbuckle's still makes a good cup of coffee!"[15]

In his year-end report for 1904, Mose Drachman had to write Arbuckle Brothers to explain why his sales had dropped off in Arizona Territory and how the situation could be improved:

I have delayed somewhat in making my report for the year 1904 on account of being away considerable of the time.

The sales of Ariosa for 1904 in Arizona show a decrease but a corresponding increase in New Mexico. An increase needs no explanation, so we will take up the matter of decrease.

The main industries of Arizona, as you are well aware, are mining, cattle raising, and in the irrigated section agriculture. The drought of 1904, the worst in the history of the Territory, practically ruined the cattle business and caused heavy losses to the farmers. For nearly a year there was hardly any rain whatever, and when the drought was broken in July last it saved what few cattle were still alive. Had it lasted thirty days longer there would have been none to save. The losses . . . were from twenty-five to fifty per cent of the holdings.

Then the mining business which is our main stay in our future last year was not as prosperous on account of the price of copper not being as high as it is now. Our mines are principally copper, this being a distinct copper section. The price of copper has been very low for about three years, culminating last year in a complete closing down of some of such plants, here for instance Helvitia, thirty miles from Tucson, where two or three years ago there was a population of about two thousand, had only a watchman for a year or more until the latter part of 1904. Copper is now up in price again and in demand and Helvitia as well as many other camps is feeling and showing the benefit thereof.

The prospects for this year and the next few years is just the reverse of twelve months ago. Then again we have had plenty of rain the last month and I look forward to the year 1905 to regain all the lost ground of the year before.

Some of the lost trade I attribute on account of the building of a railroad from El Paso to Bisbee which cut off considerable trade that used to be supplied from Tucson. Now this trade goes to El Paso and the jobbers of El Paso are supplying Ariosa to this section which formerly was supplied by Tucson, and this was brought about on account of the railroad rates which enabled El Paso jobbers to sell Ariosa at a less price than the Tucson jobbers. This territory includes the towns: Bisbee, Douglas, Naco, Cananea, and other small points.

BISBEE:

I have explained to you in former letters the condition existing at Bisbee so that it will not be necessary to go into this fully at this time. We are not getting the business from this section that we are entitled to. The Copper Queen Company will not handle our coffee. There is a demand for our coffee by the consumer and we ought to take some steps to see that they can get Ariosa. This territory is neglected for the reason that I am unable to sell the coffee. Your El Paso agent does not push the sales of Ariosa in this section for if he did he would antagonize the Copper Queen Company and as the Copper Queen Company is his largest customer in the other lines that he represents it would not be in his interest to do anything that would hurt them. This Copper Queen Company guard very jealously their interest and if your El Paso man would attempt to push Ariosa they would retaliate by refusing to purchase his other lines, and he represents a great many firms which you no doubt know.

I think the best plan to handle this is as I wrote you a few days ago, to place the handling of our brand in the hands of Buxton Smith Company, exclusively. They will push the sale of Ariosa and as they call on the retail trade regularly and are in a position to do some business.

I trust that I have made myself clear as to the peculiar condition existing in this section, and that you will decide to grant my request. This is the best section of Arizona, and I am anxious to secure more business from that point, but I have been handicapped as you can readily see.

CLIFTON AND MORENCI:

The towns of Clifton and Morenci, being in Arizona I have always felt that that trade properly belonged to me, and that the commissions therefrom should be credited to my account. However, the trade already is such that it costs less to ship from El Paso to these points than from any Arizona Depot, and of course I don't get the business.

Now what I wish you would do is this: give me permission to go to Clifton and make up car-load quantities, same to be shipped direct from New York. If you grant this I will go there at once, and I believe I can get the business. Kindly advise as to this.

YUMA:

The trade of Yuma and points adjacent thereto I have handled through E. F. Sanguinetti; that is I would quote them direct adding 50 cents a case as profit and this would go to Mr. Sanguinetti, the different parties having the impression that they were getting their coffee direct.

By shipping in car-load lots to Yuma and distributing from there the coffee costs considerable less than if shipped by the local freight. I failed to make up my last car at Yuma as you remember as Sanguinetti wanted you to consign 50 cases out of the car to him which you refused to do. I think Mr. Sanguinetti feels hurt on account of being placed on a cash basis, and he resented as he believed you are afraid to trust him with these 50 cases. The reason for placing Mr. Sanguinetti on a cash basis was a report which you received about four and a half years ago that matters were not right through your Mr. Shirller. Now it may be possible that since then conditions have changed and Mr. Sanguinetti might be in a position that would warrant you in extending him a line of credit. I wish you would kindly look into this matter and if he is entitled to any credit grant it to him. It would create a better feeling if you do so.

Now, in the event that Mr. Sanguinetti does not show a disposition to be friendly I think it would be a good plan, in fact I recommend it, to establish a storage depot at Yuma, and advise the selling direct of Ariosa to the parties to whom we have sold in the past through Mr. Sanguinetti. Yuma and the territory attributary thereto will be very prosperous as the government is about to build a dam for the storage of water and this will increase the population considerably.

COMPETITION:

There is some other package coffee sold in my territory but the percentage is small. The brand Yosemite I think sells the most on account of costing from $1.50 to $2.50 a case less than ours, but even at that they have been unable to make much of an inroad on our trade. I think it is safe to say that we are getting 90 per cent of the package coffee business in Arizona. The population of Arizona is estimated at 140,000. Cut out the section of Arizona that we do not sell would cut down the population that I am selling to to about 100,000 and last year we sold over 700,000 pounds, so even though there is a decrease I think this is a good record.[16]

Arbuckle Brothers demanded strict compliance with their established policies. They did not trust Western banks and maintained absolute control over which jobbers should be allowed credit. Henry C. Schuetz in the bookkeeping department was Mose Drachman's nemesis. Letters from the home office were liberally sprinkled with admonitions and recriminations from Schuetz:

We wrote you two letters on August 16th relative to delivery slips that had not been mailed as indicated by the postmarks on the envelopes and the dates on the delivery slips, and requested an explanation. Up to the present writing, we have not heard from you. Please note that the delivery slips must be mailed on the day the order is received by you, and you in turn giving an order to the dealer on your stock. This is of prime importance.

. . .

We return herewith your Bowie delivery slip No. 5 $^1/_2$ of July 27th, covering 5 cases Ariosa shipped Buxton-Smith Co., Bisbee, A.T., for the reason that you show the price as 14.47 instead of 14.43. This also changes the extension for the slip from $72.35 to $72.15. Please render us a corrected delivery slip and Buxton-Smith Co. a corrected invoice in case the original was made out incorrectly.

. . .

. . . please call Mr. McCanna's attention to the fact, that when a shipment arrives in the future in a damaged condition, with a hundred or more packages damaged he is not to purchase new packages to take the place of all the damaged packages, but should consolidate the good packages in the damaged cases into complete cases and then only purchase a sufficient number of new packages to complete one case. He should sell the loose coffee as bulk coffee at the best price obtainable, deducting the amount received from the bill for the new packages purchased. In the event that he receives more for the loose coffee than the cost of the new packages purchased he should remit the excess to you, which you in turn should remit to us. Of course, the paid railroad expense bill should bear notation of the railroad agent showing the loss and damage.

. . .

Referring to your reports of comparative delivery prices dated March 31st, in which you state that the price at Flagstaff is $14.81 for Lion as against $15.31 for Ariosa, and at Bowie $14.83 for Lion as against $15.43 for Ariosa, would ask that you endeavor to obtain a recent invoice covering Lion Coffee, showing the above prices, or if it is not possible to obtain an invoice, get one of their recent quotation cards.

. . .

Referring to the enclosed envelope addressed by you to Magdalena, N.M., would suggest that you write in full the word "New Mexico" in the future, at any rate make it a little plainer than noted on this envelope.

. . .

In an envelope postmarked Tucson, August 25th, 7 P.M., we received a number of Flagstaff Delivery Slips dated August 18th and August 19th, and attached thereto were stubs showing that the orders were lodged August 8th, 18th and 19th. We cannot understand these transactions at all. Why should it take on one instance 17 days, another 7, and another 6 for mail to reach you at Tucson from this depot? In view of the change in price and your knowledge that there would be some question as to the price of these transactions, did you save the envelopes containing these stubs indicating that deliveries and shipments had been made? How long does it take in the usual course for a letter to reach you in Tucson from Flagstaff?

. . .

We cannot accept Slips Nos. 8, 9 and 10 at the 14 cent basis price since they were not mailed by you within a reasonable time after the change in price of August 19th. . . . We return Slips Nos. 8, 9 and 10 to you herewith.

. . .

We have since obtained an agency report, and find that the party's rating is not such as to warrant our extending credit, so, while you may continue to honor Gleason's orders, you are not at liberty to do so, without having exchange in hands to cover.

. . .

We wish to call your attention, in this connection, to the fact that we have had more than one complaint recently from the trade relative to unsatisfactory billing. It occurs to us that possibly this is due to the fact that you have not an efficient assistant in your office to look after clerical details when you are absent on a trip. This matter should be remedied. It is not so much the question of cash discount alone that is involved, but, furthermore, the annoyance to the trade and ourselves in these We should like to hear from you on the subject, with assurances that we may expect a radical improvement.[17]

As Mose frequently told his wife, "This isn't going to be all beer and skittles."[18]

Mose was always on the alert to expand his territory. On July 21, 1904, he wrote Arbuckle Brothers:

There is a matter which I have given much thought lately, and I desire to present it to you. I would like that you would place me in charge of a territory bounded by certain points, which I will state more fully later on. That you are to appoint me as your representative for the said district at a fixed salary and traveling expenses when out on a trip. I believe I can demonstrate to you that there will be many advantages in my plan, and that the cost would be but very little more than you are now paying for handling your business in this section; and furthermore it would not require any radical changes. I will not now take up your time by going into full details as to why I think it would be advantageous to you, as I first want to know if you would consider any such proposition. If this appeals to you it would give me great pleasure to go over the ground in full detail. The territory in question would be embraced within the following points:—

Commencing at Los Angeles, Cal. then East on the Southern Pacific R. R. to El Paso; then East on Texas Pacific R. R. to Tehas, Tex.; then North on the Tehas Valley & East. R. R. to Amarillo, Tex; thence North on the Colorado & South. R. R. to Trinidad Colo; thence South on the Atchison & Topeka to Albuquerque, N. M.; thence West on Atchison & Topeka to Los Angeles Cal., which completes the circuit. Of course this is to include all points tributary to the aforesaid railroads.

Trusting to receive a favorable reply, I remain,[19]

Mose did not get any of Texas or California, but he did get a substantial section of New Mexico. He received credit for some orders placed with depots in Los Angeles, Fort Worth, and Dallas. There is no record of his being placed on a salary basis.

On February 13, 1905, he wrote a letter to a Sig. Harris outlining his duties as they were to be handled by Harris during Drachman's absence:

The manner in which you are to handle the coffee business while I am gone will be as follows:

We have the following supply depots where stocks of coffee are always carried: Tucson, Phoenix, Prescott, Flagstaff, Bowie Station, Roswell, New Mexico, Albuquerque, New Mexico, and Los Angeles, California.

The names of the warehouse men for the different depots you will find in the book I am leaving with you.

The present price for Ariosa in New York is 14 cents. In making out bills you will add the price above . . . the New York price, which makes the present price at the different depots as follows: Tucson $16.54 a case; Phoenix $16.73; Prescott $16.73; Flagstaff $16.31; Bowie Station $16.43; Los Angeles $15.37; Roswell $15.69 and Albuquerque $15.85.

The discount is $1.50 per case less two per cent for cash. By looking at one of the invoices you will find full particulars as to terms. When an account is marked cash, you are not to order coffee shipped *unless you have funds in your hands.* When local checks are sent exchange should be added. All exchange must be in favor of Arbuckle Bros.

New York prices change sometimes of which you will be advised by wire then you must change the prices and notify the trade. Sales slips are numbered beginning with No. 1 for each shipment on the first of each month.

BOWIE STATION: All orders that you receive which are to be shipped from Bowie Station you are to mail to Solomon & Wickersham, Bowie Station.

LOS ANGELES: Any orders to be filled from Los Angeles, write to Johnson-Carvel Company, Los Angeles, make no sale slip but send bill to the party ordering. Send the New York exchange covering the amount ordered to Arbuckle Bros. direct.

FLAGSTAFF: Trade that is to be supplied from Flagstaff you will draw orders on Babbitt Bros., Flagstaff, mailing these orders to Babbitt Bros. You will in turn receive from them notices of delivery which you will keep on file. In fact these notices you will receive from all of our storage depots.

PRESCOTT: All Prescott trade is supplied direct and billed direct at Prescott, and when you receive notices of delivery all that you have to do is to make out sale slips.

JEROME, ARIZ: T. F. Miller & Co. of Jerome, Arizona will order coffee direct and on receipt of their order you will write to Prescott Transfer Company, Prescott, Arizona, ordering the amount of coffee shipped them. You will make out sale slip and send duplicate bills to T. F. Miller Company.

PHOENIX: Goldman & Company and M. Jacobs at Phoenix will write to you for coffee. You will send then an order for their wants on the Pioneer Transfer Company, mailing the order to them with their invoice.

I have furnished E. S. Wakelain Grocery Company with a supply of orders for their wants and when you receive notices from the Pioneer Transfer Company that they have delivered Wakelain any coffee you may charge them up with amount and mail invoices.

You will also receive from the Pioneer Transfer Company New York exchange in payment for coffee delivered to J. W. Dorris, on receipt of same charge and bill it attaching draft to sale slip.

On receipt of any orders from the Congress Consolidated Mines, Congress, Arizona, and Octave Commercial Company, Octave, Arizona, mail orders for same to the Pioneer Transfer Company sending bills to the parties direct and sale slip as usual.

TUCSON: The Tucson trade will call upon you for orders which you will issue to them direct as they will get their own coffee. Charge and bill the coffee the same day that you give them the order. Any trade outside that is supplied from the Tucson depot you will make out the order and take it down in person to A. Steinfeld & Co. and turn it over to Mr. Hoffeister.

ROSWELL, NEW MEXICO: The trade at Roswell will be supplied with blank orders, that is you will fill in the amount of coffee they are to receive signing same but you are not to date these orders. When you receive the stubs showing that a delivery has been made then you are to charge this coffee and bill it dating both the date that is shown on the stub. When you receive letters asking for these orders send as follows:

To Joyce Pruitt Company—5 orders of 25 each;

Coleman-Lysaght-Blair Company—5 orders of 15 each;

Jaffa Prager Company—5 orders of 5 each.

FORT WORTH, TEXAS: You will receive orders from McCord Collins Company, Fort Worth, Texas. Do not send them supply of orders, just honor their requisitions charging the coffee the date that you receive their orders sending them an order for amount that they desire. In billing them their coffee you will use the one per cent cash discount billheads.

DALLAS, TEXAS: Schneider-Davis Company will send you their orders you will handle these exactly as you handle the Fort Worth business.

All orders must be charged and billed on the day that you receive them and mailed that day, this is imperative and a deviation from this rule will cause a letter from Arbuckle Bros. asking for an explanation.

ALBUQUERQUE, NEW MEXICO: The trade at Albuquerque, New Mexico is supplied direct and charged and billed direct so you have nothing to do except on receipt of the slips to enter them in the book.

TELEGRAMS: Forward all telegrams to me, excepting those ordering coffee. Also send me all letters.[20]

Considering Drachman's somewhat vague instruction, unless Sig. Harris was already familiar with his operation, it is small wonder that Schuetz found fault with activities during Mose's absence. However, when the occasion warranted, Schuetz could be congratulatory.

In 1908, Arbuckle Brothers introduced a new brand, Seven Day Coffee, to fill the need for a less expensive coffee than Ariosa:

You will note by the sample, that nothing that can compare

with SEVEN DAY Coffee has been offered to the jobbing trade to fill this long-felt want. In our opinion it simply distances all competitors in the two essentials of quality and price. In offering the two brands to the trade—

ARIOSA and SEVEN DAY—we wish you to emphasize as much as possible that ARIOSA, being removed from the class of the so-called standard brands, is a high-grade coffee such as is sold at a much higher price by competing roasters throughout the country. Do not lose an opportunity to impress this point upon the trade.[21]

During the month of March agents were offered a special introductory commission of twenty-five cents per hundred pounds "to fully cover such special work as you may be doing in introducing Seven Day Coffee." Mose Drachman got right to work. He distributed fifty-six pounds from a sample case and told the New York office he would sell the remaining forty-four pounds. His labors generated a substantial number of orders, and Schuetz wrote to congratulate him and tell him that the special twenty-five-cent commission would be extended through the month of April.

In 1905-06, Mose Drachman was servicing seventy-four jobbers in Arizona. The list included some of the most famous trading firms of the Territory: Buxton-Smith of Bisbee; Babbitt Brothers of Flagstaff; Norton-Morgan and Soto Brothers of Willcox; J. W. Dorris of Phoenix; E. G. Carruthers of Gila Bend; Rand Trading Company of Winslow; Solomon and Wickersham of Bowie, Safford, and Solomonville; Shattuck and Desmond of Mesa; Old Dominion Commercial Company of Globe; Wingfield and Sons of Camp Verde; and L. Zeckendorf and Company of Tucson.

His commissions were computed upon the number of 100-pound cases sold from various depots. September 1906, was a typical month:

DEPOTS	CASES	COMMISSION
Prescott	50	10.00
Phoenix	125	25.00
Flagstaff	75	15.00
Bowie	76	15.20
Tucson	55	11.00
Albuquerque	270	54.00
Socorro	70	14.00
Roswell	85	8.50
Safford	240	48.00
		$200.70

Through twenty-one years of Mose Drachman's ups and downs, Arbuckle Brothers provided the sinecure which augmented his finances or rescued him from disaster. In lean times, usually in November when taxes were due, Arbuckle Brothers would advance him three hundred dollars to be deducted from his commissions at the rate of fifty dollars per month. Toward the end of his tenure, his commissions totaled an average of $250 a month, "which at that time was remarkably good pay," as he later commented in his memoirs.[22]

After Mose Drachman relinquished his post with Arbuckle Brothers, about 1910, he devoted himself to other business interests and civic activities. As a member of the Arizona Pioneers' Historical Society, he pursued his principal hobby, the early history of Tucson and the Southwest. After a short illness, on October 2, 1935, Mose died of a heart attack while lying in bed reading a newspaper.

BUCKLES

TRADE

ARBUCK

ROASTED COFFEE

ORK — PITTSBURGH — CHIC

BUCKLES

TRADE

9
HOSTEEN COHAY:
"MISTER COFFEE"

Long before the manufacturer of a coffee maker thought of capitalizing upon the popularity of Joe DiMaggio by dubbing him "Mr. Coffee" to advertise the product, the Navajos knew about "Mister Coffee": *Hosteen Cohay*—"Mister Coffee" in the Navajo tongue—was Arbuckles' Ariosa, and nothing else would do.

Only briefly during John Arbuckle's fight with the sugar trust was the dominance of Ariosa challenged. Sales people from the Woolson Spice Company spread the story on New Mexico and Arizona Indian reservations that because of the picture of a lion on the Lion Coffee package those who drank the potion would attain the strength of a lion. Mose Drachman, the Arbuckles' representative for the area, countered the attack.

He assembled Indian chiefs. Were they not aware, he asked, that there was a picture of an angel on the Arbuckle package? Was not an angel stronger than ten thousand lions? The devout Indians switched back to Ariosa.

"If Lion wants to beat my angel they'll have to put on their label a picture of God himself," Drachman told his wife.[1]

The Navajos and Hopis drank prodigious quantities of coffee, well-sweetened. They liked it strong and black, boiled in the pot. A blackened coffeepot was a perpetual fixture on a bed of cedar coals in every hogan or outdoor summer camp. Every visitor received a cup of coffee and perhaps a piece of fried bread if it was close to mealtime.

Indian trader Joseph Schmedding spent seven years at the Keams Canyon trading post in Arizona. He learned that it did not pay to attempt to substitute other brands for Arbuckles' Ariosa, even if they were cheaper. If the Indians could not get Ariosa they would buy no coffee at all.[2]

Wool, sheep, skins, and rugs were the principal mediums of exchange. During the Depression years of 1930-33, when Navajos asked why they

*Mose Drachman convinced the Navajos that Arbuckles' Ariosa angel
was stronger medicine than the picture of a lion on the Lion Coffee package,
and Arbuckles' Ariosa emerged the premier brand on the reservation.*

got so little for their products, the expression *"Peso Etin* (no money) in Washington" was the answer. During lean times, a good five-foot square rug brought about six dollars, and a nine-by-twelve-foot not over twenty dollars. However, in those days Arbuckles' coffee was twenty cents a pound and a twenty-five-pound sack of flour sold for a dollar. The Indians supplemented a steady diet of mutton and goat meat with fried bread and Arbuckles' Ariosa. Traders at isolated posts had to buy hundreds of rugs and truck them to dealers in Gallup, Winslow, and Flagstaff.

After the Roosevelt administration established the Civilian Conservation Corps, the Navajos brought in their checks to shop for luxuries such as canned peaches and pears, and the traders told them, *"Peso doh-haiyui* (much money) in Washington."[3]

During the heyday of the coupon redemption campaign, a traveler on the Navajo reservation visited the homes of a number of Indian traders. He noticed a similarity in furnishings—dishes, lace curtains, cooking utensils, silverware, bedspreads. He asked if all these items came from the same wholesale house. The wife of the trader at Inscription House Trading Post in Arizona explained:

"Traders' living quarters at posts are furnished with signature premium coupons that come on packages of Mr. Arbuckle's coffee. If it weren't for Mr. Arbuckle, we would have to do without many nice things out here in the back country."[4]

Traders bought the coupons back from the Indians for a stick of candy or a penny and redeemed them for home furnishings and stock for their shelves. Stock for stores included steel files, butcher knives, baby blankets, towels, gloves, and piece goods— better quality merchandise than they could get from wholesalers. The traders sent coupons to the Arbuckles Notion Department in bundles of eight to ten thousand. However, Maurice Kildare remembered one Navajo who had saved his coupons and wanted to order from the premium catalogue. He turned the pages until he found a picture of a simple wedding band:

"Get me that," he said. "I want my wife to wear one just like a white woman!"[5]

Beginning a couple of months before the end of the school term in June, the Indians would begin to save their coupons in order to have money with which to treat their children on their return from the government schools. They exchanged their signatures for nickels and dimes. They met the buses bringing their children home from the schools and gave them money with which to buy apples, oranges, gum, candy, and soda pop. The coupons were also a common medium of exchange used by young men at squaw dances to pay the forfeit when they were chosen to dance by girls.[6]

Arbuckles' coupons became legal tender on the reservation. When a trading post changed hands, the inventory included the number of signatures on hand, valued at a penny each. Initially, Arbuckles coupons were printed on coffee packages without a value designation, but when merchants in the West began to use them as legal tender in place of small change, the value designation was added to prevent overcharging.

On one occasion a Navajo bought a two-hundred-dollar Studebaker wagon from the trader at the Inscription House post. After the Indian sold his wool in the spring, he still lacked ninety- two dollars to pay off his debt, but he promised that he would be back in four days. He was. On the evening of the fourth day he came in and threw a bulging flour sack on the counter.

"There it is!" The bag contained 9,200 Arbuckles coupons.[7]

On one occasion a new trader on the scene decided he was going to corner the Navajo trade in his area. He started paying two cents for "Arbuckle Bros." signatures instead of the officially established value. This did not set well with his nearest competitor, a trader of many years' experience. The old hand prepared a mixture of lampblack and kerosene. Then, by using the unprinted areas of Arbuckles' sacks, he managed to counterfeit several thousand coupons which he gave to the Navajos to sell to the upstart trader. Shortly after the new trader sent the bogus signatures to the Notion Department of Arbuckle Brothers, a representative of the firm called at his trading post to learn why anyone would counterfeit something worth only a penny, and the trader stopped buying coupons from Navajos at any price. Shortly after that, the "Arbuckle Bros." signature was printed against a mottled red background to forestall counterfeiting.[8]

A price war erupted between the Inscription House post and a competitor twenty miles away at Shonto. At that time Arbuckles coffee was wholesaling at forty-eight cents a pound or forty- eight dollars a case, plus five dollars freight from Flagstaff. Traders sold the coffee at sixty cents a pound. In order to garner more business, the Shonto trader began to sell Ariosa as a loss-leader, three packages for a dollar, less than the wholesale cost, claiming this brought in customers and he could recoup the loss on other merchandise.

Gladwell Richardson, the Inscription House trader, told about bringing the errant Shonto trader back into line. He gave his Navajo friends the largest rugs he had and sent them to Shonto to barter for coffee in case lots. It was late fall, when Navajos laid in supplies for the winter, so the Shonto trader did not get suspicious of the sudden rush of business. It took two months for the proprietor of the Shonto post to wise up. In the meantime, the Inscription House trader filled his warehouse with coffee at a price much below the wholesale cost.[9]

Arbuckles coffee crates were even more important on the Indian res-

ervations of the Southwest than elsewhere in the West. Charles G.
Newcomb, a long-time trader, told of his arrival at a lonely trading post:

> The store building and living quarters were made of logs and
> were about twenty by sixty feet and maybe eight feet high—hard
> to tell, as the sand had drifted so heavily up against the walls.
> There was the store, rug room, wareroom, living room, two bed-
> rooms and a kitchen—all under a flat roof of sheet iron. The
> barn, henhouse, woodshed, and the other little house were made
> either wholly or partially of Arbuckle coffee boxes, roofed with
> sheet iron.
>
> Next to the tin can, Arbuckle coffee boxes did more for the
> Southwest than anything. They were nice big boxes with wide,
> smooth boards. Most traders opened them very carefully so they
> would not split the boards. As the Navajos hardly ever bought
> any coffee but Arbuckles, traders generally had enough boards
> on hand; so if the trader's wife suddenly wanted a henhouse,
> porch, or wash shed, the lumber was right there to build it with.[10]

A fine example of a wall paneled with Arbuckle crates has survived
in the storeroom of the Red Lake Trading Post—now called Old Red
Lake Trading Post—on the Navajo Reservation near Tonalea, Arizona.
The post was established in 1881, in the northwest corner of the reserva-
tion. It moved to its present location in 1891 under the ownership of the
Babbitt Brothers Trading Company of Flagstaff.

The storeroom wall, a melange of boards from Arbuckle crates, dis-
plays countless signatures and brands of customers at the trading post.
Zane Grey visited the store periodically, and the first chapter of his novel
Rainbow Trail (1915) is set at the Red Lake Trading Post.

An Arbuckles shipping case was the most prized gift an Indian trader
could bestow upon an expectant mother. In one case a new mother
brought her baby girl in to show a trader, on a carrier made of Arbuckle
boards. The trader pointed to the letters "Ariosa" and said that would
be a nice name for the baby. The mother agreed. However, her daughter went through life with her name pronounced "Aliosa," because the
Navajos could not make the "r" sound.[11]

It was often noted that a Navajo baby began its life in a cradle made
of Arbuckles boxes and, if the baby died, the cradle was immediately
converted into a coffin. Arbuckles cases were frequently used to make
coffins for adults. The late Dr. Irving McNeil, a long-time reservation
physician, told of his experiences:

I have seen adults buried in many a coffin built of wood from Arbuckles boxes, and more often than not a package of coffee would be put into the coffin along with other personal effects to ease the trip to the Happy Hunting Ground. I remember one time, a woman was watching as the lid was about to be nailed on her husband's coffin. Suddenly, she stopped the proceedings, grabbed out the package of coffee and ran to a coffee grinder in the kitchen. She poured the beans into the hopper, ground them, and put the coffee back into the bag, tears streaming all the while. "He never likes to grind coffee," she explained.[12]

Archaeologist Albert E. Ward, director of the Center for Anthropological Studies in Albuquerque, is an ardent student of Arbuckles coffee memorabilia, in part because of his love of things western and in part because of their archaeological and historical value. During his work of supervising the excavation and documentation of historic Navajo sites, ahead of oncoming construction projects, he learned to use Arbuckles coffee cans and crates to help date the earlier abandoned sites. He also found that the wooden crates were commonly used for Navajo caskets, and has reported several examples for the ethnographic literature. One grave contained the body of a child buried in an Arbuckles coffee crate, complete with grave offerings. If Ward could establish from markings on a crate the window of time during which that crate was used, he could make a closer estimate of the date of burial.[13]

Though few were aware of it at the time, April 6, 1914, was a sad day for the Indian traders and their customers. That was when the Interstate Commerce Commission ruled that railroads could no longer discriminate against the use of fiber boxes. Prior to that, railroads charged a penalty on merchandise shipped in cardboard boxes. Both railroads and lumber interests fought the measure to no avail; the newly burgeoning fiber box industry won. General Foods Corporation, which soon acquired a number of Arbuckle Brothers' brands, switched to cardboard shipping containers.[14]

Worse and more of it, the familiar paper bags of Arbuckles' Ariosa were on the way out, to be replaced by coffee in metal canisters. During World War II, life for the Navajos changed as they obtained work on and off the reservations, as they augmented their lives with radios, washing machines, and cars and trucks. The trading posts changed. Gladwell Richardson told about his return after the war:

> The first day I walked into Inscription House Trading Post after the war, the change had moved far toward what it was to become. One thing proving it most was the absence of a particular

In this 1880s photography of the Hubbell Trading Post's storeroom Lorenzo Hubbell is seated on a sack of wool. The photograph shows sacks of flour, Arbuckles coffee crates, pelts, wool sacks, horse trappings, etc. (Courtesy U.S. Department of the Interior, National Park Service, Hubbell Trading Post NHS, HUTR 2178)

Arbuckles coffee crates on display in the visitors' center of the old Hubbell Trading Post at Ganado, Arizona. (Courtesy U.S. Department of the Interior, National Park Service, Hubbell Trading Post NHS)

item on the shelves. Vacuum-packed coffee in all sizes of containers and assorted brands occupied space once filled with ground and whole-bean Arbuckle Brothers Ariosa Coffee. The absence of the Navajo's long favorite *Hosteen Cohay* (Arbuckle Coffee) seemed to signal the end of the glamorous, even romantic period of adventurous barter-trading.[15]

One of the most historic trading posts on the Navajo reservation was the Hubbell Trading Post at Ganado, Arizona. John Lorenzo Hubbell began trading with the Indians in Ganado in 1876. He was Don Lorenzo to the whites; Old Mexican or Double Glasses to the Navajos. Besides being a merchant-trader, Hubbell guided the Navajos in their problem of understanding the ways of white men. He translated and wrote letters for them, settled family quarrels, explained government policy, and helped the sick. He influenced Navajo rugweaving and silversmithing by promoting excellence in craftsmanship.

As a result, Hubbell built a trading empire that included stage and freight lines as well as trading posts. At various times, he and his two sons owned twenty-four trading posts, a wholesale house in Winslow, Arizona, and other businesses and ranch properties. He participated in politics, helping guide Arizona to statehood. He died November 12, 1930, and was buried on Hubbell Hill, overlooking the trading post he had started more than half a century before.

The Hubbell Trading Post still operates, now as a National Historic Site, administered by the National Park Service. About the only difference is that, like many other trading posts, it is self-service. Today Navajos who patronize the old post are joined by tourists from across the nation. The tourists study turquoise-studded silver earrings, bracelets, and necklaces with an eye to purchase, while Navajo customers frequent the jewelry cases in appreciation of the craftsmanship of their fellow artisans.

Hosteen Cohay is no longer available from the grocery shelf of the Hubbell Trading Post, but it is honored by an exhibit in the middle of the lobby of the visitors' center to the historic site. The exhibit consists of Arbuckles' Ariosa crates and memorabilia.

Somewhere in the Great Beyond or the Happy Hunting Ground—depending upon which of the participants are white eyes or long- hairs—there must be a campfire around which are gathered Navajos, Indian traders, cowmen, and homesteaders. The homesteaders are arguing with the cowmen about whether eggshells or a dash of cold water is better to settle coffee grounds in a freshly boiled pot, and the Navajos and Indian traders are lamenting the replacement of Hosteen Cohay with an abomination of weak-kneed blends of vacuum-packed coffee.

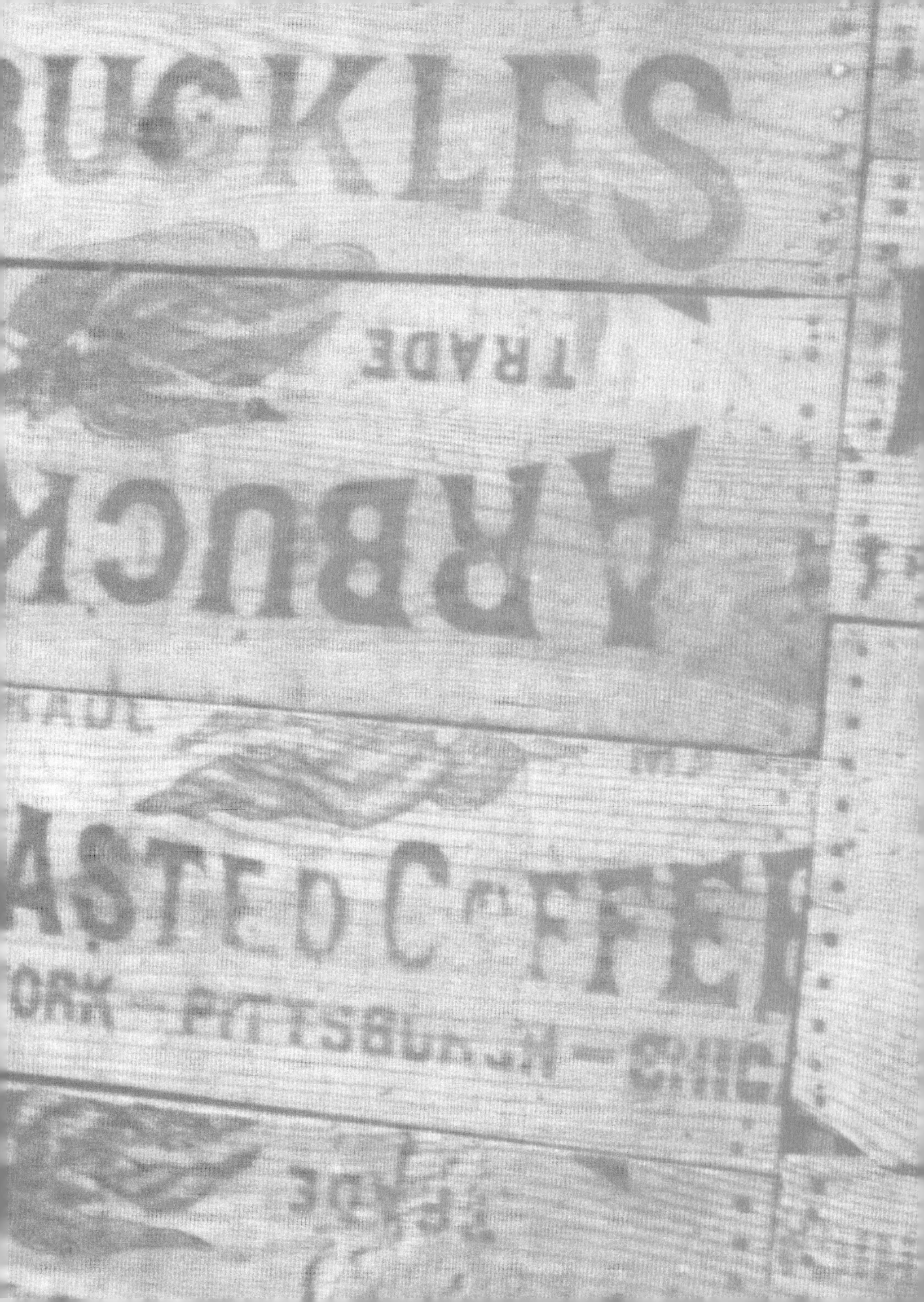
UCKLES
TRADE
PITTSBURGH

10
ARBUCKLES COFFEE TRADE CARDS

Tradesmen's cards, or trade cards as they are more commonly called, originated in Great Britain during the seventeenth century and came into general use during the eighteenth century. Initially they were printed on sheets of paper of varying size. The front announced the trader's name, his sign and his address or location, and a listing of his wares or services. In some cases, the back of the sheet did double duty as an accounting or billing form, with space to show from whom the dealer purchased or to whom he sold merchandise. The reinforced variety on pasteboard was not generally used until the Victorian era, although a few examples date from as early as 1780.

The dealer's sign, usually a hanging sign projecting out over the street in front of his business establishment, was the equivalent of today's trademark or logo. A shop's location would be designated by such statements as "at the Sign of the Black Boy, and Hatt, near Red Lion Street, in High Holbourn, London." As their supports deteriorated, hanging signs became a hazard to wayfarers. In London, hanging signs were abolished in 1762, when numbering of buildings and houses began to take their place. Gradually, merchants succumbed to the newfangled notion of numbering. After that, shopkeepers illustrated trade cards with pictures of their business establishments and items of their trade.

Trade cards are of historical, ethnological, and sociological interest. They reflect changes in fashion and architecture, show industrial development, and depict social customs, attitudes, and prejudices.[1]

The first printed advertisement in the English language for coffee appeared in 1652, in the form of a shop-bill or handbill for London's first coffee house: "Made and Sold in *St. Michaels Alley* in *Cornhill*, by *Pasqua Rosée*, at the Signe of his own Head." The handbill was more in the nature of ballyhoo for a patent medicine than an advertisement for coffee as a social drink. It promised coffee would cure dropsy, gout, scurvey, the King's Evil, and other ailments. A copy is preserved in the British Museum. The complete text is reproduced in Appendix A.

In the American colonies, shopkeepers began to announce the availability of coffee as early as 1714, generally included among a list of items such as teas, spices, almonds, rum, and brandy. In 1790, the first newspaper advertisement in the United States solely for coffee appeared in a New York paper:

New Coffee Manufactory.
Highly necessary in this City,

The subscriber informs the public that he has provided himself with proper utensils at a considerable expence, to burn, grind and clarify Coffee on the European plan, so as to give general satisfaction; this useful Manufactory would save the inhabitants, on reflection, considerable, in that article, as it is often thro' want of knowledge or wrong management injured and spoiled by trusting to careless servants; whereas one making it his business to serve the citizens with coffee ready prepared would be able to make it better and sell it cheaper than it could be bought in the grain, besides loss of time, waste and expence. This undertaking invites the public to try the experiment, as it may be had in pots of various sizes from one to twenty weight, well packed down either for sea or family use, so as to keep good for twelve months, and be clear, strong and well tasted, from a proper receipt. Apply at No. 4, Great Dock Street. Feb. 9.[2]

This was virtually the same approach John Arbuckle would take almost a century later in the first multicolored handbill for packaged coffee.

In colonial America, the trend in trade cards followed the pattern set in England. They were chiefly copper-plate engravings with an occasional wood-block print, usually simple lettering announcing the name of the tradesman with occasionally a vignette to illustrate the goods sold or the service performed. One of the earliest was an engraving by Paul Revere portraying a bell and cannon and advertising "Paul Revere & Son, At their Bell and Cannon foundry, at the North Part of Boston."[3] Subsequently, as a copper-plate engraver, Paul Revere designed and printed trade cards for a number of colonial business establishments.[4]

With the development of lithography, trade cards became elaborate, extravagantly drawn and highly colored. They were made expressly to be collected. Most were designed to appeal to children, but young and old collected and treasured them. They were included in containers of staples obtained from the grocery store, given in exchange for coupons included in the packages, or doled out by the grocer. Victorian parlor tables would contain a scrapbook of trade cards along with the inevitable family Bible, a family album, and a postcard album.

The backs of cards issued by the New Orleans Coffee Company noted: "Your Grocer will present *FREE* with each pound of our *Fine Bulk Coffees* one handsome Souvenir Art Gem like sample (100 varieties) and it is a guarantee that you receive the Celebrated Genuine French Market Roasted Coffees." On the backs of other cards, the New Orleans Coffee Company attempted to fight the effect of John Arbuckle's glazing process:

French Market Roasted Coffee
HAS STOOD THE TEST OF
POPULAR APPROVAL.
A PERFECT BLEND.
NO GLAZING.
GLAZING ONLY ADDS TO THE WEIGHT OF COFFEE AND
DETRACTS FROM THE DRINKING QUALITIES.
ABSOLUTELY PURE.

Arbuckle Brothers countered the claims for French Market Coffee on the backs of their Ariosa trade cards:

GRIND YOUR COFFEE AT HOME.

It will pay you well to keep a small coffee-mill in your kitchen and grind your coffee just as you use it, one mess at a time. Coffee should not be ground until the coffee-pot is ready to receive it. Coffee will lose more of the strength and aroma in one hour after being ground than in six months before being ground. So long as

ARIOSA

remains in the whole berry, our glazing, composed of choice eggs and pure confectioners' A sugar, closes the pores of the coffee, and thereby are retained all the original strength and aroma.

ARIOSA COFFEE

has during 25 years set the standard for all other roasted coffees. So true is this that other manufacturers, in recommending their goods, have known no higher praise than to say, "It's just as good as Arbuckles'."

The McLaughlin Coffee Company also used their trade cards to go to bat for glazed coffee. Their glazing compound of corn starch and rectified sugar settled coffee grounds and was "perfectly healthful." Not using eggs realized a saving of from five to ten cents a pound, they said. For a two-cent stamp and the fronts of twelve XXXX coffee wrappers, one could get a set of twelve National Pictures "without any printing" in the shape of an album, "an ornament in every house." Another series of McLaughlin cards warned against unglazed coffee:

> Coffee is a vegetable fibre containing oil known as caffeine. This oil makes the taste and smell of coffee and evaporates quickly after the coffee is roasted. When the oil has evaporated nothing remains but a woody substance. The glazing on XXXX seals the pores of the coffee and prevents the oil from evaporating. If you wish to buy coffee, buy XXXX which is glazed. If you want to buy wood, ask for an unglazed coffee that has lost most of its oil.

Trade cards fell into four general categories: First, simple "business cards": printed announcements of the manufacturer, wholesaler, or dealer. Second, similar business cards with portrayals of the place of business or wares; some of these also had colorful lithographs on the reverse sides, often pictures from the lithographer's stock which had no relationship to the business being advertised. Third, extravagantly colored illustrations of the place of business or wares to be sold. Fourth, colorful lithographs of subjects or scenes which had no bearing on the business but which appealed to collectors.[5]

Issuance in numbered sets encouraged collectors to try to complete their collections. The McLaughlin Coffee Company may have set the record for a single series with 225 cards portraying children engaged in assorted wholesome activities.[6] In a special appeal to children, McLaughlin's produced die-cut cardboard dolls, nursery story characters, and animals with flaps which could be bent to make stands for them. For Lion Coffee, the Woolson Spice Company issued seasonal greeting cards: Easter, Christmas, and Midsummer. The backs bore a legend: "These Beautiful Easter Greetings are found only in the one pound packages of Lion Coffee." The front was unsullied by advertising.

Arbuckle Brothers featured Noah's Ark, a handsome set of die-cut animals obtainable as a premium with signatures from Arbuckles' packages. The set consisted of twelve pairs—elephants, camels, deer, horses, cattle, donkeys, goats, lions, bears, tigers, dogs, and cats—ranging downward in size from the seven-inch elephant. The colorful display stretched across many a Victorian era mantel.

The Woolson Spice Company countered Arbuckle Brothers' trade cards with holiday greeting cards and eventually implemented a premium program, giving premiums in exchange for lion's heads cut from Lion Coffee packages.

The American Indian, having long served in European art as a symbol of America, became important on trade cards in the portrayal of trade and commerce and the resources of America. Indians became such an exotic, romanticized abstraction for so many Americans that they were a natural vehicle for advertising, often portrayed in incongruous manners and situations.

The Indian Princess emerged as an allegorical figure in the American colonies, perhaps as an outgrowth of the Pocahontas story, and was used to lend credence to assorted products. Purveyors of patent medicines capitalized upon the Indians' communion with nature to promote various potions and remedies on the assumption that their efficacy stemmed from secrets which had been learned from Indians.[7]

About 1880, Libby, McNeill & Libby Meat Products produced a trade card to advertise corned beef which has to be an all-time front-runner for poor taste in advertising. It portrays a ravaged covered wagon. One of the erstwhile occupants is lying on the ground with an arrow sticking from his chest. In the foreground gloating Indians are pillaging a box of corned beef, declaring it to be "Heap Good."

In one of a series of trade cards entitled "History of the Sports and Pastimes of all Nations," Arbuckle Brothers described Indians as having admirable traits:

AMERICAN INDIANS

No hardier or more rugged race than the Indians of North America ever existed. Their endurance and tenacity were more than human, their stoicism was remarkable, their courage shrank from nothing, and their skill and agility were the development of generations of outdoor life. They were nomads, and dwelt in tents and often changed their habitations. Their sports and pastimes were of outdoor character, and many in number. In hunting and fishing they employed canoes.

Canoes were made either of birch bark or of hollow logs, and in the extreme West of cedar logs with extended prows and curious figures painted on the sides. They were propelled by paddles, and glided noiselessly and swiftly down the forest-fringed streams.

Foot-racing was universally popular, and so too was horse and pony-racing.

Hunting the buffalo was the favorite sport of the chase. Of all game this was the most exciting and dangerous to attack. Bears, panthers and the numerous other denizens of the wilds fell prey to the Indians skill, but none were so welcome as the shaggy monster of the plains.

La Crosse, now universally adopted by the Canadians, was played by the Indians from a very early time. Two sides of twelve each were chosen. Each player was armed with a stick or crosse—an implement somewhat like a racket in tennis, but longer. At each end of the playing field were two goals. Each side facing one of these and its object was to propel a solid rubber ball through the opponent's goal. The war-dance, principal of their terpsichorean exercises was more horrible than graceful, and suggested the sanguinary atrocities of bloodshed. The Indian was the original smoker of tobacco and the pipe (Calumet) their peace offering.

During the westward expansion from 1880 until 1889, as the railroads brought civilization and settlers to the American West, the farmer and the western settler became prime subjects for trade-card illustrations, most often portraying serenity and pastoral beauty which bore little resemblance to the actuality of life in the West, not by intent but because most trade cards were produced by Eastern artists who knew absolutely nothing about rural life in the West.[8]

Trade cards generated some shabby racial stereotypes and grotesque caricatures, particularly of blacks. Since before the Civil War, blacks had been a subject of white humor. Black and white minstrels portrayed the black man as a mincing, frolicking fool. By the 1870s, advertising and packaging of merchandise often showed blacks with saucer lips and bulging eyes.

Black fictional characters such as Sambo, Uncle Remus, Aunt Jemima, and Stepin Fetchit perpetuated the idea that blacks were suited only for menial jobs. Actually, it was into the 1950s before Dick Gregory and others came to the rescue of the black race as harbingers of change. Arbuckle Brothers' 1893 trade-card portrayal in the "History of the Sports and Pastimes of all Nations" series was somewhat less offensive than most characterizations of that period:

AMERICAN NEGROES

The American Negro is a child of nature, and one of the most entertaining, interesting and happy of beings. His disposition is sunny, he is a born humorist, and has an inexhaustible fund of good-nature and spirits. There is infection to laughter even in the unctuous tones of his rich voice. He is fond of display, gorgeous in his choice of colors and happy-go-lucky.

'Possum hunting is much practiced in the warmer portions of this country by the negroes. The opossum is the daintiest of dishes to their taste. To catch one requires great skill, for these animals are very tricky, and even simulate death so well, when caught, as to deceive the novice. It is the object to capture the opossum without injuring his hide, as this has a market value. 'Possums are oftenest `treed,' but they are also caught in traps; the former method is sportsmanlike, and generally requires an arduous chase.

The cake-walk is one of the most original and entertaining of amusements. This is an exhibition participated in by as many couples as may choose to compete. The idea is based upon the simple desire of being pronounced the most graceful and best of walkers. Human nature is so constituted that this challenge is accepted by most of the young negroes of a community. Judges are appointed, and before them pass in serious and sober fashion, to the accompaniment of music, couple after couple. They award the prize, a cake, to the best deserving, to the envy of the rest.

The banjo is the favorite instrument of the negro and adds to gayety of his home life in his cabin. Here while thrumming the notes, and beating time with his foot, he teaches his young pickaninnies to make their crude steps in harmony with the music. The bones and the tambourine, rude and elementary as they are, played by negroes as accompaniments to their vocal music, add much that is pleasing to the effect.

Most principal manufacturers of foods and household staples issued trade cards. The concept of the "insert card" was borrowed from highly successful European firms during the last two decades of the nineteenth century. Most American firms included pictures of their products in illustrations on their cards. Some coffee companies, including Arbuckle Brothers, were unique in using only the backs of their cards to proclaim the superiority of their brands.

John Arbuckle joined the trend during the mid-1880s with trade cards for his Ariosa brand. He put Henry E. Smyser to work developing a packaging machine capable of "automatically inserting a card or a sheet into the package in upright position alongside the material therein." (Appendix B-14)

While John Arbuckle did not originate the idea of the trade card, he certainly improved upon it. Early trade cards were unnumbered series: Children at play, smacking of the Victorian era; fruits without recipes; birds; boats; flowers; colorfully uniformed individuals and British horsemen and women; miscellaneous scenes, mostly British such as Kirkstall Abbey, Cuckfield in Sussex, and the Old Norman Staircase of King's School in the Cathedral Precincts at Canterbury; and religious scenes illustrating Bible verses and passages from *The Pilgrim's Progress*.

An early series consisted of cartoons taken from various joke magazines of the era. A second series likewise consisted of jokes from such publications as *Judge, Puck*, and *Texas Siftings*, but differed from the first in that they carried a line "From _____ by permission." It can be assumed that Arbuckle received complaints from publishers for failure to get permission to use their material.

There was no mention of coffee on the fronts of these cards, but the backs of most were filled with advertising—the "four points" which for fifty years formed the core of Arbuckle's constant advertising campaign:

Arbuckles' Ariosa Coffee
COSTS MORE AND IS WORTH
MORE THAN OTHER BRANDS OF COFFEE
W H Y ?

1st. It is made from green coffee of higher grade and better drinking quality; and it is glazed at an actual cost to us of three-eighths of a cent per pound.

2d. Its entire strength and aroma are retained by our process of glazing coffee.

3d. The ingredients used in glazing are the choicest eggs and pure confectioners' "A" sugar; in testimony of this fact, see our affidavit on each package of coffee bearing our name.

4th. The glazing, composed of eggs and sugar, not only retains the full strength and aroma of our coffee, but gives to it a richness of flavor unknown to other coffees; besides it saves the expense of eggs used in settling unglazed coffee.

BEWARE of buying low-grade package coffee, falsely purporting to be made of Mocha, Java and Rio; this being a cheap device, employed by the manufacturers, to deceive unwary consumers.

ARBUCKLE BROS. COFFEE COMPANY,

NEW YORK.

It did not take Arbuckle Brothers long to realize the value of catering to collectors by issuing trade cards in a numbered series and urging owners to complete their sets. "If you chance to get two cards of one kind, your neighbor also may have two of a kind, in which case you can exchange with each other." Encouraging exchange between collectors abetted John Arbuckle's goal of getting people to talk about Arbuckles coffee.

"And Joseph dreamed a dream, and he told it to his brethren, and they hated him yet the more."

Gen. XXXVII.5.

COPYRIGHT 1889 BY ARBUCKLE BROS. COFFEE CO.

Above: This demure Victorian serving maid portraying "coffee" in the "Cooking Notes" series to advertise Arbuckles' Ariosa is hardly what one would expect as promotion for a robust coffee which appealed to cattlemen and Indians. (Courtesy Warshaw Collection of Business Americana, Smithsonian Institution)

Top left: Arbuckle Brothers issued a colorful set of numbered bird trade cards, but the birds were neither identified nor annotated. (Courtesy Warshaw Collection of Business Americana, Smithsonian Institution)

Bottom left: "Religious Series" of trade cards may have been standard Sunday school cards converted to commercial usage. The scenes illustrate Bible verses and passages for The Pilgrim's Progress. (Courtesy Warshaw Collection of Business Americana, Smithsonian Institution)

Two series of numbered cards—1-50 and 51-100—were issued simultaneously. Thus, each package in a one-hundred-pound case of Ariosa Coffee would contain a different card. In 1889, Arbuckle Brothers issued a "State Maps" series. In addition to the ubiquitous "four points," the backs of the cards noted:

> This series of cards is at once the most interesting, instructive and artistic, yet offered as an advertisement. Every card is a study in itself, and affords an object lesson for both young and old. The series consists of fifty cards, each one of which shows a correct map (properly bounded) of one State, or Territory. The pictures illustrating the peculiar industries and scenery of the States and Territories are entirely new, and by the very best American artists.

Cards in this series omitted information about the states. That, it turned out, was available in a separate atlas which could be obtained by purchasing more Arbuckles' Ariosa.

In addition to a message extolling the value of Ariosa, the backs of some cards touted the educational value of the trade cards: "Teachers in the public schools are unanimous in their praise of object lesson cards, and pronounce them one of the happiest and most impressive mediums, for imparting instruction to all classes of students."

There is evidence that this was a successful ploy, both as a sales technique and an educational tool. In 1949, the author received a letter from Arthur Dandridge, at that time living in Kansas City, Missouri:

> Yes indeed! I remember Arbuckles coffee. When I was in the fifth grade, my parents almost drowned in it. That was back in 1889.
>
> I grew up in Wichita, Kansas. My fifth grade teacher was Miss Grove. Her father owned a grocery store and she had us getting our parents to buy Arbuckles' coffee from him for our geography lessons because each package had a little card in it with a map of a state. While we looked at the cards, Miss Grove would tell us about the state. We were studying two states a day.
>
> Well, I took down with the measles. My mother was a schoolteacher before she married my father, and she wasn't going to have me miss any schooling. She had books for Reading, Writing, and Arithmetic, but she didn't have anything to keep me up in Geography. She went to see Miss Grove, and Miss Grove said her father would give her a book that had everything in it I would need to know.

Arbuckles' Illustrated Atlas of the United States of America *containing the "State Maps" series of trade cards, was issued in 1889.* (Courtesy James E. Sherman)

The backs of some of Arbuckle Brothers' early trade cards portrayed the firm's waterfront complex and boasted of production.

He did! He sold mother a whole case of Arbuckles coffee and gave her a copy of the book Miss Grove used to tell us about the states: *Arbuckle's Illustrated Atlas of the United States of America.*

By the time mother got through reading to me and drilling me, I was able to make 95 in Geography when I got back to school. (Momma said I should have known Miss Grove would ask us about the population of Kansas.) Later, when my little sister was coming along, mother hid the book away in the attic for fear it would give her measles. The atlas has served its purpose. I would like for you to have it. I guess it won't give you measles after fifty years.[9]

It will be noted that, in addition to imparting geographical information, John Arbuckle's copywriter found a way, albeit lefthanded, to sing the praises of Arbuckles' Ariosa. The write-up about Missouri, where the Gasconade River flows, probably takes first prize: "But it is not gasconading to say that `Arbuckles' Ariosa Coffee' is the best in the world." Then there is West Virginia, where "The State is very healthy, the death rate is less than one per cent, which is largely owing to the general use of `Arbuckles' Ariosa Coffee'."

Had Mrs. Dandridge read and believed the remarkable message printed inside the back cover of the atlas, she would have known that the case of coffee she had to purchase from Grove's grocery was providing ample security not only from the spread of measles but other contagious maladies. The story purported to have been taken from the *Boston Herald:*

COFFEE AS A DISINFECTANT.
A German Physician has found out that Coffee Kills Bacteria.

An old negro living in a district where the disease often prevailed once told the writer that one of the best preventive measures against yellow fever was an infusion of coffee. Some years ago he passed through an epidemic of that grave malady under the worst possible conditions. For at least a month he occupied the quarters of a large number of sufferers, passing night and day among them, eating and sleeping in their midst.

Recalling the homely advice given him, he faithfully tried coffee as an antiseptic and drank freely of a very strong infusion five or six times a day, and continued the practice all the time he was under exposure. He was fortunate enough to escape contagion, but never attached much importance to the use of the coffee. Considering the results of recent developments, it would seem that the old negro was right in attributing antiseptic properties to it.

A series of experiments conducted by a German professor has proved that they are quite marked. Several different forms of intestinal bacteria were experimented upon, and their development and growth were found in all cases to be interfered with by the addition of a small quantity of coffee infusion to nutrient gelatin. In pure infusion the bacteria were rapidly destroyed.

The question as to what constituents exercise the antiseptic effect cannot yet be fully determined. The caffeine is certainly active in only a slight degree; the tannin to a somewhat greater extent; but, presumably, of greatest importance are the substances that are developed by roasting. It is interesting to note that a cup of coffee, left in a room for a week or more, remains almost free from micro-organisms.

Write-ups for a couple of states intimated the prophylactic effect of Arbuckles' Ariosa Coffee was saving the residents from the ravages of disease.

In 1892, Arbuckle Brothers issued a series of trade cards entitled "Pictorial History of the United States and Territories." Both the lithography and the artistry are excellent. The set was produced by Donaldson Brothers of New York, premier lithographers of the time. Unfortunately, names of the artists are unknown. Unlike the "State Maps" series, two-thirds of the back of each card in this series was devoted to a write-up of the state's history.

After the passage of a century and prior to obvious attempts by Arbuckle Brothers to court collectors by numbered cards, it is impossible to determine which groups of trade cards were planned as series and which were randomly issued, perhaps as selections from a lithographer's stock merely to appeal to purchasers and to serve as a medium for advertising on the reverse sides.

Arbuckle Brothers issued thirteen or perhaps fourteen sets of trade cards between the mid-1880s and 1893. The first five were not numbered, and the backs were entirely occupied with advertising, either the "four points" or an illustration showing Arbuckle Brothers' sprawling factory complex. There were two series of comic illustrations, one of religious illustrations, and a set devoted to sports with comic overtones. A set of bird portraits was numbered, but the birds were neither identified nor annotated. The same was true of sets portraying flowers, children, and costumes.

Beginning in 1889, except for those series which were accumulated into book form, from one-half to one-third of the backs were devoted to textual descriptions of the illustrations:

Subjects on Cooking

Numbered series 1-50 and 51-100, issued in 1889. The illustrations were either children with animals, pastoral scenes, or large illustrations of fruits, vegetables, and fish. The backs contained recipes or "cooking notes." Printed by Knapp & Co., Lith., New York.

From Arbuckle Brothers, one would have expected more attention to their product on No. 11 in the series: "Coffee." The illustration portrayed an attractive girl, presumably a housemaid, carrying a coffee service down a staircase. The back of the card contained a brief recipe for preparing Ariosa and instructions for care of the coffeepot:

Coffee

To make strong coffee, use one-half teacup of ARIOSA Coffee, add five or six (according to strength required) teacupsful of boiling water, stir the coffee and the water well at first, and then boil twenty minutes. After taking it off the stove, pour in one-quarter of a teacup of cold water and let it stand a minute, then you will have coffee as clear as amber—for ARIOSA requires nothing to settle it.

Notes

Never scour the inside of your coffee pot, as by doing so you will wear the tin off and expose the iron. A bit of iron the size of a carpet tack will render unfit to drink five gallons of the best coffee ever produced, if permitted to come into contact with the coffee after the water is put on it.

Clean the inside of your coffee pot with hot water only and dry it in the open air.

State Maps

Numbered series 51-100, issued in 1889. Maps of the states and territories of the United States surrounded by illustrations depicting activities in the states. The backs of the cards contained a list of states in the series but no descriptive text. A companion atlas contained textual material. Printed by Donaldson Brothers, New York.

Fifty Nations of the World

Numbered series 51-100, issued in 1889. Sometimes referred

to as "National Geographical." Maps of the various nations are surrounded by scenes from the nations and pictures of inhabitants in their native dress. This series was issued as a companion to the "Zoological" series. Text on the back praised the educational value of the cards but did not include information about the subjects. A separate atlas was produced: *Arbuckles' Illustrated Atlas of Fifty Principal Nations of the World*, printed by Donaldson Brothers, New York.

Zoological

Numbered series 1-50, issued in 1890. Assorted exotic animals from Aard Vark to Zebu, "a true picture drawn (drawn by an eminent artist) of one of the most interesting specimens of the animal kingdom, and giving the classical appellation, together with the English name, of each animal portrayed." This was a companion set to the "National Geographical" series. Their backs contain a list of subjects in the series, but no text regarding them. Printed by Knapp & Co., Lith., New York.

However, simultaneously Arbuckle Brothers published the *Arbuckles' Album of Illustrated Natural History* containing beautifully rendered pictures of all fifty animals in the series as well as textual descriptions of the animals and their habitats. The back pages of the book contained a brief but somewhat inaccurate history of the origin of coffee.

Views from a Trip Around the World

Numbered series 1-50, issued in 1891. Cards portray scenes from the various countries and include pictures of inhabitants in their native dress. Half of the backs are devoted to text about the subjects. Printed by Joseph P. Knapp, Lith., New York.

Pictorial History of the United States and Territories

Numbered series 1-50, issued in 1892. Cards portray scenes from the various states and territories. Half of the backs are devoted to textual matter, and titles identify the illustrations on the fronts. Printed by Donaldson Brothers, New York.

History of Sports and Pastimes of all Nations

Numbered series 1-50, issued 1893. This was the last series produced by Arbuckle Brothers. Subjects vary from portrayal of social activities to sports in the various countries. The lithography and artistry are particularly good. Two-thirds of the backs are devoted to text. Printed by Kaufmann & Strauss.

During the pre-Prohibition era, ladies of the Winona, Minnesota, WCTU trundled coffee carts through the saloon district to sober up inebriates and hopefully, wean their addiction from demon rum to caffeine. (Courtesy Winona County Historical Society)

Around the turn of the century coffee purveyors discontinued trade cards and turned their attention to using magazines in order to reach the adult population. Advertising took a rather vicious turn as manufacturers of substitutes were attempting to invade the coffee market. At one time there were almost a hundred coffee-substitute concerns engaged in a bitter campaign directed against coffee. William H. Ukers noted in his history of coffee:

> The burden of the cereal-faker's song was that coffee was the cause of all the ills that flesh is heir to, and that by stopping its use for ten days and substituting his panacea, these ills would vanish.[10]

In the meantime, coffee was getting a boost from the Women's Christian Temperance Union. During the pre-Prohibition era the ladies were using coffee to fight demon rum. They manned coffee carts to sober up inebriates. Winona, Minnesota, was a typical example. There were eighty saloons in town, and members of the WCTU circulated among them with two coffee wagons in an effort to convince patrons that the effect of caffeine was better than that of alcohol.

In the meantime the coffee industry went on the defensive: "If coffee works havoc with your nerves and digestion, it is because you are not using a fresh roasted, thoroughly cleaned, correctly cured coffee." . . . "Our coffee is free from the dust and bitter tannin—the only injurious property in coffee."

Following the turn of the century, Arbuckle Brothers advertised in such publications as *Needlecraft* and *Farm and Ranch*. For the rural audience, the thrust was on quality of the product: Arbuckles' coffee "should not be classed with the inferior imitations sold at a cent a pound less than Arbuckles'. It has a quality greatly superior to these imitations and makes many more cupfuls to the pound." Advertising directed toward female readers concentrated on the bonus of premiums available from the Notion Department.

In 1920, the Joint Coffee Trade Publicity Committee of the United States launched a campaign with series of advertisements titled "The Case for Coffee," in which they used the opinions of doctors, both dead and alive, to tout the beneficial qualities of caffeine:

> We owe to Pavlov, and other eminent seekers after psychological truth, the knowledge of the value of mental stimulation in producing the so-called "appetite juice" without which gastric digestion cannot be efficiently performed.[11]

Obviously, such messages would not fit onto the backs of three-by-five-inch trade cards. Magazines and newspapers profited, and it was well into the twentieth century before manufacturers rediscovered the avidity of trade card collectors. In 1946, the *Saturday Evening Post* published a two-page editorial signaling the return of "the card craze." Collectors were trading Frank Sinatra cards for those featuring Hedy Lamarr and eagerly seeking specimens from yesteryear.[12] Again, in 1979, The *New York Times* reported a revival of the craze: "Trade cards have long been lionized by art directors of advertising agencies and commercial artists. The boom in collecting for the general public began in the past four or five years and numbers thousands of followers today."[13]

Not long after that, advertisers rediscovered the value of courting customers, both young and old, with trade cards featuring sports figures. Today dealers in collectibles are doing a thriving business in this revival of trade cards.

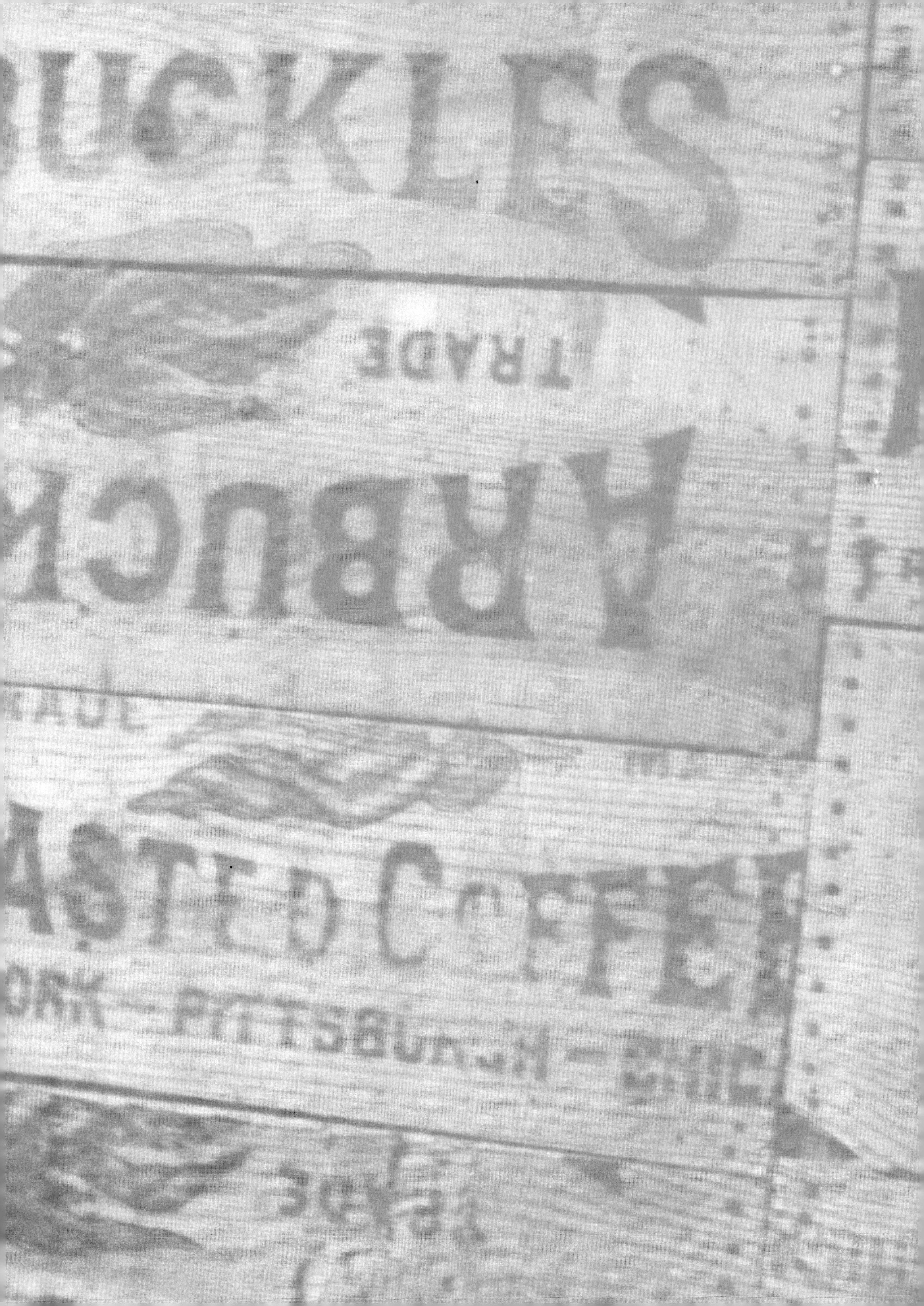
UCKLES
TRADE
ARBUC
ASTED C FFE
ORK – PITTSBURGH – CHIC

11
THE ARBUCKLES
MYSTIQUE

Arbuckles Coffee has come back to life!

The resurrection of the historic brand was accomplished in 1974 by Denney Willis and associates when they started a specialty coffee company in Harrisburg, Pennsylvannia. An employee, who later became a partner, was named Arbuckle, inspiring them to see whether the name was available for a coffee enterprise; it was and they registered it as their own. They relocated in Fort Lauderdale, Florida, then in Tucson, Arizona, where Willis and his wife, Patricia, now operate Arbuckle Coffee. [Their mailing address is P.O. Box 31176, Tucson Arizona 85751]

The contemporary Arbuckle (without the "s") enterprise does no retailing. It concentrates on preparing special blends for restaurants, coffee houses, and office coffee providers. The private blend label usually shows the name of the restaurant and "Arbuckle Coffee." In 1994 the firm was setting up new distributorships in several cities, starting with Chicago. Sales extend across the continental United States and as far away as Guam and Korea.

In 1988, around the time this book was in preparation, a Scottsdale business, Old West Outfitters, revived the Arbuckles' Ariosa brand in a coffee line prepared by Willis's wholesale house. The label carried the Arbuckle angel. Old West closed its doors, however, and the Ariosa Specialty is no longer produced.

Willis said he never found good enough art work to reproduce the Arbuckle angel to his satisfaction, so his firm developed its own logo, a steaming cup of coffee on a bed of roasted beans.

Coffee currently is produced in about forty countries, each with a dozen or more distinct regions, according to Willis. Arbuckle Coffee roasts a wide variety of specialty coffees "from Sumatra to Zimbabwe, from A to Z." For about twenty years, an agreement between producers and consuming nations kept coffee prices fairly stable, he said, but that ended under the Bush administration. Now the free market offers its

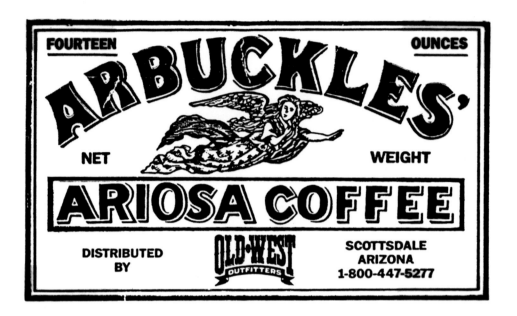

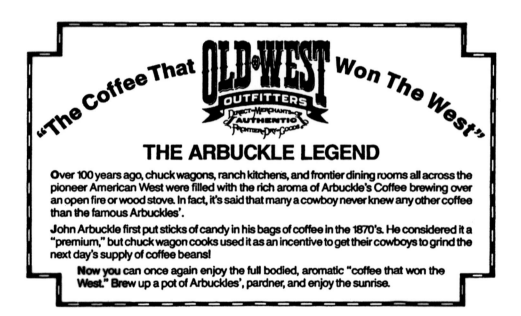

Old West Outfitters, of Scottsdale, Arizona brought Arbuckles' Ariosa back.

share of surprises in price changes.

Besides the regular wholesale customers, Arbuckle Coffee has a very dedicated group of fans. Members of the Arbuckle family hold annual reunions in several states and call Tucson beforehand to order up enough coffee for their get-togethers. They can also request tee-shirts and mugs labeled "Arbuckle" to further their drinking pleasure.

The success of the revival brings up the question, why was Arbuckle Brothers able to dominate the western market in the first place? The answer does not stem from a single reason. Perhaps it started with John Arbuckle's bold statement "Arbuckles' Ariosa Coffee costs more and is worth more than other brands of coffee." Perhaps it was the quality of the coffee. Many old-timers have testified that a pound of Arbuckles' in a three-gallon coffeepot boiling over an open fire spread an aroma that reached out for a mile or more across the prairie.

Maurice Kildare, an Indian trader at the Inscription House trading post in Arizona, attributed the success of Arbuckles among the Navajos to its strength: "They liked it blacker than mud." Across the Southwest, Arbuckles' Ariosa became known as "'Sheepherders Delight'—two cups and you *had* to walk all day. Even if he possessed nothing to eat, the Navajo always had Mr. Arbuckle's product."[1]

Dr. B. Ira Judd and John Matthews attributed the early success to the brand consciousness of Westerners: "When a man put his mark on a steer, it meant something. Arbuckles brand of coffee guaranteed 'good beans inside'."[2] Western author Matt Dodge agreed. In an article entitled "Arbuckles' Branded the West," he noted: "Without Arbuckles Coffee, no cowpuncher could have grown to manhood, and no chuck wagon could have ever bumped out on a roundup."[3]

The quality of the product was abetted by the convenience of preroasted coffee and the utility of sturdy shipping boxes which served a multitude of purposes in prairie country where wood was scarce. Innovative marketing techniques gave users a reason to select Arbuckles. Both cowboys and children could look forward to a stick of candy when the package was opened. Premiums gave users a bonus; the redemption of 108 million signature coupons a year speaks for success of the program. And the colorful trade cards added still another plus.

But what has kept the brand name alive for more than half a century after it faded from the marketplace?

In part it is because virtually every old-time ranch has had at least one Arbuckles crate on the premises as a reminder, a reminder that set old-timers to talking and passing down memories of roundups and trail-driving days. Attics have yielded scrapbooks of Arbuckles trade cards which were collected by grandmas. And rarely does one find a museum featuring Western memorabilia which does not display an

Arbuckles crate. All of this, coupled with the nostalgia which infects collectors, has made Arbuckles memorabilia prime items in antique shops across the West.

Lee Cravens of Unique Antiques in Oklahoma City, stated, "I don't know why, but anything with Arbuckles' name on it sells." Norm Sturgess, of Inland Empire Postcards in California, believes a "sense of history" has something to do with it. He noted that trade cards sell better in San Francisco than in Los Angeles because, generally speaking, people in San Francisco have a more highly developed interest in history.

Arbuckles' trade cards are back in the classroom, but John Arbuckle would shudder at the use to which they are being put. Some innovative high school history teachers are displaying examples of the "Pictorial History of the United States and Territories" series to their classes. Then they distribute copies of the historical write-ups from the backs and encourage research techniques by offering a prize to the student in a class who can find the most errors.

Collectors are variously motivated. Some of the most avid collectors of western historical relics are transplants to the West. In 1961, James E. Sherman of Tucson, Arizona, obtained a degree in mining engineering in Wisconsin and went to Arizona to pursue his profession. As a spinoff from his interest in mining, within two years Sherman and his wife were gathering material for books on ghost towns. They wrote two: one on Arizona and another on New Mexico.[4]

Sherman's interest in Arbuckles coffee was sparked during the 1970s with the discovery of a virtually intact Arbuckles' Ariosa wrapper in the underground workings of a mine at the ghost town site of Chance City, southwest of Deming, New Mexico. He was teaching engineering classes at Pima Community College in Tucson. An ancillary course in ghost towns developed into a two- semester series entitled "Living History of the Old West," covering such subjects as prospecting, the soldier's life during the Indian wars, professional medicine, and trash and bottle identification. His students get hands-on experience in areas such as chuckwagon cooking, black-powder shooting, and clothes construction. Of course, a lecture and slide show on Arbuckles coffee is part of the curriculum.

The collecting bug bites deep. Albert E. Ward, director of the Center for Anthropological Studies in Albuquerque, New Mexico, pursues Arbuckles memorabilia with a passion which far outreaches his professional interest in using antique containers to date archaeological finds. In any discussion of the subject he will lament not having purchased a rare Arbuckle Brothers' peanut butter jar when he had the opportunity.

Bill Dakan of El Dorado, Texas, operates a chuckwagon cooking enterprise and deals in antiques. When he stages a barbecue, his serving tables are supported by Arbuckles crates.

The interest of Mrs. Hollace Arbuckle Brassfield of Trenton, Missouri, was sparked by her maiden name. After she traced her ancestry back to the area of Scotland from which John Arbuckle's father emigrated, Mrs. Brassfield became an ardent collector of Arbuckles memorabilia.

Harold R. Belsher, an Arizona history buff residing in Scottsdale, has accumulated a splendid collection. His treasures include a rare sugar sack in mint condition which somehow escaped use as a dishtowel or apron. Belsher also likes to display a street sign from the intersection of Coffee and Arbuckle Drives in Sedona, Arizona, near a prominent red rock mountain known as Coffee Pot. Many years ago the developer of the property below that formation named his streets after coffee-related items, including various brands.

Indian trader Al Packard of Santa Fe, New Mexico, collects Indian pictorial rugs. One of the highlights of his collection is a rug portraying the Arbuckles flying angel. It was acquired by his father during the 1920s.

Memories of Arbuckles have survived in the vernacular of the West. For example, in the Texas Panhandle there is an expression of unknown origin used by people to indicate that they have already had too much coffee to drink. If you ask a person, particularly an old-timer from off the range, to join you at coffee, he is likely to refuse with the excuse that he has the "Arbuckle Thumps."

Tourists to Navajoland are being indoctrinated in the lore surrounding Arbuckles' Ariosa. At the Hubbell Trading Post National Historic Site, Ganado, Arizona, they find an exhibit in the visitors' center, and they can purchase replicas of the colorful package. At the Tuba City Indian Trading Post they can buy Arbuckles T-shirts and return home with the historic Flying Angel trademark emblazoned across their chests.

Arbuckles coffee continues to hold its place in Western literature. In the February 1988 issue of *The National Tombstone Epitaph*, Western poet Robert Dyer perpetuated the legendary strength of Arbuckles' coffee:

ARBUCKLE'S

Build up a good fire,

in early mornin' light.

Boil up the water

until it gets just right.

Grab up a handful

of good ol' Arbuckle's.

Toss it in, listen,

'til the water chuckles.

Pour it in your cup,

then toss a dollar in.

If the dollar floats,

it's good coffee, my friend!

In a recent novel, *Deadwood Dick and the Code of the West*, Bruce H. Thorstad dubbed his black hero Coffee Arbuckle:

"Ain't you never heard of Arbuckle's Coffee?" Coffee said, astonished. "Arbuckle's is the most famous brand there is." He shook his head wonderingly. "You had some here this morning. I drunk it all through the war—least- ways when I could get real coffee 'stead of burnt acorns. `Arbuckle Coffee, best closest to the spout,' folks say."[5]

In his award-winning Western novel, *The Homesman*, Glendon Swarthout had Mary Bee Cuddy feed the circuit-riding preacher a sumptuous meal which included Arbuckles' Ariosa:

Then she served them a feast—antelope steaks, fried potatoes, corn bread and molasses, dried-apple pie, and Arbuckles' Ariosa coffee, which his wife had informed him went for thirty-five cents the pound. When she sat down, he bowed his head. Mary Bee bowed hers.[6]

In his eulogy to coffee, western poet Wallace McRae included Arbuckles among the brands as he said:

The feller who invented coffee

Rates pretty high in my book.

You could prob'ly run the Tongue for a week

With the gallons that I've partook.[7]

Cowboy Flint Cosby may have best summed up motivation behind the Arbuckle mystique back in the 1920s on the Long S range of the south plains of Texas in a variant of the song "Make Me a Cowboy Again":

Under the star-studded canopy vast,

Arbuckles' Coffee and comfort at last;

144

Bacon that sizzles and crisps in the pan,

After the roundup smells good to a man.

Tales of the ranchman and rustlers retold,

Over the pipes as embers grow cold;

These are the tunes that memories play,

So, make me a cowboy again for a day.[8]

EDITOR'S NOTE:

Francis Fugate died unexpectedly on December 31,1992, while seated at his computer putting finishing touches on the manuscript of this book.

His lifelong interest in the subject that led to an article, published in *American West*, that won the 1984 Spur Award for Best Nonfiction Short Subject in the annual competition of Western Writers of America. Fugate was the first WWA president to serve a two-year term, 1986 to 1988, and at the time of his death was the organization's secretary-treasurer.

Born in Ottumwa, Iowa, in 1915, he was a graduate of the University of Missouri, School of Journalism. He was a writer and editor for newspapers and magazines before serving in the military during World War II. In 1949 he joined the faculty of Texas Western College (now the University of Texas at El Paso). There he taught writing and was an administrator for a research laboratory. He retired in 1978 as associate professor emeritus of English.

Fugate's first book was also the first publication to carry the imprint of Texas Western Press, still the publishing arm of the University of Texas at El Paso. The 1952 work, *The Spanish Heritage of the Southwest*, was illustrated by José Cisneros and marked the beginning of the author's long association with Carl Hertzog, founder of the press and internationally known book designer. Fugate also wrote *Frontier College*, a history of Texas Western College, designed by Hertzog, and annotated another Hertzog-designed book, *The King Ranch* by Tom Lea. In collaboration with his wife, Roberta, he wrote a book about Erle Stanley Gardner's writing techniques and roadside histories of New Mexico and Oklahoma. She preceded him in death in 1991.

With Roberta's passing, Fugate lost interest in writing projects he had set aside during her illness, among them a book about Arbuckles. But when he started to get rid of various files, he discovered she had amassed much more information on coffee than he had known about—so he changed his plan and got to work on the book. Their daughter, Roberta Treece of Frederick, Maryland, cooperated with Texas Western Press in seeing that her parents' goal of publishing the story of Arbuckles was realized.

Nancy Hamilton

BUCKLES

TRADE

ARBUCK

ASTED C FFEE

ORK — PITTSBURGH — CHIC

BUCK

TRADE

Color Illustrations

Arbuckles' Ariosa coffee in one-pound packages.

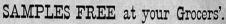

These Arbuckle Brothers' handbills from about 1872 were the first use of color in advertising a packaged coffee. (Photos by James E. Sherman)

Top: About 1880 the White Steamer Company of New York, capitalized on summer weather conditions by issuing a trade card which compared the plight of children who remained in the city with those who took a White Steamer to Rockaway Beach. (Courtesy Prints and Photographs Division, Library of Congress)

Bottom: Arbuckle Brothers' first two series of trade cards were jokes reprinted from various publications.

Above and right: Typical Arbuckle Brother's Trade cards in the 1889 "Cooking Notes" series featured large illustrations of fish, vegetables, and fruits. These three contained instructions for preparing tomatoes, lemons, and salmon on the reverse sides.

ARBUCKLE'S
Ariosa Coffee

COSTS MORE AND IS WORTH MORE THAN OTHER BRANDS OF COFFEE.

WHY?

1st. It is made from green coffee of higher grade and better drinking quality, and it is glazed at an actual cost to us of three-eighths of a cent per pound.

2d. Its entire strength and aroma are retained by our process of glazing coffee.

3d. The ingredients used in glazing are the choicest eggs and pure confectioners' "A" sugar; in testimony of this fact, see our affidavit on each package of coffee bearing our name.

4th. The glazing, composed of eggs and sugar, not only retains the full strength and aroma of our coffee, but gives to it a richness of flavor unknown to other coffees; besides it saves the expense of eggs used in settling unglazed coffee.

BEWARE of buying low-grade package coffees, falsely purporting to be made of Mocha, Java and Rio—this being a cheap device, employed by the manufacturers, to deceive unwary consumers.

ARBUCKLE BROS.

Coffee Company,

NEW YORK.

KNAPP & CO. LITH. N.Y.

No. 37

COOKING NOTES.

Lemon.

LEMON PIE.—One large lemon; grate off only the yellow and squeeze all the juice. Then add one teacup heaping full of sugar, one teacup and a quarter of water, a pinch of salt, a half teacup of raisins and two teaspoonsful of corn starch. Have upper and lower crust.

Top crust: two teacupsful of flour, one-half teaspoonful of salt, two-thirds teacupful of lard. Rub all together till mixed thoroughly, then add cold water, teaspoonful at a time, being careful to get it just moist enough to roll without adding more flour, and don't knead or press it more than just to get it together to roll it.

LEMON PUDDING.—Wash half a pound of butter till all the salt is extracted, then mix it well with half a pound of powdered white sugar and a wine-glass of brandy (wine may be used, but it is not as good); grate the rinds of three ordinary size lemons, squeeze their juice; beat together six fresh eggs and stir them into the butter and sugar, after which add the prepared lemons. Lay a border of puff paste around the pudding dish, then bake from half to three-quarters of an hour. Serve it cold, and grate over it white sugar mixed with a little nutmeg. The latter ingredient, however, is not generally preferred.

LEMON CAKE.—Whip well two and a half cups of sugar and one-half cup of butter; stir in three well-beaten eggs, one grated lemon, a little mace, four cups of flour, one cup of milk, in which a teaspoonful of super-carbonate of soda has been dissolved; mix this well, and bake immediately, half an inch thick, in buttered tins.

LEMONS can be purchased at almost any season in the year, and are grown mostly in the West Indies and Mediterranean Islands.

151

This is one of a Series of 50 different Subjects on Cooking.

ARBUCKLE'S
Ariosa Coffee

COSTS MORE AND IS
WORTH MORE THAN OTHER
BRANDS OF COFFEE.

WHY?

1st. It is made from green coffee of higher grade and better drinking quality, and it is glazed at an actual cost to us of three-eighths of a cent per pound.

2d. Its entire strength and aroma are retained by our process of glazing coffee.

3d. The ingredients used in glazing are the choicest eggs and pure confectioners' "A" sugar; in testimony of this fact, see our affidavit on each package of coffee bearing our name.

4th. The glazing, composed of eggs and sugar, not only retains the full strength and aroma of our coffee, but gives to it a richness of flavor unknown to other coffees; besides it saves the expense of eggs used in settling unglazed coffee.

BEWARE of buying low-grade package coffee, falsely purporting to be made of Mocha, Java and Rio—this being a cheap device, employed by the manufacturers, to deceive unwary consumers.

ARBUCKLE BROS.

Coffee Company,

NEW YORK.

KNAPP & CO. LITH. N.Y.

COOKING NOTES.

Rabbit.

RABBIT STEW.—Skin a pair of rabbits, and cut in small pieces, keeping the blood that is found inside. Take a good-sized pot, put in half a pound of bacon, cut in half inch squares; let it brown nicely, and then put in the rabbit, a heaping teaspoon of salt, about seven cloves, seven allspice, seven black peppers and two bay leaves. Let it boil for half an hour, stirring often. Then add two cups of boiling water, one cup of red wine and the blood from rabbit. Let it boil one and one-half hours more. Before serving, add browned flour enough to thicken the sauce.

LARDED RABBIT.—After removing its skin and head, divide the body into joints; lard with slips of fat pork, put into a frying pan and fry until half done. In the meantime prepare some strained gravy, made from veal or beef. Put the rabbit into a saucepan with a little sweet herb, minced onion and pepper, over which put a tight cover, and stew for about half an hour. Then take out the rabbit and lay in a hot covered dish. Strain the gravy, add a tablespoonful of butter, juice of a lemon, and thicken with flour; and after boiling this pour it over the meat.

RABBIT PIE.—Take two small rabbits, cut them into joints, and lay them in a saucepan with two carrots, two onions, garlic, a bunch of herbs and a pound of pickled pork (the belly). Boil in a very little water for half an hour; take out the rabbits and drain them, also drain the pork and place it at the bottom of a well-buttered pie-dish, and then lay the pieces of rabbit in it. Pour on a wine-glass full of Sauterne or other wine, and strew over it a little spice. Pour in some good batter, and bake in a quick oven for half an hour. Reduce the liquor in which it was cooked, and add the strained juice of a lemon. The sauce should be handed with it.

No. 3

Other trade cards in the "Cooking Notes" series featured either pastoral scenes or children involved with the subjects of the foods treated on the backs.
This little girl obviously does not know that her trusting pet rabbit can be turned into rabbit stew, larded rabbit or rabbit pie.

This is one of a Series of 50 different Subjects on Cooking.

ARBUCKLE'S

Ariosa Coffee

COSTS MORE AND IS
WORTH MORE THAN OTHER
BRANDS OF COFFEE.

WHY?

1st. It is made from green coffee of higher grade and better drinking quality, and it is glazed at an actual cost to us of three-eighths of a cent per pound.

2d. Its entire strength and aroma are retained by our process of glazing coffee.

3d. The ingredients used in glazing are the choicest eggs and pure confectioners' "A" sugar; in testimony of this fact, see our affidavit on each package of coffee bearing our name.

4th. The glazing, composed of eggs and sugar, not only retains the full strength and aroma of our coffee, but gives to it a richness of flavor unknown to other coffees; besides it saves the expense of eggs used in settling unglazed coffee.

BEWARE of buying low-grade package coffee, falsely purporting to be made of Mocha, Java and Rio—this being a cheap device, employed by the manufacturers, to deceive unwary consumers.

ARBUCKLE BROS.

Coffee Company,

NEW YORK.

COOKING NOTES.

Milk.

This is an article that all of us are, or have been at some stage in our lives, familiar with, and there is practically little that can be said about its various uses but what is already quite well known in every household in the land. A few words, however, from the advice of a prominent physician, in reference to the use of milk in a medical way, may be of value to some of our patrons. Good, pure, sweet, wholesome milk is a natural food, and should be used by both old and young. Drinking a large cup or glass of cold milk on a hot day is almost as harmful as doing the same thing with ice water. To get the full benefit of milk, drink it moderately and slowly. There are some persons whose stomachs are so sensitive that they cannot retain milk; let such persons add a little lime water to the milk, and they will find it has a very beneficial effect.

MILK OR EGG NOG.—Break a fresh egg into a bowl with two tablespoonfuls of fine white sugar, which beat together until it is very light and frothy; then pour in half a pint of ice-cold new milk, stir the whole well, and grate upon it a little nutmeg; use it immediately.

A spoonful of grated horse radish will keep a pan of milk sweet for days.

No. 4

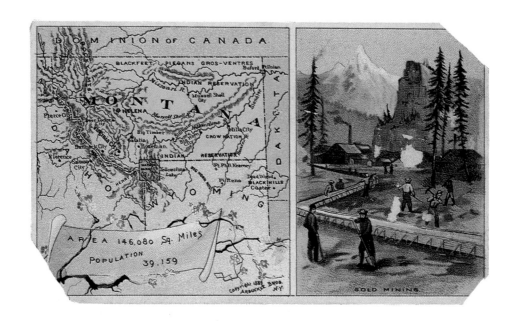

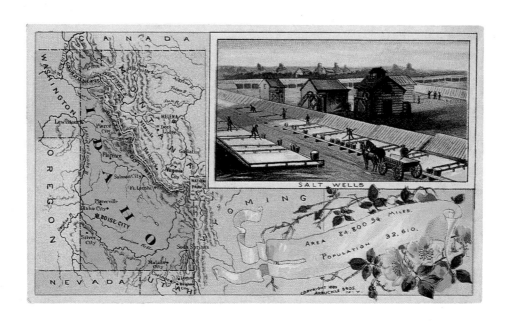

"State Maps," numbered series 51-100, issued in 1889.

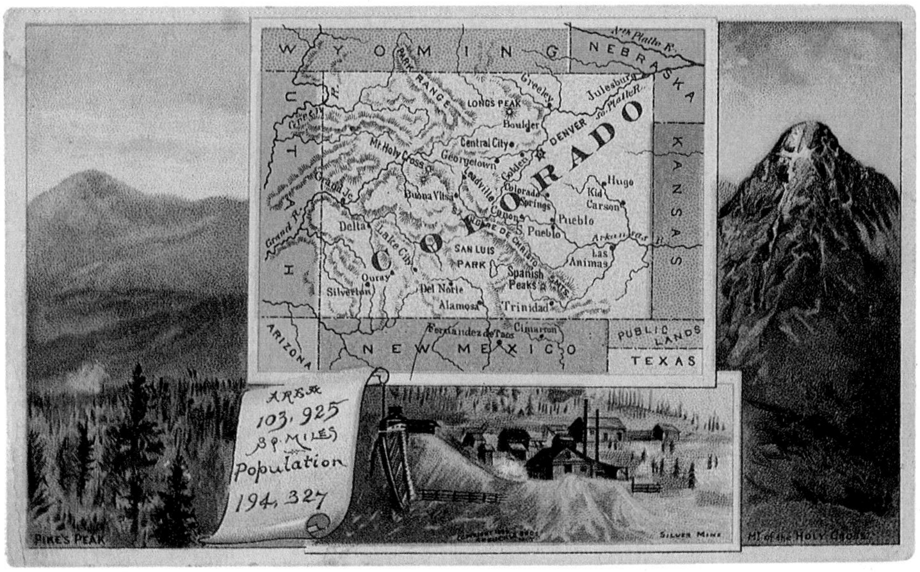
WYOMING
NEBRASKA
KANSAS
COLORADO
NEW MEXICO
TEXAS
PUBLIC LANDS
ARIZONA
UTAH
LONGS PEAK
Boulder
Greeley
Julesburg
Denver
Central City
Georgetown
Golden
Leadville
Buena Vista
Colorado Springs
Pueblo
Hugo
Kit Carson
Las Animas
Delta
Lake City
SAN LUIS PARK
Spanish Peaks
Ouray
Silverton
Del Norte
Alamosa
Trinidad
AREA
103,925
SQ. MILES
Population
194,327
PIKE'S PEAK
SILVER MINE
MT. of the HOLY CROSS

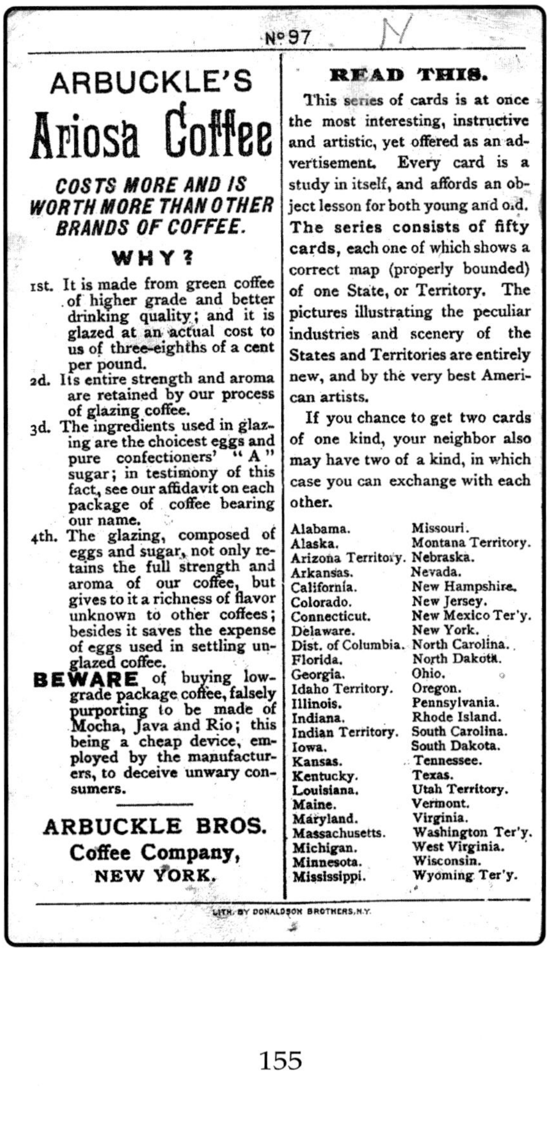

Nº 97

ARBUCKLE'S
Ariosa Coffee

COSTS MORE AND IS WORTH MORE THAN OTHER BRANDS OF COFFEE.

WHY?

1st. It is made from green coffee of higher grade and better drinking quality; and it is glazed at an actual cost to us of three-eighths of a cent per pound.

2d. Its entire strength and aroma are retained by our process of glazing coffee.

3d. The ingredients used in glazing are the choicest eggs and pure confectioners' "A" sugar; in testimony of this fact, see our affidavit on each package of coffee bearing our name.

4th. The glazing, composed of eggs and sugar, not only retains the full strength and aroma of our coffee, but gives to it a richness of flavor unknown to other coffees; besides it saves the expense of eggs used in settling unglazed coffee.

BEWARE of buying low-grade package coffee, falsely purporting to be made of Mocha, Java and Rio; this being a cheap device, employed by the manufacturers, to deceive unwary consumers.

ARBUCKLE BROS.
Coffee Company,
NEW YORK.

READ THIS.

This series of cards is at once the most interesting, instructive and artistic, yet offered as an advertisement. Every card is a study in itself, and affords an object lesson for both young and old. **The series consists of fifty cards**, each one of which shows a correct map (properly bounded) of one State, or Territory. The pictures illustrating the peculiar industries and scenery of the States and Territories are entirely new, and by the very best American artists.

If you chance to get two cards of one kind, your neighbor also may have two of a kind, in which case you can exchange with each other.

Alabama.	Missouri.
Alaska.	Montana Territory.
Arizona Territory.	Nebraska.
Arkansas.	Nevada.
California.	New Hampshire.
Colorado.	New Jersey.
Connecticut.	New Mexico Ter'y.
Delaware.	New York.
Dist. of Columbia.	North Carolina.
Florida.	North Dakota.
Georgia.	Ohio.
Idaho Territory.	Oregon.
Illinois.	Pennsylvania.
Indiana.	Rhode Island.
Indian Territory.	South Carolina.
Iowa.	South Dakota.
Kansas.	Tennessee.
Kentucky.	Texas.
Louisiana.	Utah Territory.
Maine.	Vermont.
Maryland.	Virginia.
Massachusetts.	Washington Ter'y.
Michigan.	West Virginia.
Minnesota.	Wisconsin.
Mississippi.	Wyoming Ter'y.

LITH. BY DONALDSON BROTHERS, N.Y.

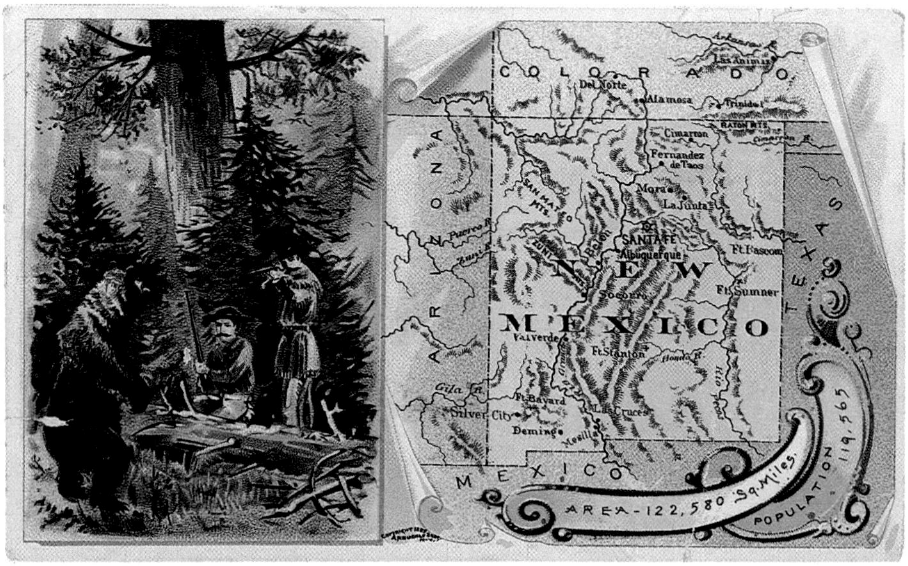
COLORADO
Arkansas R.
Las Animas
Del Norte
Alamosa
Trinidad
RATON MTS.
Cimarron
Fernandez de Taos
Mora
La Junta
SANTA FE
Albuquerque
Ft. Bascom
Ft. Sumner
NEW
MEXICO
ARIZONA
TEXAS
Valverde
Socorro
Ft. Stanton
Gila R.
Ft. Bayard
Silver City
Deming
MEXICO
AREA-122,580 Sq. Miles
POPULATION 119,565

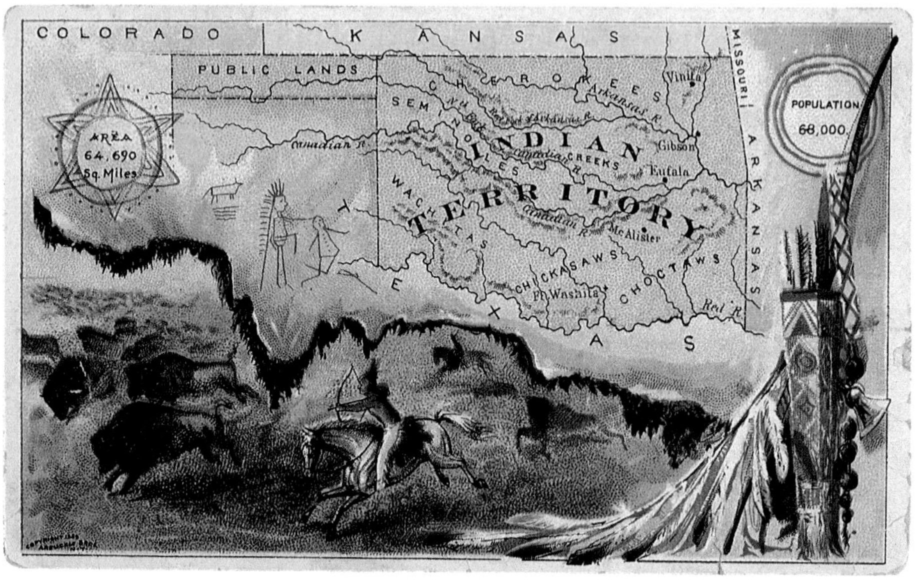
COLORADO
KANSAS
PUBLIC LANDS
MISSOURI
ARKANSAS
Vinita
POPULATION 68,000
AREA 64,690 Sq. Miles
Canadian R.
INDIAN
TERRITORY
Gibson
Eufala
Mc.Alister
CHICKASAWS
CHOCTAWS
Ft. Washita
Red R.
TEXAS

COLUMBIA
WASHINGTON, T
PACIFIC OCEAN
Portland
Columbia River
SALEM
Baker City
OREGON
SAGE PLAIN
INDIAN RES.
Diamond Peak
Jacksonville
Klamath Lakes
Christmas Lake
Silver City
IDAHO
CALIFORNIA
NEVADA
SALMON
SALMON
AREA IN
SQ. MILES
96,030.
SALMON FISHERIES
POPULATION 174,768

WHEAT FIELDS
AREA
77,000
SQ. MILES
POPULATION
67,588
CANADA
MONTANA
MINNESOTA
NORTH
DAKOTA
Mandan
BISMARCK
Jamestown
Grand Forks
Fargo
Wahpeton
Aberdeen
SOUTH
DAKOTA
Ft. Sully
Watertown
SOWING
REAPING

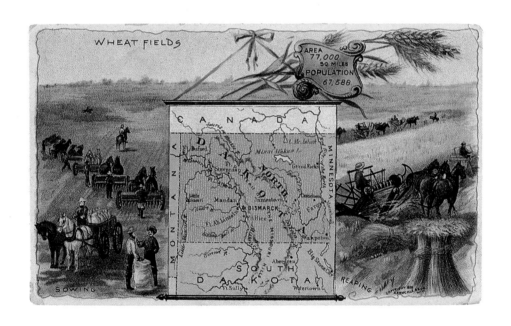

UTAH
NEVADA
CALIFORNIA
ARIZONA
COLORADO
NEW MEXICO
MEXICO
St. George
Rockville
Callville
WHITE MESA
COLORADO PLATEAU
PRESCOTT
Aubrey City
Wickenburg
La Paz
Eureka
Ft. Yuma
Yuma
Florence
Tucson
Tubac

MONTANA
DAKOTA
IDAHO
UTAH
NEBRASKA
COLORADO
WYOMING
NATIONAL PARK
Ft. Phil. Kearney
Union Peak
Fremont's Peak
So. Pass City
Bryan
Evanston
Rawlins
Carbon
Laramie City
Sherman
CHEYENNE
AREA 97,890 Sq. Miles
POPULATION 20,789
CATTLE
HORSES AND

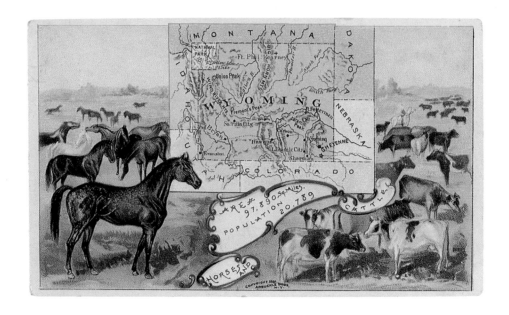

NEW MEXICO
INDIAN TERRITORY
ARKANSAS
LOUISIANA
CORN, CATTLE COTTON & WOOL
TEXAS
MEXICO
GULF OF MEXICO
Ft. Stanton
Clarksville
Red River
Canadian R.
Brazos R.
Colorado R.
Henrietta
Sherman
Dallas
Jefferson
Henderson
AUSTIN
Houston
Fredricksburg
San Antonio
Galveston
Matagorda
Eagle Pass
Rio Grande City
Brazos Santiago
Rio Grande del Norte
AREA, 265,780 Sq. Mile
Population 1,591,749

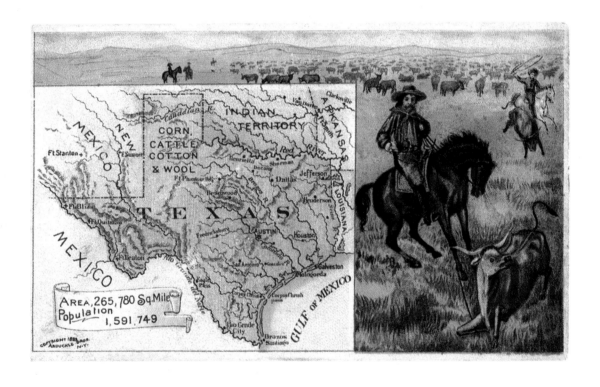

*Top: Arbuckle Brothers issued an atlas containing the "National Georgraphical"
series of trade cards:* Arbuckles' Illustrated Atlas of Fifty Principal Nations
of the World. *It contained textual matter concerning the various countries
and teachers were courted to utilize its "educational value."* (Courtesy James
E. Sherman)

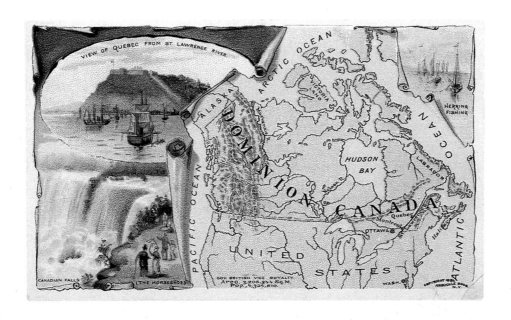

Examples of the "Fifty Principal Nations of the World" series of trade cards issued in 1889. Backs of this series did not contain information about the countries; they touted the educational value of the cards and the advantages of grinding coffee at home. The fronts gave the population, area, and form of government of the various countries. Arabia's form of government was noted as "despotism," Turkey's "absolute despotism," Canada's "British vice royalty."

161

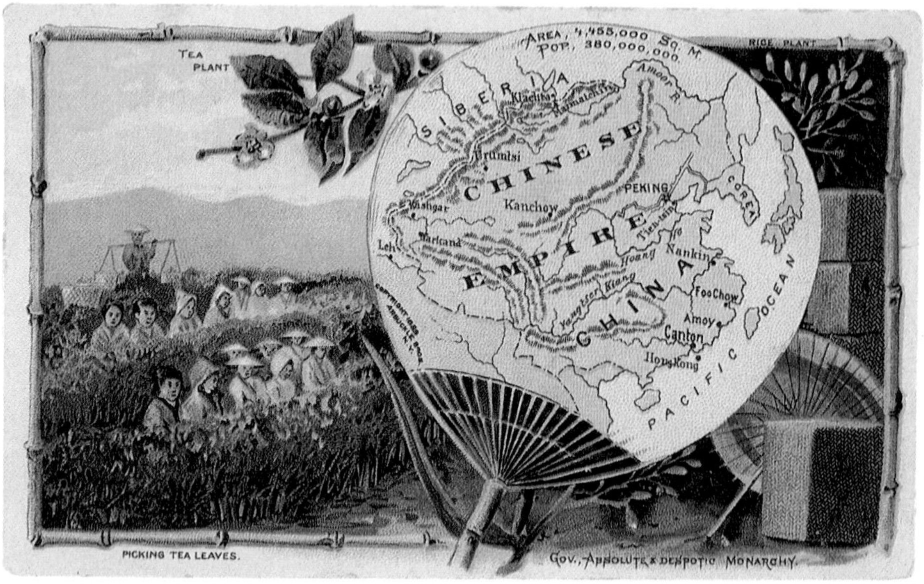
Tea Plant
Area, 4,455,000 Sq. M.
Pop. 380,000,000.
Rice Plant
Siberia
Amoor R.
Chinese Empire
China
Peking
Kanchow
Kashgar
Leh
Corea
Nankin
FooChow
Amoy
Canton
Hong Kong
Pacific Ocean
Picking Tea Leaves.
Gov., Absolute & Despotic Monarchy.

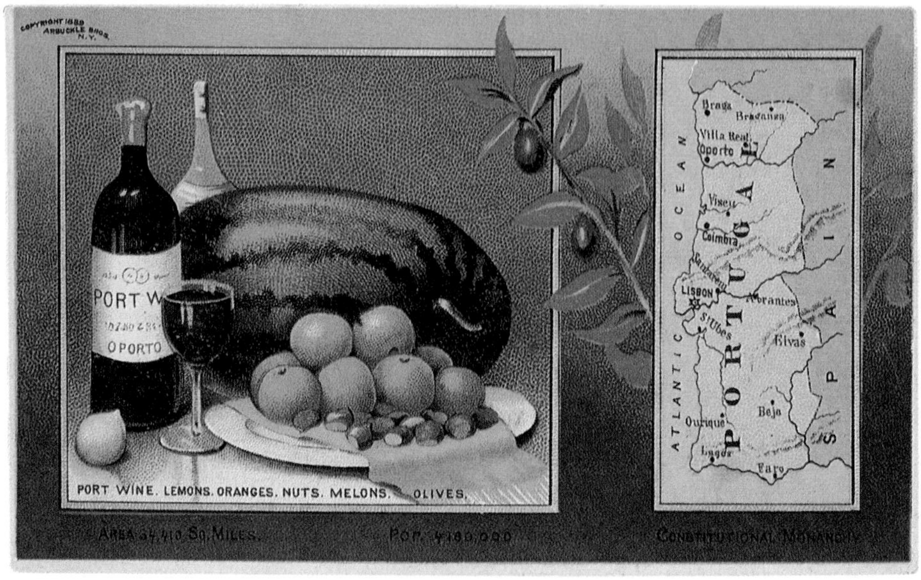
Copyright 1889 Arbuckle Bros. N.Y.
Port W
Oporto
Port Wine. Lemons. Oranges. Nuts. Melons. Olives.
Braga
Braganza
Villa Real
Oporto
Viseu
Coimbra
Lisbon
Abrantes
Elvas
Beja
Ourique
Lagos
Faro
Atlantic Ocean
Portugal
Spain
Area 34,410 Sq. Miles.
Pop. 4160,000
Constitutional Monarchy

Area, 1,425,700 Sq.M.
Pop. 255,000,000.
BRITISH VICE ROYALTY.
AFGHANISTAN
CHINA
HIMALAYA MTS
Lahore
Delhi
Lucknow
Benares
Kurrachee
INDIA
CALCUTTA
BURMAH
Bombay
Surat
BAY of BENGAL
Rangoon
Madras
Calicut
CEYLON
Colombo
INDIAN OCEAN
COPYRIGHT 1889 ARBUCKLE BROS. N.Y.
OPIUM PLANT

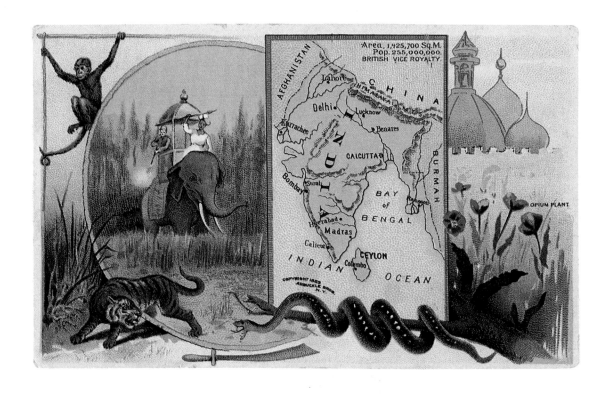

Top: Arbuckles' Album of Illustrated Natural History *was issued in 1890, containing the "Zoological Series" of trade cards with textual information about the animals.* (Courtesy James E. Sherman)

Bottom: The "Zoological Series" of Arbuckle trade cards, numbered 1-50, issued in 1890, featured fifty exotic animals.

REINDEER
(Rangifer tarandus)

VLACKE VARK
(Sus scrofa)

OTOCYON
(Otocyon lalandii)

GRIND

YOUR COFFEE

AT HOME.

It will pay you well to keep a small coffee-mill in your kitchen and grind your coffee just as you use it, one mess at a time. Coffee should not be ground until the coffee-pot is ready to receive it. Coffee will lose more of its strength and aroma in one hour after being ground than in six months before being ground. So long as

ARIOSA

remains in the whole berry, our glazing, composed of choice eggs and pure confeotioners' A sugar, closes the pores of the coffee, and thereby are retained all the original strength and aroma.

ARIOSA COFFEE

has during 25 years set the standard for all other roasted coffees. So true is this that other manufacturers, in recommending their goods, have known no higher praise than to say, "It's just as good as Arbuckles'."

ARBUCKLE BROS.

Coffee Company,

NEW YORK CITY.

KNAPP & CO. LITH. N. Y.

EXPLANATORY.

The series of cards to which this one belongs consists of 50, each card of which shows a true picture (drawn and colored by an eminent artist) of one of the most interesting specimens of the animal kingdom, and giving the classical appellation, together with the English name, of each animal portrayed. Every package of Arbuckle's Coffee contains either one of these cards, or one of our series of 50 National Geographical cards, an equal number of which are used in conjunction with the Zoological cards—both series being so distributed that every pound package, in each 100 pound case, contains a card different from those contained in all the other packages. Teachers and parents unanimously agree in declaring our cards to be the best conceived and executed object lessons for young people.

Names of Animals Represented.

Aard Vark	Leopard
Alpine Hare	Lion
Angora Goat	Llama
Aye-Aye	Mullingong
Asiatic Elephant	Opossum
Badger	Orang-Outang
Beaver	Otocyon
Big-Horn	Ounce
Bison	Panda
Blotched Genett	Phatagin
Buansuah	Polar Bear
Cacomixle	Puma
Camel	Reindeer
Cheetah	Rimau-da-han
Ermine	Spring Haas
European Lynx	Taguan
Galago	Tanreo
Gems-Bok	Tatou
Giraffe	Tiger
Gnu	Vlacke Vark
Gorilla	Whallabee
Ind'n Rhinoceros	Yak
Jackal	Zebith
Jaguar	Zebra
Kuda-Ayer	Zebu

No. 43.

ZIBETH
(Viverra zibetha)

GEMS-BOK
(Oryx gazella)

"Views from a Trip Around the World" series, numbered 1-50, issued in 1891.

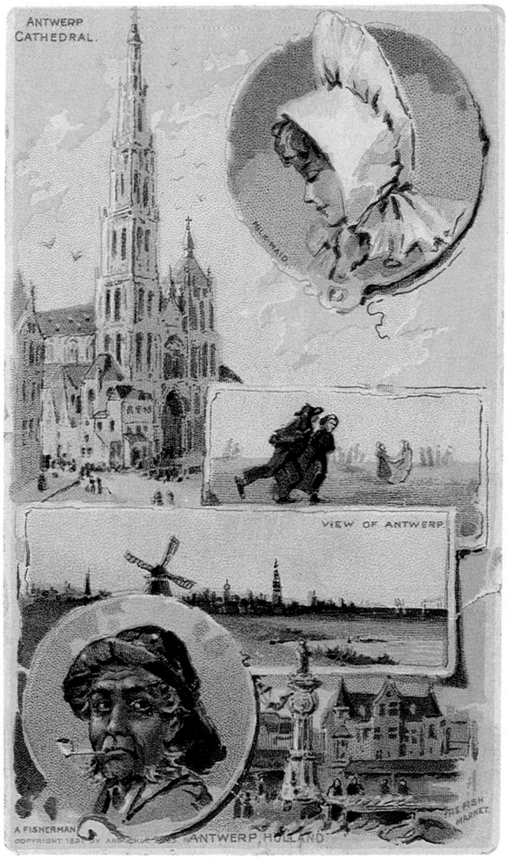
ANTWERP CATHEDRAL.
VIEW OF ANTWERP
A FISHERMAN
THE FISH MARKET
ANTWERP, HOLLAND

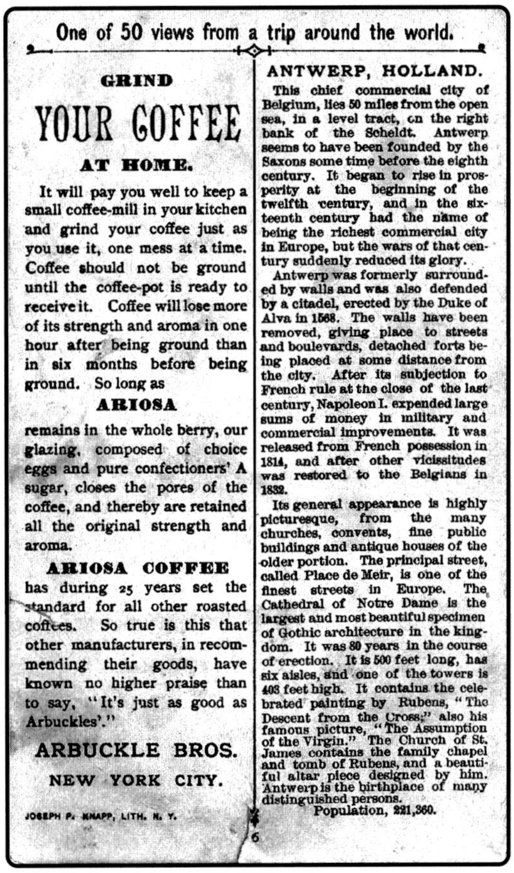

One of 50 views from a trip around the world.

GRIND

YOUR COFFEE

AT HOME.

It will pay you well to keep a small coffee-mill in your kitchen and grind your coffee just as you use it, one mess at a time. Coffee should not be ground until the coffee-pot is ready to receive it. Coffee will lose more of its strength and aroma in one hour after being ground than in six months before being ground. So long as

ARIOSA

remains in the whole berry, our glazing, composed of choice eggs and pure confectioners' A sugar, closes the pores of the coffee, and thereby are retained all the original strength and aroma.

ARIOSA COFFEE

has during 25 years set the standard for all other roasted coffees. So true is this that other manufacturers, in recommending their goods, have known no higher praise than to say, "It's just as good as Arbuckles'."

ARBUCKLE BROS.

NEW YORK CITY.

JOSEPH P. KNAPP, LITH. N. Y.

ANTWERP, HOLLAND.

This chief commercial city of Belgium, lies 50 miles from the open sea, in a level tract, on the right bank of the Scheldt. Antwerp seems to have been founded by the Saxons some time before the eighth century. It began to rise in prosperity at the beginning of the twelfth century, and in the sixteenth century had the name of being the richest commercial city in Europe, but the wars of that century suddenly reduced its glory.

Antwerp was formerly surrounded by walls and was also defended by a citadel, erected by the Duke of Alva in 1568. The walls have been removed, giving place to streets and boulevards, detached forts being placed at some distance from the city. After its subjection to French rule at the close of the last century, Napoleon I. expended large sums of money in military and commercial improvements. It was released from French possession in 1814, and after other vicissitudes was restored to the Belgians in 1832.

Its general appearance is highly picturesque, from the many churches, convents, fine public buildings and antique houses of the older portion. The principal street, called Place de Meir, is one of the finest streets in Europe. The Cathedral of Notre Dame is the largest and most beautiful specimen of Gothic architecture in the kingdom. It was 80 years in the course of erection. It is 500 feet long, has six aisles, and one of the towers is 403 feet high. It contains the celebrated painting by Rubens, "The Descent from the Cross;" also his famous picture, "The Assumption of the Virgin." The Church of St. James contains the family chapel and tomb of Rubens, and a beautiful altar piece designed by him. Antwerp is the birthplace of many distinguished persons.

Population, 221,360.

6

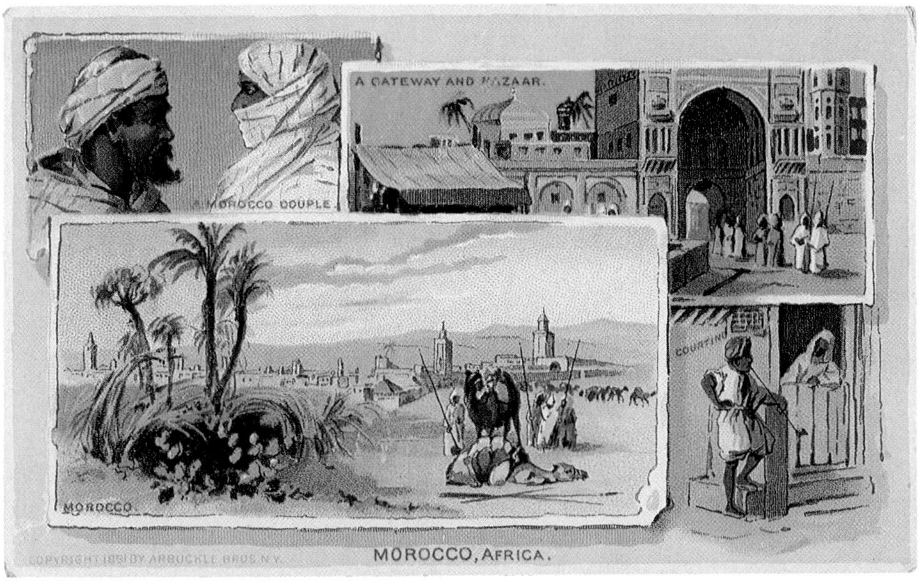
A MOROCCO COUPLE.
A GATEWAY AND
COURTING
MOROCCO.
COPYRIGHT 1891 BY ARBUCKLE BROS. N.Y.
MOROCCO, AFRICA.

Pictorial History of the United States and Territories series, numbered 1-50, issued 1893. Actual size 3" by 5".

Above: Mormon Temple, Tabernacle and Assembly Hall, Salt Lake City; Completion of the Pacific Railroad, 1869; An Indian attack on an Emigrant Train.

Early Potter; Friar Padilla, Missionary, 16th Century; Settlers, 1849.

John Brown's Cabin at Ossawatomie; The Border Ruffians invading Kansas in 1855; Sacking of Lawrence in 1863.

Mount Tacoma; Indians on their way to Hop-Picking; Big Lumber.

Sam Houston Wild Horses of Texas; Houston at San Jacinto, 1836; De la Salle landing in Texas, 1685.

Cabeza de Vaca discovering "First Habitations"; a Zuni of To-Day Decorating Pottery; The Conquest of Cibola.

*Mormon Camp Stopping-Place, afterwards Genoa; Rush to the Silver Mines;
Cornerstore in Death Valley.*

Arcadians, 1775; Bienville, Founder of New Orleans, 1718; Battle of New Orleans, 1814; La Salle at the Mouth of the Mississippi, 1682.

ARBUCKLES : THE COFFEE THAT WON THE WEST

Mountain of the Holy Cross; Cliff Dwellings; Garden of the Gods and Pike's Peak.

General Miles attacking the Forces of Geronimo in the Mountain Passes, 1890;
Spanish Explorers Discovering Cave Dwellings, 1540.

GRIND YOUR   No. 28

COFFEE

AT HOME.

It will pay you well to keep a small coffee-mill in your kitchen and grind your coffee just as you use it—one mess at a time. Coffee should not be ground until the coffee-pot is ready to receive it. Coffee will lose more of its strength and aroma in one hour after being ground than in six months before being ground. So long as Ariosa remains in the whole berry, our glazing, composed of choice eggs and pure confectioners' A sugar, closes the pores of the coffee, and thereby all the original strength and aroma are retained. Ariosa Coffee has, during 25 years, set the standard for all other roasted coffees. So true is this, that other manufacturers in recommending their goods, have known no higher praise than to say: "It's just as good as Arbuckles'."

ARBUCKLE BROS.,

NEW YORK CITY.

→PATAGONIA.←

THE Patagonians are all born Nimrods. They are brought up to become brave, active and efficient men. Idleness is not tolerated. They are wonderful horsemen, and singularly expert in the use of their weapons. They lead lives of constant wandering and dwell consequently in habitations which can readily be removed. A few Patagonian tribes consist of men and women of great stature. It is a characteristic of this people that they are even greater nomads than the Arabs. Though but a half-civilized race, the various tribes live in amity, and the provocation must indeed be great, which incites to war.

The panther is one of the favorite species of game, this animal, a species of leopard becomes very desperate when attacked and it requires great watchfulness and accuracy of aim to save oneself from danger. But the Patagonians are cool and collected, and it is seldom they are victims of even the most ferocious of these animals. Ostrich and guanaco hunting are much indulged in. These species are captured more easily by rounding them up, than by individual effort.

Even the children's thoughts run to hunting and to similar sports. Their first impulse when they become old enough to toddle off by themselves, is the robbing of birds' nests.

So too, there seems to be a wonderful affinity between these children, and the tamer wild animals which infest the forests and streams of Patagonia. Often young children are found at play with flamingoes by the brookside.

Games of manual dexterity are very popular among the Patagonians. So are horse-racing and gambling, but the latter is very fairly conducted. Bull-fights, too, are frequently indulged in.

The Patagonian women embroider beautifully, and ornament their mantles, made of guanaco-skins with the best of taste.

This is one of a series of Fifty (50) Cards giving a pictorial History of the Sports and Pastimes of all Nations.

"History of Sports and Pastimes of All Nations" series, numbered 1-50, issued in 1893.

TURKEY.

ESQUIMAU.

Australia.

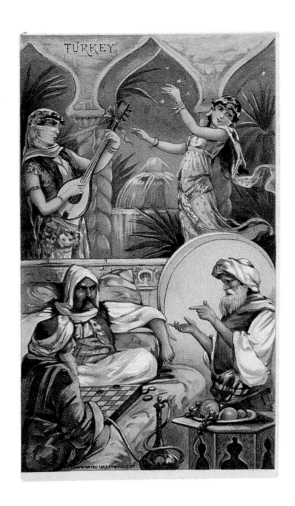

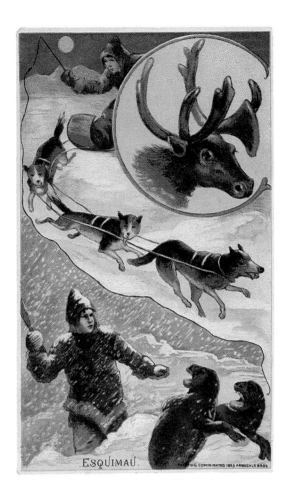

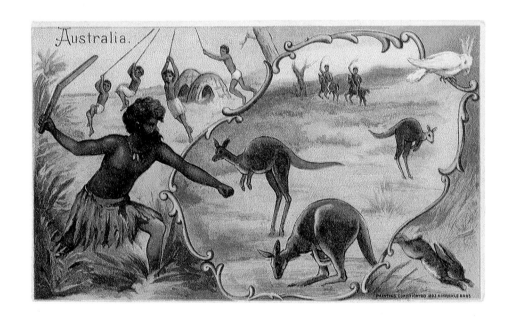

PAINTING COPYRIGHTED 1893 ARBUCKLE BROS.

⇾POLAND.↜

THE unhappy land of Poland preserved until very recently even after it had lost its nationality, a distinctive national life. Poland was a nation that deserved to be free, for under condi-tions most depressing, it struggled patriotically for that end; but fate and its unfavorable position decreed otherwise. Nevertheless that struggle of centuries left its impress on the national character. For Poland has a generous people, brave, high minded, light-hearted and liberal.

If there is one national characteristic impelling them to pleasure, it is their love for dancing. In the women especially this is a pas-sion. The rhythmical genius of the Polish people has produced three forms of dance music, the Mazurka, the Polonaise and the Craco-vienne. These have been adapted or imitated by every modern composer.

Late in August the polish peasantry celebrate their Harvest-Home. This is a national festival throughout the country, and young and old participate in the rolicking pleasures. The celebra-tion is not an informal one, but is preceded by some ceremonies, and a song of praise. A favorite game with Polish children is "Hoops" decorated with red and white ribbons (their national colors) dexterously thrown and caught with the aid of sticks.

Spearing fish by moon-light is a favorite mode of fishing practised by the Polish. A torch light is set at the stern of the boat and a grate at the bow. These throw sufficient light over the water to attract the fish. Two men armed with spears await the game. Quick eyes and strong and steady arms soon suffice to give an ample supply.

Hunting finds many devotees in Poland, since game is very plentiful. The boar is the favorite animal of the chase.

ROME.

OF ALL the nations prior to modern times, none has so filled the pages of history as imperial Rome. Time was indeed, when "to be a Roman was greater than a king." And before their fall for many centuries Romans were kingly men, broad in intellect, wise in debate, fearless in war. In some respects, their manly sports resembled those of the Greeks, the aim being to develope to the highest the physical possibilities of their young men.

The Circensian games were among the earliest and most popular festivals. They were at first especially designed for chariot-racing. The circus was a long narrow enclosure generally situated in a suitably shaped valley, where the slope could serve for spectators. The old race-course of the Circus Maximus was nearly one-half mile long. A race consisted of a number of rounds. At one end were the pens whence the chariots started. A low wall along the centre divided the space into parallel courses. In later days the four-horse chariot-race was by all odds the favorite.

Wrestling, the sport in which one person tries to throw another to the ground, was a great Roman favorite. It formed a part of the Circensian games and later on was also adopted in the Amphi-theatre, as also were boxing, foot-racing, the evolutions of companies of trained horses, animal hunts and gladiatorial combats. In the Amphitheatre, theatrical performances were also given.

The Roman ladies were great embroiderers. Embroidery work was much esteemed, and a visit to the home of any thrifty Roman matron during the hours when drudgery was completed, would discover that lady and her handmaidens, at work that would be a credit to our modern housewives.

Throwing the *discus*, the Roman quoit was practised by most young Romans. The *discus* had no hole in it, but was solid like a plate.

Arbuckle Brothers' premium catalogues were upgraded over the years with covers printed in brilliant colors. (Courtesy James E. Sherman)

In an appeal to children, the McLaughlin Coffee Company issued a series of die-cut dolls and animals with flaps which could be bent to make stands for them.

185

Top: A McLaughlin trade card with adult appeal.

Bottom: This trade card illustration portraying the statue of liberty was used by a number of firms. This one advertised Jersey Coffee, packed by the Dayton Spice Mills Co., of Dayton, Ohio.

Top: Some companies gave dealers small booklets to distribute to purchasers of coffee. This 1898 "The History of our American Flag" was imprinted by Chase & Sanborn for John Parris, a dealer in Walnut, Texas.

Bottom: This Lion Coffee trade card portrays "The Sleeping Beauty" and has a brief rendition of the fairy tale on the back.

Top: Many trade cards portrayed foreign children in their native dress. This one was issued by the New Orleans Coffee Co. to promote French Market Roasted Coffee.

Bottom: The storeroom wall in the Red Lake Trading Post on the Hopi Reservation near Tonalea, Arizona, is paneled with Arbuckles coffee crates.

Top: The old Arbuckles' thermometer is prized by collectors. In 1990 Mrs. Bertha Wilson of Atlanta, Georgia, wrote: "Mine still gives the correct temperature. I guess that says something for Arbuckles." (Courtesy Albert E. Ward)

Bottom: Arbuckle Brothers furnished retailers with colorful banners to advertise premiums. (Courtesy Harold R. Belsher)

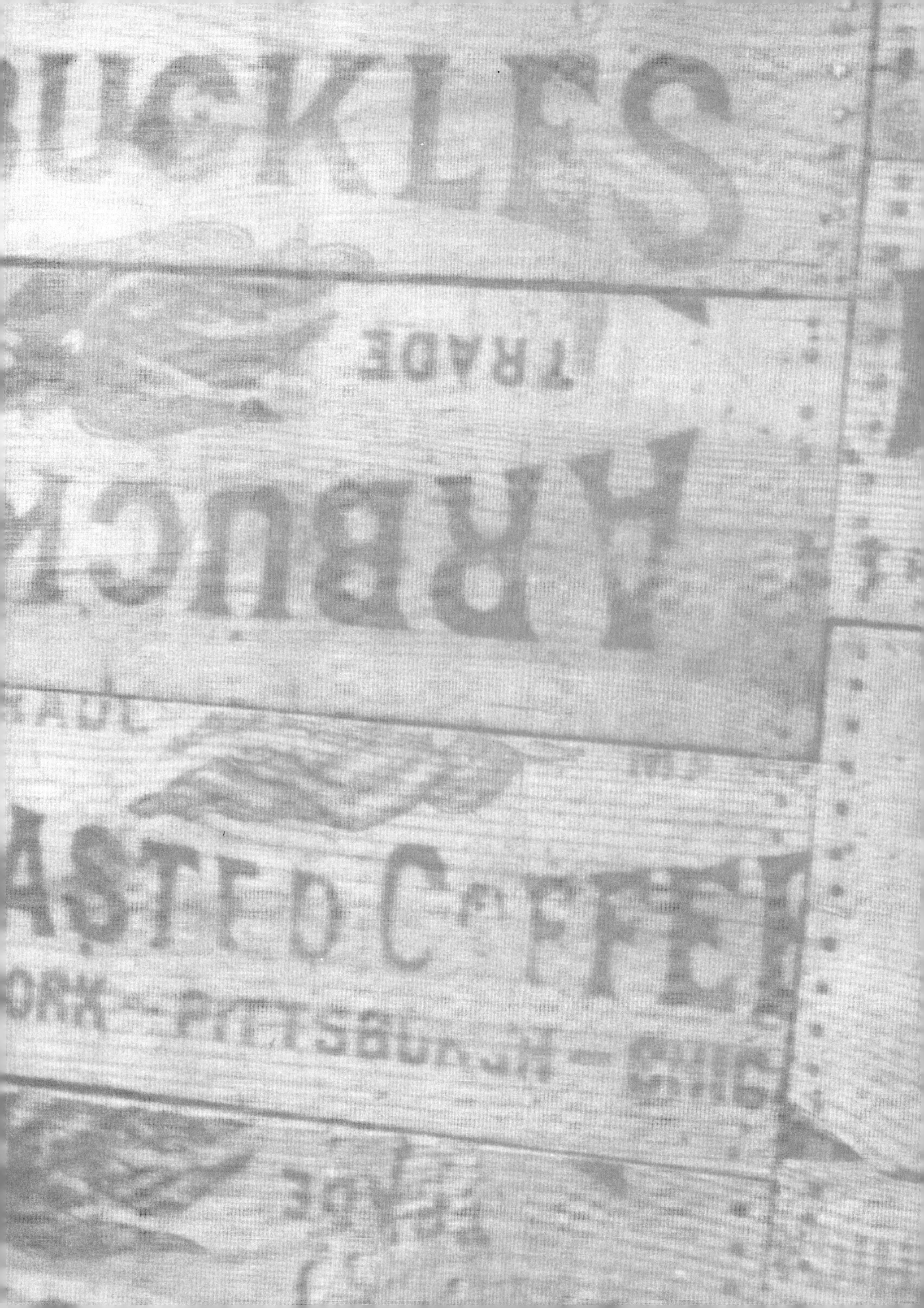
TRADE

APPENDICES

Appendix A
First Advertisement for Coffee in the English Language.

The Vertue of the COFFEE Drink.

First publiquely made and sold in England, by *Pasqua Rosée.*
The Grain or Berry called *Coffee,* groweth upon little Trees, only in the *Deserts of Arabia.*
It is brought from thence, and drunk generally throughout all the Grand Seigniors Dominions.
It is a simple innocent thing, composed into a Drink, by being dryed in an Oven, and ground to Powder, and boiled up with Spring water, and about half a pint of it to be drunk, fasting an hour before, and not Eating an hour after, and to be taken as hot as possibly can be endured; the which will never fetch the skin off the mouth, or raise any Blisters, by reason of that Heat.
The Turks drink at meals and other times, is usually *Water,* and their Dyet consists much of *Fruit,* the *Crudities* whereof are very much corrected by this Drink.
The quality of this Drink is Cold and Dry, and though it be a Dryer, yet it neither *heats,* nor *inflames* more than *hot Posset.*
It so closeth the Orifice of the Stomack, and fortifies the heat within, that it's very good to help digestion, and therefore of great use to be taken about 3 or 4 a Clock afternoon, as well as in the morning.
It much quickens the *Spirits,* and makes the Heart *Lightsome.* It is good against sore Eys, and the better if you hold your Head over it, and take the Steem that way.
It suppresseth Fumes exceedingly, and therefore good against the *Headach,* and will very much stop any *Defluxion of the Rheums,* that distil from the *Head* upon the *Stomack,* and so prevent and help *Consumptions*; and the *Cough of the Lungs.*
It is excellent to prevent and cure the *Dropsy, Gout,* and *Scurvy.*
It is known by experience to be better than any other Drying Drink for *People in years,* or *Children* that have any *running humors* upon them, as *the King's Evil.* &c.
It is very good to prevent *Mis-carryings in Child-bearing Women.*

191

It is a most excellent Remedy against the *Spleen, Hypocondriack Winds,* or the like.

It will prevent *Drowsiness,* and make one fit for busines, if one have occasion to *Watch;* and therefore you are not to Drink of it *after Supper,* unless you intend to be *watchful,* for it will hinder sleep for 3 or 4 hours.

It is observed that in Turkey, where this is generally drunk, that they are not troubled with the Stone, Gout, Dropsie, or Scurvey, and that their Skins are exceedingly cleer and white.

It is neither *Laxative* nor *Restringent.*

Made and Sold in *St. Michaels Alley* in *Cornhill,* by *Pasqua Rosée* at the Signe of his own Head.

Appendix B
Patents Granted to John Arbuckle and / or Under the Control of Arbuckle Brothers

B-1. PROCESS FOR COATING ROASTED COFFEE (Pat. No. 73,486)

John Arbuckle, Jr., Allegheny, Pa.—Roasted Coffee. The roasted coffee is coated with a preparation composed of the following: Irish moss, 1/2 ounce; gelatine, 1/2 ounce; isinglass, 1/2 ounce; white sugar, 1 ounce; eggs, 24. The first three are boiled in water, and the moss strained.
Claim.—Coating roasted coffee with any glutinous or gelatinous matter for the purpose of retaining the aroma of the coffee, and also act as a clarifying agent, as herein described and set forth.—*Patent Gazette,* January 21, 1868.

B-2. COFFEE CLEANERS AND GRADERS (Pat. No. 155,001)

J. Arbuckle, Jr. Filed June 24, 1874.
Brief.—Coffee fed into vertical spout is carried upward by a blast of air, and falls onto inclined side of spout, from which it passes through a spout into grading cylinder, while the chaff and other light impurities are blown out through the upper end of spout.—*Patent Gazette,* September 15, 1875.

B-3. PROCESS FOR SEPARATING STONES, &c., FROM GRAIN, &c. (Pat. No. 196,178)

John Arbuckle, Brooklyn, N. Y. Application filed April 4, 1877.

The within-described process of separating stones or other like impurities from grain, corn, coffee, or other similar materials, by heating said materials and dumping the kernels or beans while hot into a tank containing water, whereby the stones or other like impurities are caused to sink down, while the kernels or beans can be skimmed off from the surface of the water, substantially as set forth.—*Patent Gazette,* October 16, 1877.

B-4. APPARATUS FOR CLEANING GRAIN, &c. (Pat. No. 226,471)

John Arbuckle, Brooklyn, N. Y. Filed August 6, 1879.
Claim.—In an apparatus for cleaning Grain, & c., the combination of the chamber E having an upper foraminous partition, an inclined bottom, and a discharge spout, the escape flue, passing through said inclined bottom, and the air flue of a less diameter than the escape flue, and having a flaring mouthpiece, for receiving the grain & c. . . . .—*Patent Gazette,* April 13, 1880.

B-5. FIRE-PROOF BUILDING (Pat. No. 253,658)

John Arbuckle, Brooklyn, N. Y.

Brief.—The wooden parts of the building are covered by outer metallic plates and an inner layer of cement, secured so as to leave an air-space between the wood and the cement.—*Patent Gazette*, February 14, 1882.

B-6. SAFETY-SIGNAL FOR RAILROAD TRAINS (Pat. No. 262,722)

John Arbuckle, Brooklyn, N. Y.

Brief.—A signal is drawn in rear of a train to prevent a following train from colliding therewith, each train also being provided with a device traveling in the path of said signal, whereby, should the engineer of the train fail to see the signal of the train ahead, an alarm will sound upon his locomotive.—*Patent Gazette*, August 15, 1882.

B-7. MITTEN, &c. (Pat. No. 406,690)

John Arbuckle, Brooklyn, N. Y. Application filed December 6, 1888. (No model)

This invention relates to coverings for the hands—such as gloves, mittens, and similar articles; and it consists in providing them with inlet-valves, which permit air from the mouth to be forced into the interior of the glove or mitten for the purpose of warming the fingers when cold, as fully described in the following specification, reference being had to the accompanying drawings. —*Patent Gazette*, July 9, 1889.

B-8. FEED MECHANISM FOR WEIGHING-MACHINES (Pat. No. 470,146)

Henry E. Smyser, Philadelphia, Pa., assignor to Arbuckle Brothers, New York, N. Y. Filed April 29, 1891. (No model)

Claim.—1. In an automatic-weighing machine, the combination, with a series of scale-pans, of a series of chutes leading to the respective pans, a corresponding series of measures, a supplyhopper, and the means for actuating the measures, as described, and so that they shall alternately communicate with the supplyhopper and the chutes.

2. In an automatic weighing machine, a combination, with a series of scale-pans, of a series of chutes leading to the respective pans, a reciprocating box divided into measuring-compartments corresponding to the chute series, a supply-hopper arranged above the box, a platform to support and guide the box having at one end a series of holes corresponding to the divisions of the box and connecting to the chute series, and mechanism arranged to actuate the box, moving it to and from a position over the holes in the platform. —*Patent Gazette*, March 1, 1892.

B-9. PAPER-FEEDER (Pat. No. 492,374)

Henry E. Smyser, Philadelphia, Pa., assignor to Arbuckle Brothers, New York, N. Y. Filed April 4, 1892.

A method of feeding paper in single sheets from a pile, obviously to be used to handle packing material and inclosures.— *Patent Gazette*, February 21, 1893.

B-10. AUTOMATIC WEIGHING-MACHINE (Pat. No. 493,795)

Henry E. Smyser, Philadelphia, Pa., assignor to Arbuckle Brothers, New

York, N. Y. Filed April 15, 1891. (No model)

Claim.—1. In an automatic weighing machine, the combination of a series of stationary scales, of a series of receptacles adapted to receive the weighed charges from the scales, and mechanically-driven mechanism for automatically dumping the receptacles in regular succession.—*Patent Gazette*, March 21, 1893.

[This highly complex piece of assembly-line equipment required almost two pages in the patent application to delineate its operation.]

B-11. AUTOMATIC WEIGHING-MACHINE (Pat. No. 493,796)

Henry E. Smyser, Philadelphia, Pa., assignor to Arbuckle Brothers, New York, N. Y. Filed May 22, 1891.

Claim.—1. The combination with an intermittently-revolving series of scales, of an intermittently-discharging measuring device comprising a measuring box and mechanism for filling it and discharging it, and a chute leading therefrom to one of the stopping points in the travel of the scales, so that the scalepans receive the measured charges at said point in succession, and means for feeding additional material to the scales to bring the charges to full weight.—*Patent Gazette*, March 21, 1893.

B-12. AUTOMATIC WEIGHING-MACHINE (Pat. No. 493,797)

Henry E. Smyser, Philadelphia, Pa., assignor to Arbuckle Brothers, N. Y. Filed August 15, 1892.

Claim.—1. The combination with a series of scales and a corresponding series of stationary receptacles arranged to receive charges of the material to be weighed and deliver them into the scalepans, of a movable slide beneath the receptacle having openings registering with the respective receptacles, and movable to bring said openings out of register therewith to close the receptacles, or to bring said openings into register therewith to discharge the receptacles.—*Patent Gazette*, March 21, 1893.

B-13. FEEDING DEVICE FOR WEIGHING-MACHINES (Pat. No. 493,798)

Henry E. Smyser, Philadelphia, Pa., assignor to Arbuckle Brothers, New York, N. Y. Filed April 15, 1891. Renewed February 20, 1893.

Claim.—1. In a weighing machine, the combination with a feedhopper and a series of scales, of means for feeding graduated streams of material to the scales consisting of chutes leading to the scales from discharge openings in said hopper, and a reciprocating slide having perforations moving over said openings, and arranged to be filled with material from said hopper and by the movement of the slide to carry the material over said openings and discharge it through them into said chutes.—*Patent Gazette*, March 21, 1893.

B-14. CARD-FEEDER FOR PACKAGE-FILLING MACHINES (Pat. No. 505,858)

Henry E. Smyser, Philadelphia, Pa., assignor to Arbuckle Brothers, New York, N. Y. Filed October 10, 1892. Renewed August 16, 1893. (No model)

Claim.—1. The combination with an automatic package filling machine of a mechanism for automatically inserting a card or a sheet into the package in upright position alongside the material therein.—*Patent Gazette*, October 3, 1893.

B-15. PACKAGE MAKING AND FILLING MACHINERY (Pat. No. 544,697)
Henry E. Smyser, Philadelphia, Pa., assignor to Arbuckle Brothers, New York, N. Y., Filed September 8, 1893.
Claim.—1. In a bag forming mechanism, a former, and a matrix for wrapping a sheet of paper around three sides of the former preparatory to the formation into a tube.—*Patent Gazette*, August 20, 1895.

B-16. GLUING MECHANISM (Pat. No. 560,009)
   Henry E. Smyser, Philadelphia, Pa., assignor to Arbuckle Brothers, New York, N. Y. Filed February 1, 1895. Renewed September 25, 1895.
   A device for applying glue on an assembly line basis.—*Patent Gazette*, May 12, 1896.

B-17. MECHANISM FOR APPLYING ADHESIVES TO PAPER (Pat. No. 561,141)
   Henry E. Smyser, Philadelphia, Pa., assignor to Arbuckle Brothers, New York, N. Y. Filed November 16, 1894. Renewed September 25, 1895.
   A device for applying glue to paper during folding.—*Patent Gazette*, June 2, 1896.

B-18. BAG-MAKING AND PACKAGING MACHINE (Pat. No. 564,722)
   Henry E. Smyser, Philadelphia, Pa., assignor to Arbuckle Brothers, New York, N. Y. Filed March 4, 1895.
Claim.—1. In a packaging machine, the combination of a mechanism for making bags, means for filling the bags with material, and mechanisms for closing the tops of the bags, with carrying devices comprising a series of pockets adapted to receive the bags, to retain them until dry, and to carry them to the filling and top-closing mechanisms, and retain them during the filling and top-closing operations, whereby the bags are dried before being filled.—*Patent Gazette*, July 28, 1896.

B-19. FEED MECHANISM FOR WEIGHING MACHINES (Pat. No. 570,109)
Henry E. Smyser, Philadelphia, Pa., assignor to Arbuckle Brothers, New York, N. Y. Filed March 22, 1895.
   A device for weighing material and dumping it into containers on an assembly line basis.—*Patent Gazette*, October 27, 1896.

B-20. PACKAGING-MACHINE (Pat. No. 609,472)
   Henry E. Smyser, New York, N. Y., assignor to Arbuckle Brothers, same place. Filed March 27, 1897.
Claim.—1. In a packaging-machine, the combination with means for operating on and delivering packages, of an endless movable carrier for receiving the packages delivered therefrom having top and bottom plates adapted to receiving the folded ends of the packages between them and thereby hold them closed, and means for transferring the successive packages to the carrier by pushing them between said plates.—*Patent Gazette*, August 23, 1898.

B-21. BAG OR SACK (Pat. No. 686,847)
   William N. Green, Chicago, Ill., assignor to Arbuckle Brothers, New York, N. Y., a Firm. Filed August 7, 1901.

Claim.—1. A bag consisting of two thicknesses of woven fabric forming outer and inner bags, combined with a sheet of paper between them and uncemented to them, forming an intermediate bag.

. . .

5. A bag consisting of a continuous piece of woven fabric larger than four times the area of the bag to be made, folded together . . .

6. A bag consisting of a continuous piece of toweling fabric, folded double with a sheet of paper between its thickness, and sewed together, whereby the bag is formed of inner and outer layers of fabric and an intervening thickness of paper, and the fabric is adapted by ripping its seams to constitute a towel.— *Patent Gazette*, November 19, 1901.

B-22. APPARATUS FOR ROASTING COFFEE (Pat. No. 719,717)

John Arbuckle, Brooklyn, N. Y., assignor to Arbuckle Brothers, New York, N. Y., a Firm. Original application filed Apr. 22, 1897. Divided and this application filed April 25, 1900. (No model)
Claim.—1. An apparatus for roasting coffee consisting of a revolving drum having means for elevating the coffee and showering it in a distributed rain of beans through a current of hot firegases, so as to substantially fill the free space within the drum with falling beans, combined with a furnace and blower for circulating the hot fire-gases therefrom through said drum whereby to roast the beans individually while falling through the hot gases. —*Patent Gazette*, February 3, 1903.

B-23. APPARATUS FOR EXTRACTING STRANDED VESSELS (Pat. No. 721,851)

John Arbuckle, Brooklyn, N. Y. Filed April 26, 1902. (No model)
A plow with a capacity for discharging fluid alongside a vessel and cables to pull the vessel loose.—*Patent Gazette*, March 3, 1903.

B-24. FEEDING DEVICE (Pat. No. 1,012,016)

Eugene Seavey, New York, N. Y., assignor to Arbuckle Brothers, a Firm. Filed June 25, 1910.
A feeding device for assembly line use with an agitator to agitate the materials being fed.—*Patent Gazette*, Dec. 19, 1911.

B-25. MEANS FOR RAISING SUNKEN VESSELS (Pat. No. 1,016,213)

John Arbuckle, New York, N. Y., Christina Arbuckle and Charles A. Jamison, administrators of said John Arbuckle, de- ceased. Filed July 13, 1910.
A series of piles and jacks around a sunken vessel.—*Patent Gazette*, May 6, 1913.

B-26. PACKAGE-FORMING MACHINE (Pat. No. 1,133,857)

Paul H. Grimm, Glen Cove, and Frank L. Cocks, New York, N. Y., assignors to Arbuckle Brothers, New York, N. Y., a Firm comprising William A. Jamison, Catherine A. Jamison, and Christina Arbuckle. Filed March 23, 1914.
A device for holding and folding sheets to be pasted and formed into multilayer packages.—*Patent Gazette*, March 30, 1915.

B-27. PACKAGE-FORMING MACHINE (Pat. No. 1,133,858)

Paul H. Grimm, Glen Cove, and Frank L. Cocks, New York, N. Y., assignors to Arbuckle Brothers, New York, N. Y., a Firm comprising William A. Jamison, Catherine A. Jamison, and Christina Arbuckle. Filed March 23, 1914. Divided and this application filed July 13, 1914.

A device for forming sheets around a matrix to make a package.—*Patent Gazette*, March 30, 1915.

B-28. PROCESS OF RECONDITIONING BONE-BLACK (Pat. No. 1,177,725)

John W. Scott, Englewood, N. J., assignor to Arbuckle Brothers, a Firm comprising William A. Jamison, Catherine A. Jamison, and Christina Arbuckle, New York, N. Y. Filed December 19, 1914.

1. The reconditioning of bone-black by adding lime thereto and then calcining . . . repeating the process . . . and finally washing.—*Patent Gazette*, April 4, 1916.

B-29. PROCESS FOR PRODUCING SOLUBLE CONCENTRATED COFFEE (Pat. No. 1,393,045)

John W. Scott, Englewood, N. J., assignor to Arbuckle Brothers, New York, N. Y., a Firm composed of William A. Jamison, Catherine A. Jamison, and Christina Arbuckle. Filed September 24, 1918. Ten Claims.

. . .

2. The method of producing a coffee concentrate consisting in supplying a liquid to successive vessels containing ground coffee, the liquid when at its highest temperature permeating the most spent mass of coffee, and passing at a lower temperature to masses of coffee of successively increasing strength, whereby to obtain an extract rich in aroma, and atomizing the liquor thus formed into a highly heated blast to accomplish instantaneous concentration and retain the aroma in the product.

. . .

7. A method of producing a coffee concentrate consisting in first producing a coffee extract and then atomizing such extract into a highly heated blast containing aromatic and volatile products obtained from coffee roasting. —*Patent Gazette*, October 11, 1921.

B-30. PACKAGE-WRAPPING MACHINE (Pat. No. 1,590,366)

Paul H. Grimm, Glen Cove, and Frank L. Cocks, Brooklyn, N. Y., assignors to Arbuckle Brothers, New York, N. Y., a Firm comprising William A. Jamison, Catherine A. Jamison, and Christina Arbuckle. Original application filed January 27, 1921. Divided and this application filed February 16, 1923. 78 claims.

Wrapping machine fed by a strip of paper.—*Patent Gazette*, June 29, 1926.

B-31. LABEL-APPLYING MECHANISM (Pat. No. 1,590,367)

Paul H. Grimm, Glen Cove, and Frank L. Cocks, Brooklyn, N. Y., assignors to Arbuckle Brothers, New York, N. Y., a Firm comprising William A. Jamison, Catherine A. Jamison, and Christina Arbuckle. Original application filed January 27, 1921. Divided and this application filed February 16, 1923. 10 claims.

1. Mechanism for fastening labels without subjecting to impact.—*Patent Gazette*, June 29, 1926.

APPENDIX C

Arbuckle Brothers' Labels and Trademarks in the Order of Usage

C-1. ARBUCKLES (Trade-Mark No. 50,455)

Application filed September 23, 1905. Published, Serial No. 12,939: *Patent Gazette*, March 20, 1906. Registered *Patent Gazette*, March 20, 1906.

The mark claimed consists of the word "ARBUCKLES'." The class of merchandise to which said trade-mark is appropriated is coffee. . . . Said trade-mark has been continuously used in our business since the 1st day of January, 1870. . . . that said trade-mark is used by applicants in commerce between the United States of America and foreign nations, or with Indian tribes, or among the several States of the United States, and particularly between New York and Pennsylvania. [This trademark was periodically renewed.]

C-2. FRAGAR (Trade-Mark No. 32,953)

Application filed May 1, 1899. Published and registered *Patent Gazette*, May 23, 1899.

The essential feature of our said trade mark is the word "FRAGAR." The class of goods to which said trade-mark is appropriated is groceries, and the particular description of goods comprised in such class on which it is used by us is coffee.

The said trade-mark has been used by us continuously in our business since on or about the 22d day of August, 1871. . . . used by said firm in commerce between the United States and foreign nations, Indian tribes, and particularly between the United States and Canada.

C-3. COMPONO (Trade-Mark No. 32,954)

Application filed May 1, 1899. Published and registered *Patent Gazette*, May 23, 1899.

Our said trade-mark consists of the arbitrary word COMPONO.

The said trade-mark has been used by us continuously in our business since on or about the 22nd day of August, 1871. . . .The class of goods . . . on which it is used by us is coffee.

C-4. ARBUCKLE'S (Trade-Mark No. 3,595)

Application filed March 22, 1876. Registered *Patent Gazette*, April 18, 1876.

[This trademark was for use with coffee, tea, and spices. Along with use of the word "ARBUCKLE'S" the application detailed "the representation of an angel floating in the air, clothed in a star-spangled robe, and assuming a benedictory attitude." Subsequently, the Supreme Court invalidated Congressional authority to provide for trademark registration. Arbuckle Brothers applied again on September 1, 1880, and the famous angel was registered as detailed in Trade-Mark No. 8,058 below.]

Appendix C. Arbuckle Brothers employed a variety of trademarks for their lines of coffee, tea, spices, and other grocery products.

C-5. ARIOSA (Trade-Mark No. 8,058)

Application filed September 1, 1880. Registered *Patent Gazette*, October 12, 1880.

To all whom it may concern:

Be it known that we, CHARLES ARBUCKLE and JOHN ARBUCKLE, Jr., composing the firm of ARBUCKLE BROTHERS, all being domiciled in the United States, and doing business in the county and State of New York, and at Pittsburgh, in the county of Allegheny and State of Pennsylvania, have adopted for our use a Trade-Mark for Roasted Coffee, of which the following is a full, clear, and exact description.

Our trade-mark consists of the word-symbol "Ariosa," and is arranged and printed upon the wrappers used by us for the purpose of putting up an article of roasted coffee manufactured and sold by us under the name and title of "Ariosa Coffee," as shown in the accompanying facsimile—that is to say, the wrapper or label used by us for the purpose herein set forth contains, as part and parcel of the same, our trade-mark "Ariosa," and the general design of our Ariosa label or wrapper is as follows, namely: The proprietary name "Arbuckles'" is printed, in heavy red letters, with a black outline in a curved line, upon a yellow ground, underneath which and in the center of the label or wrapper is a representation of an angel floating in the air, assuming a benedictory attitude and clothed in a star-spangled robe, with a dark red flowing mantle resting lightly upon her shoulders. At the left-hand side of the angel are the words "Sich die," ("no settling,") and on the right the words "andre seite" ("required.") Underneath the proprietary name and the angel above described, and inclosed by a red border, are the words "Ariosa Coffee" printed in Gothic letters, with a black outline upon white ground. On the upper right and left hand corners are the words "one pound," and underneath the words "Ariosa Coffee" are printed our places of business, namely "New York" and "Pittsburgh," the whole being inclosed by heavy black and red parallel lines forming an oblong space. But the representation of an angel, as above described, and the words printed upon the body of the label, and the word "Coffee," at the bottom of the label, may be changed or substituted by other words or design, or said representation or words may be omitted altogether without changing the character of our trade-mark, the essential feature of which is the word "ARIOSA."

Our trade-mark is printed upon the wrapper or cover which incloses the coffee, or upon labels, which are afterward pasted upon the packages. It may be branded or placed upon boxes or barrels containing packages of the coffee, and may also be used in our advertisements, and on bill-heads, show-cards, &c., used in connection with our business.

This trade-mark we have used in our business for seven years past. [Since "on or about the 31st day of August, 1873."]

The class of merchandise to which the trade-mark is appropriated is groceries, and the particular description of goods comprised in said class upon which we use our trade-mark is roasted coffee.

ARBUCKLE BROS.

By JOHN ARBUCKLE, JR.,

A member of the firm.

C-6. ARIOSA (Trade-Mark No. 25,847)

Application filed December 15, 1894. Registered *Patent Gazette*, January 8, 1895.

[This was a renewal of the preceding trademark with a virtually identical description, used since "on or about the 31st day of August, 1873." There were minor changes in the drawing. The description noted that the background was "light and usually yellow." The drawing submitted had a background of closely spaced, fine vertical lines. The trademark was again renewed on January 8, 1925.]

C-7. ARIOSA (Trade-Mark No. 35,419)

Application filed October 22, 1900. Registered *Patent Gazette*, November 13, 1900.

Our said trade mark consists of the word symbol "Ariosa" . . . printed in heavy Gothic letters, usually in black with a black outline . . . usually arranged, as shown, in a straight horizontal line.

This trade mark we and our predecessors have used continuously in our and their business since on or about the 31st day of August, 1873.

[Arbuckle Brothers renewed the trademark on November 13, 1930. General Foods Corporation "re-renewed" the trademark on November 13, 1950.]

C-8. "Empire City Coffee" (Label No. 624)

Application filed March 22, 1876. Registered *Patent Gazette*, March 28, 1876.

C-9. "Our Nectar Coffee" (Label No. 625)

Application filed March 22, 1876. Registered *Patent Gazette*, March 28, 1876.

C-10. "Arbuckle's Compono Coffee" (Label No. 626)

Application filed March 22, 1876. Registered *Patent Gazette*, March 28, 1876.

C-11. "Pure Broken Roasted Coffee" (Label No. 688)

Application filed April 21, 1876. Registered *Patent Gazette*, May 2, 1876.

C-12. "Roasted by the Pure Spice Mills" (Label No. 689)

Application filed April 21, 1876. Registered *Patent Gazette*, May 2, 1876.

C-13. "Quaker City Unground Roasted Coffee" (Label No. 690)

Application filed April 21, 1876. Registered *Patent Gazette*, May 2, 1876.

C-14. JAV-OCHA (Trade-Mark No. 25,823)

Application filed October 10, 1894. Published and registered *Patent Gazette*, January 8, 1895.

The essential feature of said trade-mark is the word symbol "JAV-OCHA" . . . printed on a straight line in ordinary type, and in black ink. . . . continuously used by us in our business since in or about the month of May, 1885. . . . and the particular description of goods comprised . . . is roasted coffee.

[This trademark was renewed January 8, 1925.—*Patent Gazette*, January 20, 1925.]

C-15. POND LILY (Trade-Mark No. 39,682)

Application filed October 31, 1902. Published and registered *Patent Gazette*, January 27, 1903.

[This brand name for canned fruits and vegetables was used by Arbuckle & Co., Pittsburgh, Pa., in the wholesale grocery business from 1891. The trademark was] The representation of a pond-lily blooming on the surface of water, associated with the words "POND LILY," the letters which form these words being embellished by groups of radiating lines.

C-16. DOMESTIC (Trade-Mark No. 39,533)

Application filed October 31, 1902. Published and registered *Patent Gazette*, December 23, 1902.

[This trademark for canned fruits and vegetables was used by Arbuckle & Co., Pittsburgh, Pa., in the wholesale grocery business from 1891. The trademark consisted of] The representation of a winged child and of a cornucopia containing fruits and vegetables, the word "DOMESTIC," and ornamental scroll-work. The child holds the cornucopia, and the word "Domestic" is associated with the representation of the child. The scroll work partially surrounds both the representation of the child and the word "Domestic."

C-17. CABOOLA (Trade-Mark No. 27,405)

Application filed November 11, 1895. Published and registered *Patent Gazette*, December 3, 1895.

[This trademark for tea consisted of outline letters against a dotted background. It was used by Arbuckle Brothers from October 1, 1895.]

C-18. COURT HOUSE (Trade-Mark No. 39,681)

Application filed October 31, 1902. Published and registered *Patent Gazette*, January 27, 1903.

[This brand name for evaporated fruits was used by Arbuckle & Co., Pittsburgh, Pa., in the wholesale grocery business from 1897. The trademark consisted of] A design inclosed within a rectangular border. The space within the border is divided into two fields. On the one field appear the words "COURT HOUSE," embellished with scroll ornamentation, and on the other field appears the representation of the court-house at Pittsburgh, Pennsylvania. The field in which the court-house is represented has at the four corners scroll decorations.

C-19. A deer's head (Trade-Mark No. 32,259)

Application filed November 16, 1898. Published and registered *Patent Gazette*, December 20, 1898.

[This trademark for tea was used by Arbuckle Brothers from August 10, 1898. It consisted of "the head of a hind" without verbal designation.]

C-20. A crest (Trade-Mark No. 32,955)

Application filed February 27, 1899. Published and registered *Patent Gazette*, May 23, 1899.

[This trademark for tea was used by Arbuckle Brothers from November 1, 1898. It consisted of] The representation of a bunch of branches bearing leaves and flowers, a shield having a scroll- like border, the letter "A," and a band and buckle.

C-21. ANONA (Trade-Mark No. 33,214)

Application filed June 15, 1899. Published and registered *Patent Gazette*, July 11, 1899.

[This trademark for tea consisted of the word "ANONA" printed in bold capital letters in a straight line. The application claimed use of the word by Arbuckle Brothers since May 18, 1899.]

C-22. "ANONA CHOP JAPAN TEA" (Label No. 7,683)

Application filed June 15, 1899. Registered *Patent Gazette*, July 10, 1900.

[Use of "ANONA" as a trademark was claimed from May 18, 1899. The term "chop"—meaning a seal, stamp, or brand—was borrowed from the Orient where "first chop" meant "first-rate."]

C-23. ANONA (Trade-Mark No. 118,257)

Application filed May 15, 1917. Published, Serial No. 103,809: *Patent Gazette*, June 26, 1917. Registered *Patent Gazette*, August 28, 1917.

The trade mark has been continuously used in our business on teas since on or about the 18th day of May, 1899, and on coffees since 20th day of February 1917.

[The application called attention to ownership of the name under Trade-Mark No. 33,214.]

C-24. A B C (Trade-Mark No. 122,298)

Application filed May 4, 1917. Published, Serial No. 103,522: Patent Gazette, July 31, 1917. Registered *Patent Gazette*, July 23, 1918.

A B C

[Large capital letters, used by Arbuckle Brothers as a trademark for tea since 1899.]

C-25. "MEXOJA COFFEE" (Label No. 9,446)

Application filed August 28, 1902. Registered *Patent Gazette*, September 23, 1902.

[In the subsequent application for conversion of the name into a trademark, use was claimed from September 15, 1902.]

C-26. MEXOJA (Trade-Mark No. 39,334)

Application filed October 27, 1902. Published and registered *Patent Gazette*, November 25, 1902.

This trade mark has been used continuously in our business since September 15, 1902.

The class of merchandise to which this trade-mark is appropriated is groceries, and the particular description of goods comprised in said class upon which we use the said trade-mark is coffee.

C-27. RECEPTION (Trade-Mark No. 74,037)

Application filed December 14, 1908. Published, Serial No. 39,304: *Patent Gazette*, April 13, 1909. Registered *Patent Gazette*, June 15, 1909.

The class of merchandise . . . upon which said trade mark is used is blended coffee.

The trade mark has been continuously used in our business since June 1, 1904.

C-28, 29, 30, 31. DRINKSOME (Trade-Mark Nos. 50,439; 52,053; 52,054; 54,198)

[Arbuckle Brothers filed four applications for use of "DRINKSOME" as a trademark. The first, filed October 4, 1905, resulted in Trade-Mark No. 50,439 for use on coffee, registered *Patent Gazette*, March 20, 1906. The application stated the trademark device had been used continuously since September 15, 1905. This trademark was renewed on March 20, 1926.

[Three additional applications were filed on February 2, 1906, resulting in approval of use of the trademark on "cocoa and preparations thereof" (Trade-Mark No. 52,053, *Patent Gazette*, May 1, 1906), "chocolate and preparations thereof" (Trade-Mark No. 52,054, *Patent Gazette*, May 1, 1906), "teas" (Trade-Mark No. 54,198 registered *Patent Gazette*, June 19, 1906, and renewed June 19, 1926.)]

C-32. AB (Trade-Mark No. 127,313)

Application filed December 4, 1917. Published, Serial No. 107,740: Patent Gazette, May 6, 1919. Registered Patent Gazette, November 11, 1919.

[This stylized AB, connected on the top] has been continuously used in our business on coffee, tea since January 1, 1907; on spices since October 1, 1907, and on extracts since October 1, 1907. . . . among the several States of the United States, and particularly between Illinois and Iowa.

[The trademark was renewed on November 11, 1939, by General Foods Corporation.]

C-33. "ARBUCKLES' CERTIFIED COFFEE" (Label No. 13,668)

Application filed June 22, 1907. Registered *Patent Gazette*, July 16, 1907.

C-34. "ARBUCKLES' CERTIFIED COFFEES" (Label No. 13,850)

Application filed October 3, 1907. Registered *Patent Gazette*, November 5, 1907.

[Apparently a legal technicality developed concerning the use of the label on more than one brand or blend of coffee, and "coffee" was pluralized.]

C-35. A decorative border. (Trade-Mark No. 72,086)

Application filed July 22, 1907. Published, Serial No. 28,988: *Patent Gazette*, November 3, 1908. Registered *Patent Gazette*, January 5, 1909.

[This rather simple decorative border, intended for use on coffee labels, provided a blank space in the center for text.] The trade mark has been continuously used in our business, since June 18th 1907.

C-36. "NEDRA" (Label No. 13,810)

Application filed September 5, 1907. Registered *Patent Gazette*, October 1, 1907.

[The application stated that the label was for use on tea.]

C-37. NEDRA (Trade-Mark No. 68,412)

Application filed December 7, 1907. Published, Serial No. 31,603: *Patent*

Gazette, February 4, 1908. Registered *Patent Gazette*, April 7, 1908.

NEDRA

[printed on a slant in decorative outline letters]

[The application stated that the trademark was for use on tea. Presumably its use dated from September, 1907, or before.]

C-38. PAULISTA (Trade-Mark No. 69,006)

Application filed February 8, 1908. Published, Serial No. 32,622: *Patent Gazette*, March 10, 1908. Registered *Patent Gazette*, May 12, 1908.

Said trade mark is used for coffee. . . . The trade mark has been continuously used in our business since January 21, 1908.

[This trademark was renewed May 12, 1928.]

C-39. SUGAR (Trade-Mark No. 89,978)

Application filed September 30, 1912. Published, Serial No. 66,059: *Patent Gazette*, November 19, 1912. Registered *Patent Gazette*, January 28, 1913.

[In this application for a trademark for sugar, Arbuckle Brothers claimed use of the trademark since September 19, 1912. The trademark was decorated with a picture of a suspension bridge, reminiscent of the Brooklyn Bridge. It was emblazoned on shipping crates and printed in blue on sugar sacks.]

C-40. NATURAL (Trade-Mark No. 98,737)

Application filed June 10, 1913. Published, Serial No. 71,433: *Patent Gazette*, March 3, 1914. Registered *Patent Gazette*, March 3, 1914.

[This trademark consisted of the word "Natural" in a decorative script, printed on an upward slant. It was applied to assorted spices and flavoring extracts: mustard, nutmeg, sage, mace, white pepper, allspice, cloves, cinnamon, and flavoring extracts. Usage was claimed since February 18, 1913.]

C-41. TALISMAN COFFEE (Trade-Mark No. 93,254)

Application filed February 27, 1913. Published, Serial No. 68,757: *Patent Gazette*, July 1, 1913. Registered *Patent Gazette*, September 2, 1913.

[The application for this coffee trademark claimed continuous usage since February 20, 1913. The trademark was subsequently renewed.]

C-42. FIDELITY (Trade Mark No. 108,678)

Application filed July 5, 1913. Published, Serial No. 71,524: *Patent Gazette*, December 14, 1915. Registered *Patent Gazette*, February 22, 1916.

[Arbuckle Brothers claimed use of this trademark, "particularly between Illinois and Wisconsin," for tea, coffee, pepper, and flavoring extracts continuously since April 22, 1913. The trademark was subsequently renewed.]

C-43. YUBAN (Trade-Mark No. 96,081)

Application filed November 17, 1913. Published, Serial No. 74,023: *Patent Gazette*, January 27, 1914. Registered *Patent Gazette*, April 7, 1914.

[Application to patent a trademark on John Arbuckle's private blend of coffee was filed after Arbuckle's death with the word "YUBAN" in an arc, spelled in heavy, rounded letters. Use was claimed since November 1, 1913. The trademark was again renewed by Arbuckle Brothers on April 7, 1934. The trademark was renewed by General Foods Corporation on May 11, 1954, with an amendment changing "YUBAN" to heavy squarish letters in a straight line.]

C-44. DRINKSUM (Trade-Mark No. 103,638)

Application filed March 18, 1914. Published, Serial No. 76,722: *Patent Gazette*, June 30, 1914. Registered *Patent Gazette*, April 13, 1915.

[The application for this variation of previous trademarks claimed use as a trademark for coffee since March 3, 1914, and called attention to ownership of the previous trademarks for "DRINKSOME." John Arbuckle died in 1912, and Catherine A. Jamison and Christina Arbuckle joined the firm. One cannot help but speculate that the ladies may have thought the company's trade-mark needed to be pepped up by what was at that time the beginning of a popular vogue for misspelling trade names to attract attention. This trademark was renewed April 13, 1935.]

C-45. YUBAN (Trade-Mark No. 102,995)

Application filed October 30, 1914. Published, Serial No. 82,262: *Patent Gazette*, December 29, 1914. Registered *Patent Gazette*, March 16, 1915.

[This trademark adopted the "YUBAN" symbol in heavy black rounded letters for use on sugar, cane-syrup, cocoa, chocolate, tea, pepper, cloves, and cinnamon. Use was claimed from September 25, 1914.]

C-46. SURE WIN (Trade-Mark No. 169,297)

Application filed June 28, 1922. Published, Serial No. 166,162: *Patent Gazette*, March 27, 1923. Registered *Patent Gazette*, June 12, 1923.

Be it known that we, Arbuckle Brothers, a firm composed of the following members, William A. Jamison, Catherine A. Jamison, and Christina Arbuckle, citizens of the United States of America, said firm being domiciled at and doing business under the name Arbuckle Brothers at Old Slip and Water Street, New York, N. Y.; 365 East Illinois Street, Chicago, Ill., and elsewhere, and being domiciled at and doing business under the name Arbuckles & Company, at Pittsburgh, Pa., have adopted and used the trade-mark shown in the accompanying drawing, for COFFEE . . . since March 14, 1922.

C-47. PLAINSMAN (Trade-Mark No. 172,069)

Application filed March 23, 1923. Published, Serial No. 177,348: *Patent Gazette*, May 29, 1923. Registered *Patent Gazette*, August 21, 1923.

[This trademark for coffee was used continuously by Arbuckle Brothers since January 20, 1923. It was renewed by General Foods Corporation on August 21, 1943.]

UCKLES
TRADE
ARBUCK
ASTED C FFE
ORK - PITTSBURGH - CHIC
TRADE

Notes

Chapter 1: Wine of Arabia

1. James Bruce, *Travels to Discover the Source of the Nile in the Years 1768-1773* (Edinburgh, 1804-05): "The Gallæ is a wandering nation of Africa, who, in their incursions into Abyssinia, are obliged to traverse immense deserts, and being desirous of falling on the towns and villages of that country without warning, carry nothing to eat with them but the berries of the Coffee tree *roasted* and *pulverized*, which they mix with grease to a certain consistency that will permit its being rolled into masses about the size of billiard balls and then put in leathern bags until required for use. One of these balls they claim will support them for a whole day, when on a marauding incursion or in active war, better than a loaf of bread or a meal of meat, because it cheers their spirits as well as feeds them."

2. An early Arabian writer came up with a fanciful account of King Solomon's having used coffee to treat sufferers from an affliction. According to the tale, Solomon received instructions from the Angel Gabriel to roast coffee beans from Yemen and brew a drink for the afflicted citizens of a town thereby curing them of the malady.

A seventeenth-century Italian traveler, Pietro della Valle, believed that the coffee he encountered in Constantinople was the *nepanthe* mentioned in Homer's *Odyssey*, reputed to have been obtained by Helen of Troy from an Egyptian king. It was renowned for driving away care and making people forget their woes.

3. Early Arabians apparently borrowed their name for coffee from the Ethiopians. They called the bean and the tree that bore it *bunn*; the drink, *bunchum*. Variations crop up in early discussions of the use of coffee: *ban, bon, bun, bunc, bunca, bunchem, buncheum, bunchi, bunchu, bunchum, bunchun, bunn, bunna, bunnu*. Some are an obvious result of Latinization. In Amharic, the Semitic tongue that is the official language of Ethiopia, *"bunna"* means "coffee." In Tigrinya, spoken in the northern provinces where the ancient Kingdom of Axum was located, the word is *"bun."* To this day in Addis Ababa, if you want to order coffee you say in Amharic, *"Cubbaya bunna, bakh."* ("A cup of coffee, please.")

4. Antoine Galland, *De l'origine et du progrès du café* (Paris, 1699). Galland, a

French Orientalist, translated from Arabic the first reasonably authentic account of the origin of coffee, written by Abd al-Qadir ibn Muhammad al-Ansari al-Jaziri al-Hanbali in 1587 and preserved in the Bibliothèque Nationale, Paris (Arabe, 4590).

5. Wolf Mueller, *Bibliographie des Kaffee, des Kakao der Schokolade, des Tee und deren Surrogate bis zum Jahre 1900* (Wien: Walter Krieg Verlag, 1960).

Coffee's medical usage may indeed reach far back into antiquity, as some claim. The earliest developments in medicine, surgery, chemistry, and therapeutics derived from a mixture of religion, magic, and empirically acquired ideas and practices in Asia and the Middle East. The Persians, Indians, Chinese, Assyrians, Babylonians, and Egyptians had reached a surprisingly high level of expertise in the practice of medicine before Grecian times. As Egyptian and Mesopotamian cultures colonized Greece, these practices were transplanted to the European continent where Greek and, later, Roman practitioners such as Hippocrates, Galen, Herophilus, Erasistratus, and Celsus refined and codified the knowledge in their writings. Because of this literature, many tend to look upon their works as the foundation stones of modern medicine. However, the beginnings were earlier, and all might have disappeared into the oblivion of the Dark Ages between 476 and about 1000 had it not been for the Arabs and the Persians.

During the Dark Ages, they not only preserved the medical books and practices of antiquity, but they raised the status of medicine from a menial level to that of a learned profession by establishing schools and creating a rigid system of qualifying examinations for doctors. Ancient medical colleges thrived at Ninevah, Babylon, Thebes, Memphis, Sais, Heliopolis, Silsilis, and other cities; and the model for the modern university was established at Alexandria in the fourth century B.C., drawing its sustenance from Greece.

So it is not surprising that the first writings concerning the medicinal uses of coffee came to Europe out of Arabia and Persia. Leonhard Rauwolf, an Augsburg physician, lived in the Levant from 1573 to 1576, traveling as far east as Persia. He returned to Germany to relate of his travels and record his findings in *Eigentliche Beschreibung der Raisz so er vor diser Zeit gegen Auffgang in die Morgenländer vollbracht*, published in 1582.

In 1573, Rauwolf found that the inhabitants of Aleppo had "a very good Drink, by them called Chaube, that is almost as black as Ink." Everywhere, he found people drinking coffee, and was told that it had been a familiar drink for hundreds of years. Rauwolf described how it was made of berries called *"bunnu,"* how it was sold in bazaars, and how it was used as a social drink "in the Morning early in open places before everybody, without any fear or regard, out of China cups, as hot as they can." He added that the Arabs considered its use medically efficacious, "a valuable remedy in disorders of the stomach." Rauwolf equated it with wormwood and the herbal wines then in use in Germany to alleviate stomach problems. As a student of medical literature, he commented that the berries "agree in the Virtue, Figure, Looks, and Name" with remedies cited by similar names in the writings of Avicenna and Rhazes, two early Arabian physicians.

The next to publish a report on coffee was Prospero Alpini, an Italian physician and botanist who spent three years in Cairo as physician to the Italian consul. While there, Alpini saw a coffee tree in the private garden of Hali Bey, a distinguished Turkish friend. He returned to write the first

210

description of a coffee tree and to add to the information regarding the medical uses of coffee, publishing his *De Medicina Aegyptiorum* in 1591 and *De Plantis Aegypti Liber* the following year. In his herbal he told of *"arbor bon . . . cum fructo suo buna."* The beans of the ban tree, Alpini said, were imported from Arabia Felix and used to make a black drink which the Egyptians drank in public houses instead of wine. "I have seen one of these trees, whose leaves are extremely thick and have a strong lustre. It is an evergreen." Alpini reported that the Turks not only used their coava for stomach ailments but also for constipation, congested liver, and pains in the splenic region. There is no doubt, he added, that it is a valuable remedy for inflammation of the womb. The women of Egypt sipped it, very hot in copious quantities, during menstruation, particularly when the menstrual flow was suppressed. It was a well-tested remedy.

Alpini had researched the use of coffee and found it by no means a newcomer to Arabian medicine. According to his findings, coffee was mentioned in the ninth century under the name *"bunchi"* by Rhazes (865-925), a distinguished Arabian physician who has been called the Galen of his time. *Bunchi* or *bunchum* was "hot and dry," a stomach fortifier, also appropriate to remove the bad smell of perspiration. Rhazes was born in Raj, Persia, and practiced in Baghdad, drawing many students to benefit from his teachings.

Alpini also found that Abu Ali al-Husain ibn Abdallan ibn Sina, whose Arabic name shortened by translation to "Avicenna," mentioned coffee under the name *"bon."* Avicenna, also a Persian, lived from 979 to 1037 and has been cited as the greatest Arabian philosopher in the East, the physician in whom Arabian medicine reached its culmination. Even though badly translated into Latin, Avicenna's *Canon of Medicine* was still a standard textbook of medicine as late as 1650 in the universities of Louvain and Montpellier. Avicenna said *bon* came from Yemen, one of the kingdoms in the Arabia Felix of Prospero Alpini's time. He considered *bon* "hot and dry in the first degree." It comforted the members and cleaned the skin, drying up the humidity beneath it. It gave a good odor to the body and was agreeable to the stomach.

6. Early writers attributed the origin of coffee's use as a beverage to assorted individuals: Three different sheikhs named Shadhili; Sheikh Jamal al-din ibn Abdallah, a minor Moslem magistrate of Aden; and Sheikh Shihab al-din Dhabhani. In his excellent book *Coffee and Coffeehouses: The Origin of a Social Beverage in the Medieval Near East* (Seattle: University of Washington Press, 1985) Ralph S. Hattox wrestled with the confusion without reaching a definite conclusion.

Carsten Niebuhr visited Yemen in 1763. At Mocha he learned of a Moslem saint, "Schech Schaedeli," who was discovered by shipwrecked Indian sailors on the site of what was to become Mocha. He gave the sailors coffee, which they had not known before. Eventually a village grew about the saint's hut. "An elegant mosque was raised upon the tomb of Schech Schaedeli, which stands without the walls of the present city," continued Niebuhr. "The well from which the common people draw water for drinking, and one of the city gates, bear his name. His descendents are held in honour, and enjoy the title of Schech. The people swear by him. The name of Shaedeli will be remembered as long as Mokha stands . . . Besides, Schaedeli is not only the patron of Mokha: but all the Musulmans who drink coffee mention him every morning in their Pratha, or prayer, and esteem him also as their patron. They invoke him not, but thank God for having taught mankind the use of coffee, through the mediation of Schaedeli." Carsten Niebuhr, *Travels through Arabia and other Countries in the East*, trans. by Robert Heron (Edinburgh, 1792), vol. 1, 427-29.

In its May 5, 1832, issue, *The Penny Magazine of the Society for the Diffusion of Useful Knowledge* seemed sure of its ground: "All authorities agree in ascribing [the use of coffee as an alimentary infusion] to Megalleddin, Mufti of Aden, in Felix Arabia, who had become acquainted with it in Persia, and had recourse to it medicinally when he returned to his own country."

7. Hattox, as cited above, gives a detailed account of the long Moslem controversy.

8. William H. Ukers, *All About Coffee* (New York, 1935), 469.

9. Ibid., 662.

10. Heinrich Eduard Jacob, *The Saga of Coffee: The Biography of an Economic Product* (London, 1935), 58.

11. Ukers, 18.

12. Ibid., 22.

13. Ibid., 45-47.

14. Paul Lunde, "Wine of Arabia—1," *Aramco World Magazine*, September-October 1973: 1.

15. Ukers, 48.

16. Bach's *Coffee Cantata*—in German *Schweigt stille, plaudert nicht* ("Be silent, do not talk")—is a one-act operetta. It portrays efforts on the part of a stern parent to check his daughter's addiction to the new-fashioned habit of drinking coffee. The performance ends with coffee the victor: "The cat will not give up the mouse, old maids continue `coffee-sisters!'—the mother loves her drink of coffee—grandma, too, is a coffee fiend—*who* now will blame the daughter!"

17. Frederick the Great's coffee and beer manifesto: "It is disgusting to notice the increase in the quantity of coffee used by my subjects, and the amount of money that goes out of the country in consequence. Everybody is using coffee. If possible, this must be prevented. My people must drink beer. His Majesty was brought up on beer, and so were his ancestors, and his officers. Many battles have been fought and won by soldiers nourished on beer; and the King does not believe that coffee-drinking soldiers can be depended upon to endure hardship or to beat his enemies in case of the occurrence of another war."

18. Ukers, 42-43.

19. Jacob, 104-6.

20. Ibid., 109-10.

21. Philippe Sylvestre Dufour, *Traitéz Nouveaux et Curieux du Thé, et du Chocolat* (Lyons, 1684).

22. William H. Ukers, *The Romance of Coffee: An Outline History of Coffee and Coffee-Drinking Through a Thousand Years* (New York, 1948), 49.

23. Isaac Disraeli, *Curiosities of Literature* (London, 1859), vol. 2, 321.

24. Ukers, *All About Coffee*, 685.

25. "Antonie Sherlie," usually spelled Antony or Anthony Sherley, was an English adventurer who made a trip to Persia in 1599 on a dual mission: to invite the shah to join the Christian princes against the Turks and to promote English trade. The English government had not authorized the trip. Authorities disavowed Sherley and forbade his return to England. An account of the

trip was written by William Parry, a member of Sherley's party. A copy of the book is preserved in the British Museum.

26. William Parry, *Sir Antonie Sherlies Travelles* (London, 1601), 10.

27. Jacob, 128. There is ample evidence that William Harvey used coffee in his home. Geoffrey Keynes, a biographer, doubts the widely circulated story of the bequeathal of coffee to the London College of Physicians on the ground that he found no record of the bequest in Harvey's will. Geoffrey Keynes, *The Life of William Harvey* (Oxford: Clarendon Press, 1966), 408-9. It is most likely this was an informal gift or bequest which was not recorded in the doctor's will.

28. Ukers, *All About Coffee*, 625-26.

29. Aytoun Ellis, *The Penny Universities: A History of the Coffee-Houses* (London: Secker & Warburg, 1956) contains an excellent account of the coffee houses. The designation of the coffee houses as "penny universities" came from a poem in a 1677 broadside, "News from the Coffee-House":

> So great a Universitie
> I think there ne'er was any
> In which you may a scholar be
> For spending of a Penny.

30. The ladies did not mince words. A copy of *The Womens Petition against Coffee. Representing to Publick Consideration the Grand Inconveniences accruing to their Sex from the Excessive Use of that Drying, Enfeebling Liquor. Presented to the Right Honorable the Keepers of the Liberty of Venus. By Well-Willer— London, printed 1674*, is preserved at Oxford University in the Bodelian library (Douce A. 253):

Complaint: The lusty vigour of Old England, when men got sons and daughters, has of late disappeared: "We have read, how a Prince of *Spain* was forced to make a Law, that Men should not Repeat the *Grand Kindness* to their Wives, above Nine times in a night; but Alas! Alas! Those forwards days are gone. . . .

"The Occasion of which Insufferable Disaster, after a serious Enquiry, and Discussion to the Point by the Learned of the Faculty, we can Attribute to nothing more than the Excessive use of that Newfangled, Abominable, Heathenish Liquor called Coffee. . . ." which dries up and renders men impotent.

"For the continual sipping of this pittiful drink is enough to bewitch Men of two and twenty, and tie up the Codpiece-point without a Charm. . . . They come from it with nothing moist, but their snotty Noses, nothing stiffe but their Joints, nor standing but their ears. . . ."

Another complaint: "Men by frequenting these Stygian Taphouses will usurp on our Prerogative of Tatling. . . ." All this is caused by *a "little base, black, thick, nasty, bitter, stinking, nauseous, Puddle-water. . . ."* of Turkish origin.

"At these Houses . . . meet all sorts of Animals, whence follows the production of a thousand Monster Opinions and Absurdities. . . ."

"Some of our Sots pretend tippling of this boiled Soot cures them of being Drunk. . . ." The "Coffee-house being in truth, only a Pimp

to the Tavern. . . ." Men go from ale-house to Coffee-house to hear
the news and back to drink at the ale-house "and then back again to
the Coffee-house to drink themselves sober; where three or four
dishes a piece. . . ." are imbibed. Thus "the Fopps our Husbands are
bandied to and fro all day between the Coffee-house and Tavern. . . ."
The manifesto concludes by praying that all men under sixty be prohibited
from drinking coffee.

31. Bryant Lillywhite, *London Coffee Houses: A Reference Book of Coffee Houses
of the Seventeenth, Eighteenth, and Nineteenth Centuries* (London, 1963) contains
a listing and description of 2,034 London coffee houses.

32. In 1728, *The case of the coffee-men of London and Westminster* (London: G.
Smith) was authored by "a Coffee-man." It was a vain protest against exter-
nal news sources: Instead of allowing coffee houses their virtual monopoly of
news, irresponsible persons were printing and distributing news picked up in
coffee houses which had previously enjoyed exclusivity. "Twenty years ago it
was considered that our houses were the staples of news and them the fittest
persons in the world to furnish that commodity. . . . Others were preparing to
set up papers of their own and extant newspapers stationed spies" in the
coffee houses.

Chapter 2: A Staple of the American West

1. Ukers, *All About Coffee*, 101. Smith was in Turkey in 1603. His book, *The
True Travels, Adventures, and Observations of Captaine John Smith, in Europe, Asia,
Africa, and America, from Anno Domini 1593 to 1629*, was published in 1630.

2. Esther Singleton, *Dutch New York* (New York: Dodd, Mead & Co., 1909),
132.

3. Ukers, *All About Coffee*, 103. Samuel Gardner Drake, in *History and
Antiquities of the City of Boston* (Boston: L. Stevens, 1854), mentioned a London
Coffee House as having been in business in 1689. A "British" coffee house in
Boston changed its name to "American" when things British became unpopu-
lar with the colonists.

4. J. Leander Bishop, *A History of American Manufactures, 1608 to 1860* (New
York, 1864), vol. 1, 259.

5. In 1729, the *New York Gazette* published its first reference to a coffee
house. In 1730, the *Gazette* advertised a sale of land by public auction at the
Exchange Coffee House, situated at the foot of Broad Street.

6. J. F. Watson, *Annals of Philadelphia and Pennsylvania in the oldentime*
(Philadelphia: Leary, Stuart Co., 1957), mentioned a coffee house in the
neighborhood of Philadelphia's Front and Walnut streets at which a Common
Council of the city was held in 1704.

7. Disraeli, vol. 2, 323.

8. Catherine Drinker Bowen, *John Adams and the American Revolution*
(Boston: Little, Brown and Co., 1950), 434.

9. Ukers, *All About Coffee*, 102.

10. Gen. George Washington & Marvin Kitman, *George Washington's Expense Account* (New York, 1970): "It is not widely known that during the
[Revolutionary] war Washington continued to drink tea. Some radicals
wouldn't have touched that beverage for all the tea in China. By not swear-
ing off, as others had done after the Boston Tea Party of 1773, Washington

may have been giving his opinion of the issues behind that dispute," 130-31.

11. Ibid., 151.

12. Ibid., 230.

13. Page Smith, *John Adams, I, 1735-1784* (Garden City: Doubleday & Company, Inc., 1962), 161.

14. John C. Fitzpatrick, ed., *The Diaries of George Washington 1748-1799* (Boston: Houghton Mifflin Co., 1925), vol. 3, 117.

15. Alexander Carroll & Mary Wells Ashworth, *George Washington: First in Peace* (New York: Charles Scribner's Sons, 1957), vol. 7, 73.

16. Laurence A. Johnson, *Over the Counter and on the Shelf: Country Storekeeping in America. 1620-1920* (New York: Bonanza Books, 1961), 74.

17. Franz A. Koehler, *Coffee for the Armed Forces: Military Development and Conversion to Industry Supply.* QMC Historical Studies, ser. 2, no. 5. (Washington, D.C., 1958), 5-10.

18. John D. Billings, *Hardtack and Coffee, or The Unwritten Story of Army Life,* . . . (Boston: George M. Smith & Co.), 1888, 123-26.

19. Ibid., 129-30.

20. *Rebellion Records,* (Washington; Government Printing Office), ser. 1, vol. 11, pt. 3, 349-51.

21. There is debate as to the origin of the "coffee mill" rifle. The U.S. Army Quartermaster Museum at Fort Lee, Virginia, credits design of the modification of the Sharps carbine to an ingenious workman at the St. Louis Arsenal. Authorities on the Sharps carbine say the modification was made by James McMurphy of Camden, New Jersey, on contract for the U.S. Ordnance Department. The mill has been found on Model 1853, New Model 1859, and New Model 1863 rifles. McMurphy was furnished twelve "condemned" rifles. Frank Sellers, *Sharps Firearms* (North Hollywood, Calif.: Beinfeld Publishing, Inc., 1978), 76-77.

Originals are on display at the Springfield Armory National Historic Site, Springfield, Massachusetts, and at Chickamauga National Park, in Georgia. A replica is displayed at the Quartermaster Museum, Fort Lee, Virginia, and museum staff members regularly demonstrate its workings.

22. Reuben Gold Thwaites, *Original Journals of the Lewis and Clark Expedition, 1804-1806* (New York: Antiquarian Press Ltd., 1959), vol. 2, 187.

23. Dale L. Morgan, ed., *The West of William H. Ashley, 1822-1838* (Denver: Old West Publishing Co., 1964), 168.

24. Philip St. George Cooke, William Henry Chase Whiting, Francois Xavier Aubry, *Exploring Southwestern Trails*, 1846-1854 (Glendale, Calif.: Arthur H. Clark Co., 1938), 319, 340.

25. Lewis H. Garrard, *Wah-to-yah and the Taos Trail* (Glendale, Calif.: Arthur H. Clark Co.,1938), 230, 308.

26. James Josiah Webb, *Adventures in the Santa Fe Trade, 1844-1847* (Glendale, Calif.: Arthur H. Clark Co., 1931), 121.

27. LeRoy F. Hafen, ed., *Pike's Peak Gold Rush Guidebooks of 1859* (Glendale, Calif.: Arthur H. Clark Co., 1941), 216-17.

28. Eugene Bandel, *Frontier Life in the Army, 1854-1861* (Glendale, Calif.: Arthur H. Clark Co., 1932), 97.

29. Garrard, 84.

30. H. H. McConnell, *Five Years a Cavalryman; or Sketches of Regular Army Life on the Texas Frontier* (Jacksboro, Tex.: J. N. Rogers & Co., 1889), 274-76. J.

W. Wilbarger, *Indian Depredations in Texas* (Austin, Tex.: Hutchings Printing House, 1889), 555-73.

31. Lewis Morgan, *The Indian Journals, 1859-62* (Ann Arbor: University of Michigan Press, 1959), 131, 157, 179.

32. Ibid., 198.

33. *Annual Report of the Commissioner of Indian Affairs for 1862,* (Washington: Government Printing Office, 1862), 340-41.

34. Hafen, 270-74.

35. The page from Augusta Tabor's diary is in the Colorado State Historical Society's collection.

36. George F. Willison, *Here They Dug Gold* (New York: Reynal & Hitchcock, 1946), 36-37.

37. Howard Reude, *Sod-House Days: Letters from a Kansas Homesteader 1877-78*, ed. John Ise (New York: Cooper Square Publications, Inc., 1966), 161-62.

38. Abraham Robinson Johnston, Marcellus Ball Edwards, Philip Gooch Ferguson, *Marching with the Army of the West, 1846- 1848* (Glendale, Calif.: Arthur H. Clark Co., 1936), 113.

39. [James Hildreth], *Dragoon Campaigns in the Rocky Mountains* (New York: Wiley & Long, 1836), 85.

40. Mary Elizabeth Massey, *Ersatz in the Confederacy* (Columbia: University of South Carolina Press, 1952).

41. Ukers, *All About Coffee*, 70.

42. Lillywhite, 480.

43. *Abridgements of Specifications relating to Tea, Coffee, Chicory, Chocolate, Cocoa . . . A.D. 1704-1866* (London, 1877). In 1873, an apparatus was patented for mixing pelotas berries and coffee berries in a ratio of three to one: "The berries in their green state are roasted in a coffee roaster which has two compartments separated by a perforated partition; the pelotas berries being put into the one and the coffee berries into the other, the former become thoroughly impregnated with the aroma of the coffee. The roasted berries are ground in an ordinary mill, and the mixture is ready for use."
That same year Edward Dugdale, of Griffin, Georgia, filed two applications with the United States patent office for the use of persimmon seed as a coffee substitute: "No. 143,889: As a new article of merchandise, the partially-carbonized persimmon (*Diospyros Virginiana*) seed, either reduced to minute particles or used entire, as the base or constituent element of a beverage, substantially as set forth." "No. 143,890: Process for separating persimmon (*Diospyros Virginiana*) seeds from pulp, cleansing, and partially carbonizing them for the above use."

44. Warshaw Collection of Business Americana, National Museum of American History, Smithsonian Institution. The Warshaw Collection contains a vast miscellany of advertising material, literature, and business correspondence pertaining to food products. It is particularly rich in the area of coffee.

45. P. H. Felker, *What the Grocers Sell Us. A Manual for Buyers, Containing the Natural History and Process of Manufacture of All Grocer's Goods* (New York: Orange Judd Co., 1880), 5.

46. Ibid., 5.

47. Hinton R. Helper, *The Land of Gold, Reality versus Fiction* (Baltimore: H. Taylor, 1855), 168.

48. Lt. W. H. Chatfield, *The Twin Cities of the Border and the Country of the*

Lower Rio Grande (New Orleans: E. P. Brandao, 1893), 44.

49. Marion Cabell Tyree, ed., *Housekeeping in Old Virginia* (Louisville, Ky: John P. Morton and Co., 1879), 61.

50. Bryan W. Brown, "Boyhood in Early El Paso," *Password 15* (Spring 1970): 15.

Chapter 3: The Coffee King

1. "How Arbuckle Beat the Trusts," *The Literary Digest*, April 13, 1912, 783.

2. Some early biographical sources have maintained that John Arbuckle was born in Scotland. The confusion results from the fact that John Arbuckle's father, Thomas Arbuckle, emigrated to the United States at an early age. So far no proof has come to light that John Arbuckle was not born in the United States. He was of Scottish-Irish parentage.

3. Ukers, *All About Coffee*, 451.

4. Clayton A. Coppin, "John Arbuckle: Entrepreneur, Trust Buster, and Humanitarian," *Market Process*, Spring 1989, 11.

5. Ukers, *All About Coffee*, 452.

6. Samuel E. Moffett, "John Arbuckle," *Cosmopolitan*, September 1902, 543-44.

7. "How Arbuckle Beat the Trusts," 783.

8. Moffett, 544.

9. "How Arbuckle Beat the Trusts," 784.

10. Moffett, 544.

11. *National Cyclopædia of American Biography* (New York: James T. White & Co., 1914-1916), 24-26.

12. "A New `Home for the Homeless'," *The Literary Digest*, Oct. 12, 1912, 624-25.

13. *National Cyclopædia*, 25.

14. Coppin, 14.

15. *New York Times*, Oct. 13, 1911.

16. Ramon F. Adams, *Come an' Get it: The Story of the Old Cowboy Cook* (Norman: University of Oklahoma Press, 1952), 75.

Chapter 4: Building the Arbuckle Empire

1. Joel, David & Karl Schapira, *The Book of Coffee & Tea: A Guide to the Appreciation of Fine Coffees, Teas, and Herbal Beverages* (New York: St. Martin's Press, 1975), 50-51.

2. Jabez Burns was born in London in 1826. He came to New York in 1844 and pursued invention with limited success. He began development of his coffee roaster while employed as a bookkeeper by Thomas Reid's Globe Mills, a coffee and spice firm. In 1864, he patented his coffee roaster and began its manufacture at 107 Warren Street in New York under a sign which read "Jabez Burns, Inventor." By 1878 he had developed additonal equipment and was considered an authority on processing coffee, spice, and baking powder. His publication, the *Spice Mill*, was widely read in the industry. Ukers, *All About Coffee*, 589-96.

3. Johnson, 76-77.

4. Prof. Lendal H. Kotschevar, School of Hotel, Restaurant and Institution

Management, Michigan State University, *Quantity Food Purchasing* (New York: John Wiley & Sons, Inc., 1961), 306.

5. Ukers, *All About Coffee*, 198-99.

6. Kotschever, 309.

7. Forrest Crissey, *The Story of Foods* (Chicago: Rand McNally & Co., 1917), 366.

8. The first ground-coffee package was marketed in New York in 1864 as "Osborn's Celebrated Prepared Java Coffee—put up only by Lewis A. Osborn." Jabez Burns, inventor of the first practical commercial roaster, worked for Thomas Reid's Globe Mills. Reid saw a future in packaging spices for sale to consumers. As early as 1861, he advertised in the New York City Directory "spices put up in every variety of package."

Reid was one of the first to acquire the Burns roaster, as was Arbuckle & Co., in Pittsburgh. Thomas Reid also acquired the old Osborn brand and began exploitation of packaged ground coffee as "Osborn's Old Government Java." However, compared to the Arbuckles' success in the Pittsburgh area, Reid's sales were minimal. His firm depended mainly on roasting coffee for the trade. Ukers, *All About Coffee*, 431.

9. Drachman Family Papers, Arizona Historical Society.

10. "How Arbuckle Beat the Trusts," 784-85.

11. Ibid., 785-86.

12. Ibid., 787.

13. Fred L. Israel, ed., *1897 Sears Roebuck Catalogue* (New York: Chelsea House Publishers), 1976.

14. Jacob, 341.

15. Details of the firm's operations came from "Arbuckle Brothers. A Sketch of Their History and Activities," a company history compiled by M. E. Goetzinger, a member of the Arbuckle organization, for a trade publication, *The Percolator*, February 1921.

16. Ukers, *All About Coffee*, 453.

17. Hannah Campbell, *Why Did They Name It . . .?* (New York: Bell Publishing Co., 1964), 10.

18. Goetzinger, 3.

Chapter 5: John Arbuckle v. The Sugar Trust

1. Members of pools were usually assessed fines for violating pricing agreements. Large orders tended to break up pool arrangements. A merchant would figure he could reduce a prescribed 10 percent profit margin to 5 percent in order to get a million-dollar order, admit his guilt, pay a five-thousand-dollar fine, and be forty-five thousand dollars ahead of his competitors. As the practice spread, it was not long before members of the pool were back to survival of the fittest which had reigned before the pricing deal was struck.

2. In 1888, Samuel C. T. Dodd defended the Standard Oil trust both before a Congressional committee and in a pamphlet. He argued that the trust was the outcome of a crying need for centralized control of the oil business. Out of disastrous conditions had come "coöperation and association among the refiners, resulting eventually in the Standard Oil Trust [which] enabled the refiners so coöperating to reduce the price of petroleum products and thus

benefit the public to a very marked degree." *Combinations, Their Uses and Abuses, with a History of the Standard Oil Trust* (George F. Nesbitt & Co., 1888).

After 1881, despite lower raw material prices and increased volume, coupled with technological advances, petroleum prices were not lowered in twenty years. Henry H. Rogers spoke for management: "We are not in business for our health, but are out for the dollar." Matthew Josephson, *The Robber Barons: The Great American Capitalists, 1861-1901* (New York: Harcourt, Brace and Co., 1934), 281-82.

3. *New York Tribune*, September 6, 1878.

4. *Bradstreet's Journal*, vol. 4, July 16, 1881, 43.

5. *Willett & Gray's Weekly Statistical Sugar Trade Journal*, Oct. 13, 1887.

6. *New York Times*, May 17, 1912.

7. *United States v. American Sugar Refining Co. et al.*, pretrial testimony, 1912, 7244-52.

8. *New York Times*, April 13, 1892.

9. U.S. Industrial Commission. *Reports*, vol. 1, pt. 2, 112.

10. *People v. North River Sugar Refining Co.*, 3 N.Y. Sup., 409-10.

11. *New York Times*, May 17, 1912.

12. *United States v. E. C. Knight et al.*, 156 U.S. 37 (1895).

13. U.S. Industrial Commission, *Reports*, vol. 1, pt. 2, 141.

14. *New York Times*, October 8, 1896.

15. *New York Times*, October 9, 1896.

16. *New York Times*, October 10, 1896.

17. Ibid.

18. *New York Times*, October 16, 1896.

19. Gerbracht was pardoned after serving thirty days in return for assisting the government in recovering back duties from the American Sugar Refining Company.

20. *New York Times*, May 17, 1912.

21. *New York Times*, December 4, 1896.

22. *New York Times*, "Sugar and Coffee War," December 19, 1896.

23. *New York Times*, editorial, "The Sugar-Coffee War," December 19, 1896.

24. *New York Times*, December 21, 1896.

25. *National Cyclopædia*, 275.

26. *New York Times*, December 19, 1896.

27. Coppin, 12.

28. Hardwick committee investigation, 1911, U.S. Congress, House of Representatives, Special Committee on the Investigation of the American Sugar Refining Company and Others, *Hearings*, 62d Cong., 2d sess., 1912, 2310.

29. *New York Times*, June 8, 1912.

30. Henry O. Havemeyer, Jr., *Biographical Record of the Havemeyer Family, 1603-1943* (New York, 1944).

31. For readers interested in a detailed account of the American Sugar Refining Company, see Alfred S. Eichner, *The Emergence of Oligopoly: Sugar Refining as a Case Study* (Baltimore: Johns Hopkins Press, 1969).

Chapter 6: Coffee on the Range

1. Ramon F. Adams, *Western Words: A Dictionary of the Range, Cow Camp and*.

Trail (Norman: University of Oklahoma Press, 1946), 5.

2. W. T. Brite, "When He Got Big Enough to Fight, the Indians Were Gone," *Trail Drivers of Texas* (Nashville, Tenn.: Cokesbury Press, 1925), 684.

3. Henry Fest, "Parents Were Among Early Colonists," *Trail Drivers of Texas*, 421.

4. Angie Debo, ed., *Cowman's Southwest, being the reminiscences of Oliver Nelson: freighter, camp cook, cowboy, frontiersman in Kansas, Indian Territory, Texas and Oklahoma, 1878-1893* (Glendale, Calif.: Arthur H. Clark Co., 1953), 110.

5. E. E. Dale, "Cowboy Cookery," *The Hereford Journal*, January 1, 1946, 37-38.

6. E. C. Abbott & Helena Huntington Smith, *We Pointed Them North* (New York: Farrar and Rinehart, 1939), 68.

7. Agnes Morley Cleaveland, *No Life for a Lady* (Boston: Houghton Mifflin Co., 1941), 201.

8. Adams, *Come an' Get It*, 68.

9. Adams, *Western Words*, 28.

10. Abbott, 69-70.

11. Adams, *Western Words*, 18, 36.

12. Edgar R. Potter, *Cowboy Slang* (Phoenix: Golden West Publishers, 1986), 35.

13. Dale, "Cowboy Cookery," 37-38.

14. Adams, *Western Words*, 5-6.

15. Ibid., 282.

16. Rod Gragg, *The Old West Quiz and Fact Book* (New York: Harper & Row, 1986), 122.

17. Brown, 15.

18. W. C. Holden, *Rollie Burns* (Dallas: Southwest Press, 1932), 72.

19. Adams, *Come an' Get It*, 76.

20. National Live Stock Association, *Prose and Poetry of the Live Stock Industry of the United States* (Kansas City: Franklin Hudson Publishing Co., 1905), 613.

21. Holden, 72.

22. Adams, *Come an' Get It*, 128.

23. Adams, *Western Words*, 5.

24. Frances Nimmo Greene, *The Right of the Strongest* (New York: Charles Scribner's Sons, 1913), 26.

25. Mat Ennis Jones, *Fiddlefooted* (Denver: Sage Books, 1966), 50-51.

26. Joseph Schmedding, *Cowboy and Indian Trader* (Caldwell, Idaho: Caxton Printers, Ltd., 1951), 324.

27. Maurice Kildare, "Mr. Arbuckle's Coffee," *True West* (May-June 1965): 16.

28. Barry Goldwater, letter to author.

29. Kildare, 16.

30. Cleaveland, 230.

31. Reude, 99-100.

32. William MacLeod Raine and Will C. Barnes, *Cattle* (New York: Grosset & Dunlap, 1930), 215.

33. Debo, 11.

34. Adams, *Come an' Get It*, 74.

35. Ramon F. Adams, *Cowboy Lingo* (Boston: Houghton Mifflin Company, 1936), 152.

Chapter 7: The Arbuckles Go West

1. U.S. Letter Patent No. 406 690 July 9, 1889.
2. Ellen Mueller, manuscript, Wyoming State Historical Research and Publications Division, 1-3.
3. Frank M. King, *Pioneer Western Empire Builders: A True Story of the Men and Women of Pioneer Days* (Pasadena: Trail's End Publishing Co., Inc., 1946), 121.
4. Mueller, 4.
5. Ibid.
6. Marvin Pennington to author.
7. Elvis E. Fleming & Minor S. Huffman, eds., *Roundup on the Pecos* (Roswell, N. Mex.: Chaves County Historical Society, 1979), 282-83.
8. Goetzinger, 2.
9. Mueller, 4.
10. Adams, *Come an' Get It*, 74-75.

Chapter 8: Mose Drachman: Arbuckles' Salesman in the Southwest

1. Mose Drachman, "Reminiscences," typescript, Arizona Historical Society, 5.
2. Ibid., 8, 11.
3. Ibid., 31.
4. Rosemary Taylor, *Ridin' the Rainbow: Father's Life in Tucson* (New York: McGraw-Hill Book Co., Inc., 1944), 49.
5. Ibid., 50.
6. Drachman, 32-33.
7. Taylor, 53-54.
8. Ibid., 117.
9. Ibid., 52.
10. Drachman, 32.
11. Taylor, 55.
12. Ibid., 59-62.
13. Drachman Family Papers, Arizona Historical Society, *passim*.
14. Taylor, 148-67.
15. Ibid., 64-82.
16. Drachman Family Papers.
17. Ibid.
18. Taylor, 65.
19. Drachman Family Papers.
20. Ibid.
21. Ibid.
22. Drachman, 31.

Chapter 9: *Hosteen Cohay*: "Mister Coffee"

1. Taylor, 53.
2. Schmedding, 321.
3. Elizabeth Compton Hegemann, *Navaho Trading Days* (Albuquerque: University of New Mexico Press, 1963), 274-380.

4. Kildare, 16.

5. Ibid., 16-18.

6. Ibid., 54.

7. Ibid.

8. Ibid.

9. Gladwell Richardson, *Navajo Trader* (Tucson: University of Arizona Press, 1986), 97-98. Gladwell Richardson was a member of a prominent trading family in Arizona. His great-uncles began trading with the Navajos in the late 1870s. Richardson arrived on the reservation in 1918 and spent the next forty years as a trader. His book, published posthumously, paints an excellent picture of the life of a trader.

10. Charles Newcomb, *Throw His Saddle Out* (Flagstaff: Northland Press, 1970), 50.

11. Ibid., 51.

12. Dr. Irving McNeil, letter to the author.

13. Albert E. Ward, "The Arbuckle Coffee Canister," *El Palacio* (Fall 1977): 2-9; *Navajo Graves: An Archaeological Reflection of Ethnological Reality*, Ethnological Report Series No. 2 (Albuquerque: Center for Anthropological Studies, 1980), 28-30; "Navajo Graves: Some Preliminary Considerations for Recording and Classifying Reservation Burials," *American Indian Quarterly* (November 1978).

14. Ward, "The Arbuckle Coffee Canister," 6-7.

15. Richardson, 182.

Chapter 10: Arbuckles' Coffee Trade Cards

1. Ambrose Heal, *London Tradesmen's Cards of the XVIII Century, an account of their origin and use* (London: Privately Printed, 1925), 14-15.

2. *New York Daily Advertiser*, February 9, 1790.

3. "A Short History of Trade Cards," *Bulletin of The Business Historical Society* (April 1931): 4-5.

4. Robert Jay, *The Trade Card in Nineteenth-Century America* (Columbia: University of Missouri Press, 1987), 8-10, 12, 14.

5. "A Short History of Trade Cards," 5.

6. Jefferson R. Burdick, *The American Card Catalogue* (East Stroudsburg, Pa.: Kistler Printing Co., 1960), 92-95.

7. *The Trade Card in Nineteenth-Century America*.

8. Henry Nash Smith, *Virgin Land: The American West as Symbol and Myth* (Cambridge, Mass.: 1970), 159.

9. Arthur Dandridge, letter to author, June 14, 1949.

10. Ukers, *All About Coffee*, 473.

11. Ibid., 473-76.

12. "They Called it the Card Craze," *Saturday Evening Post*, March 16, 1946, 28-29.

13. Rita Reif, "The Brisk Trade In Old Trade Cards," *New York Times*, February 18, 1979.

Chapter 11: The Arbuckle Mystique

1. Kildare, 17.
2. Dr. Ira B. Judd & John Matthews, "Arbuckles' `Ariosa': A Household Word," *Grain Producers News* (November 1974): 8.
3. Matt Dodge, "Arbuckles' Branded the West," *Real West* (May 1978): 48.
4. James E. & Barbara H. Sherman, *Ghost Towns of Arizona* (Norman: University of Oklahoma Press, 1969); James E. & Barbara H. Sherman, *Ghost Towns and Mining Camps of New Mexico* (Norman: University of Oklahoma Press, 1975).
5. Bruce H. Thorstad, *Deadwood Dick and the Code of the West* (New York: Pocket Books, 1991), 131.
6. Wallace McRae, "Coffee," *Cowboy Curmudgeon and Other Poems*. (Layton, Utah: Gibbs Smith, Publisher, 1992), 33.
7. J. Evetts Haley recorded the words for the traditional cowboy song "Make Me a Cowboy Again" for the Texas Folklore Society during the 1920s. It was copyrighted in 1934 by the Paull Pioneer Music Corp., New York.

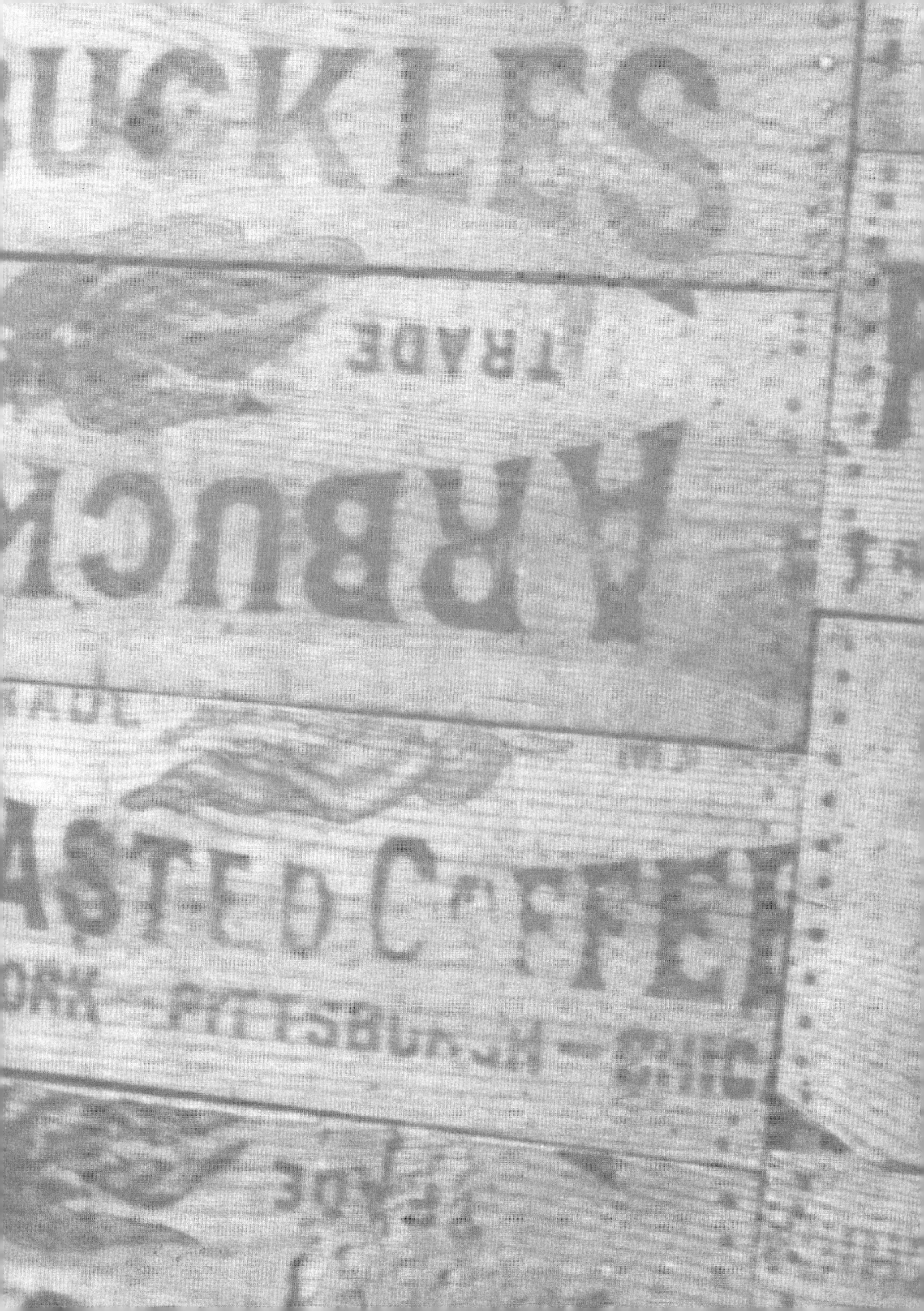
UCKLES
TRADE
PITTSBURGH

BIBLIOGRAPHY

PRIMARY SOURCES

Archival Materials

ARIZONA HISTORICAL SOCIETY, TUCSON.
Mose Drachman, correspondence with Arbuckle Brothers.
_____, "Reminiscences." MS.

BODELIAN LIBRARY, OXFORD UNIVERSITY.
The Nature of the Drink Kauhi, or Coffee. Oxford: Henry Hall, 1659. Wood 679.
"The Vertue of the Coffee Drink." (Handbill) Wood 679.
The Womens Petition against Coffee. Representing to Publick Consideration the Grand Inconveniences accruing to their Sex from the Excessive Use of that Drying, Enfeebling Liquor. Presented to the Right Honorable the Keepers of the Liberty of Venus. By Well-Willer—London, printed 1674. Douce A. 253.

BRITISH MUSEUM, LONDON.
The Alewives Complaint, against the coffee-houses, in a dialogue between a victualler's wife and a coffeeman, being at difference about spiriting each other's trade. 1675.
Coffee Houses Vindicated, in answer to the late published Character of a Coffee House, "asserting from Reason, experience and Good Authors, the excellent use and physical virtues of that liquor...which is no other than that famous black broth of the Lacedemonians as celebrated by antiquity." 1675.
Description of coffee (17th C.). MS. Sloane 3958, f.13.
The Mens Answer to the womens petition against coffee vindicating...their liquor from the undeserved aspersion lately cast upon them in their scandalous Pamphlet.
To make coffee powder and liquor (17th C.) MS. Sloane 657, F.8.

COLORADO STATE HISTORICAL SOCIETY, DENVER.
Tabor, Augusta, diary.

DEPARTMENT OF COMMERCE, WASHINGTON, D.C.
Official Gazette, Patents & Trademarks. Weekly, March 3, 1849-March 31, 1925,
Department of the Interior; April 1, 1925, Department of Commerce.
(This source is referenced in the text as *Patent Gazette*.)

LIBRARY OF CONGRESS, WASHINGTON, D.C.
Trade Cards. Prints and Photographs Division.

NATIONAL MUSEUM OF AMERICAN HISTORY, SMITHSONIAN
INSTITUTION, WASHINGTON, D.C.
Warshaw Collection of Business Americana.

PATENT OFFICE, LONDON.
Abridgements of Specifications relating to Tea, Coffee, Chicory, Chocolate, Cocoa...,
A.D. 1704-1866. London, 1877. Patents Office class 87.
Abridgments of Specifications relating to Tea, Coffee, Chicory, Chocolate,
Cocoa...,Part II, 1867-1876. London, 1883.
Patents for Inventions. Abridgements of Specifications. Class 129, Tea, Coffee,
etc. Period 1855-1930.

WYOMING STATE HISTORICAL RESEARCH AND PUBLICATIONS
DIVISION, CHEYENNE.
Ellen Mueller, "P O Ranch." MS.

Legal Cases

People v. North River Sugar Refining Co., 3 N. & Sup. 401 (1889); 6 N. Y Sup. 408
(1889; 24 N.E. 891 (1890).
U.S. Congress, House of Representatives, Special Committee on the
Investigation of the American Sugar Refining Company and Others.
Hearings. 62d Cong., 2d sess., 1912.
U.S. Department of Justice.
Official Papers, File No. 60-104-0 (*United States v. American Sugar*
Refining Co. et al., antitrust prosecution). National Archives,
Washington, D.C.
Official Papers, File No. 8247 (*United States v. E. C. Knight et al.*). National
Archives, Washington, D.C.
Official Papers, File No. 121616 (sugar customs frauds). National
Archives, Washington, D.C.
U.S. Industrial Commission. *Reports,* vols., 1, 13, and 14. Washington, D.C.:
Government Printing Office, 1900.
United States v. E.C. Knight et al., 60 Fed. 306 (1894); 60 Fed. 934 (1894); 156
U.S. 1 (1895).

SECONDARY SOURCES

Books

Abbott, E.C., and Helena Huntington Smith. *We Pointed Them North.* New
York: Farrar and Rinehart, 1939.

Adams, Ramon F. *Come an' Get It: The Story of the Old Cowboy Cook.* Norman: University of Oklahoma Press, 1952.

_____. *Cowboy Lingo.* Boston: Houghton Mifflin Company, 1936.

_____. *Western Words: A Dictionary of the American West.* Norman: University of Oklahoma Press, 1968.

Alpinus, Prosper. *De Plantis Aegypti Liber...Accessit etiam Liber de Balsamo alias editus.* Venice, 1592.

_____. *Propero Alpini De Medicina Aeygyptiorum Libri quator....* Venice, 1591.

Annual Report of the Commissioner of Indian Affairs to the Secretary of the Interior for the year 1862. Washington: Government Printing Office, 1862.

Arbuckle Brothers. *Arbuckles' Album of Illustrated Natural History.* New York: Knapp Co., Lith., 1890.

_____. *Arbuckle's Illustrated Atlas of Fifty Nations of the World.* New York: Donaldson Bros., 1889.

_____. *Arbuckle's Illustrated Atlas of the United States of America.* New York: Donaldson Bros., 1889.

Bandel, Eugene. *Frontier Life in the Army, 1854-1861.* Glendale, Calif.: Arthur H. Clark Co., 1932.

Billings, John D. *Hardtack and Coffee, or The Unwritten Story of Army Life...* Boston: George M. Smith & Co., 1888.

Bishop, J. Leander. *A History of American Manufactures, 1608 to 1860.* New York, 1864.

Bowen, Catherine Drinker. *John Adams and the American Revolution.* Boston: Little, Brown and Co., 1950.

Bruce, James. *Travels to Discover the Source of the Nile in the Years 1768-1773.* Edinburgh, 1804-05.

Burdick, Jefferson R. *The American Card Catalogue.* East Stroudsburg, Pa.: Kister Printing Co., 1960.

Campbell, Hannah. *Why did They Name It...?* New York: Bell Publishing Co., 1964.

Carroll, Alexander and Mary Wells Ashworth. *George Washington: First in Peace.* New York: Charles Scribner's Sons, 1957.

Chatfield, Lieut. W.H. *The Twin Cities of the Border and Country of the Lower Rio Grande.* New Orleans: E.P. Brandao, 1893.

Cleaveland, Agnes Morley. *No Life for a Lady.* Boston: Houghton Mifflin co., 1941.

A Coffee-man. *The case of the coffee-men of London and Westminster.* London: G. Smith, 1728.

Cooke, Philip St. George, William Henry Chase Whiting, and Francois Xavier Aubry. *Exploring Southwestern Trails, 1846-1854.* Glendale, Calif.:Arthur H. Clark Co., 1938.

Crissey, Forrest. *The Story of Foods.* Chicago: Rand McNally & Co., 1917.

Debo, Angie, ed. *Cowman's Southwest, being the reminiscences of Oliver Nelson: freighter, camp cook cowboy, frontiersman in Kansas, Indian Territory, Texas and Oklahoma, 1878-1893.* Glendale, Calif.: Arthur H. Clark Co., 1953.

Disraeli, Isaac. *Curiosities of Literature.* London, 1859.

Dodd, Samuel C.T. *Combinations, Their Uses and Abuses, with a History of the Standard Oil Trust.* George F. Nesbitt & Co., 1888.

Drake, Samuel Gardner. *History and Antiquities of the City of Boston.* Boston: L. Stevens, 1854.

Dufour, Philippe Sylvestre. *Traitez Nouveaux et Curieux du Thé et du Chocolat.* Lyons, 1864.

Eichner, Alfred S. *The Emergence of Oligopoly: Sugar Refining as a Case Study.* Baltimore: Johns Hopkins Press, 1969.

Ellis, Aytoun. *The Penny Universities: A History of the Coffee-Houses.* London: Secter & Warburg, 1956.

Felker, P.H. *What the Grocers Sell Us. A Manual for Buyers, Containing The Natural History and Process of Manufacturing of All Grocer's Goods.* New York: Orange Judd Co., 1880.

Fleming, Elvis E.l and Minor S. Huffman, eds. *Roundup on the Pecos.* Roswell, N.Mex.:' Chaves County Historical Society, 1979.

Galland, Antoine. *De l´origine et du progrés du café.* Paris, 1699.

Garrard, Lewis H. *Wah-to-yah and the Taos Trail.* Glendale, Calif.: Arthur H. Clark Co., 1938.

Gragg, Rod. *The Old West Quiz and Fact Book.* New York: Harper & Row, 1986.

Greene, Frances Nimmo. *The Right of the Strongest.* New York: Charles Scribner's Sons, 1913.

Gruner, O. Cameron, M.D. *A Treatise on the Canon of Medicine of Avicenna Incorporating a Translation of the First Book.* London: Luzac & Co.,1930.

Hafen, LeRoy F., ed. *Pike's Peak Gold Rush Guidebooks of 1859.* Glendale, Calif.: Arthur H. Clark Co., 1941.

Hattox, Ralph S. *Coffee and Coffeehouses: The Origin of a Social Beverage in the Medieval Near East.* Seattle: University of Washington, 1985.

Havemeyer, Henry O., Jr. *Biographical Record of the Havemeyer Family, 1603-1943.* New York, 1944.

Heal, Ambrose. *London Tradesmen's Cards of the XVIII Century, an account of their origin and use.* London: Privately printed, 1925.

Hegemann, Elizabeth Compton. *Navaho Trading Days.* Albuquerque: University of New Mexico Press, 1963.

Helper, Hinton R. *The Land of Gold, Reality versus Fiction.* Baltimore: H. Taylor, 1855.

[Hildreth, James]. *Dragoon Campaigns in the Rocky Mountains...By a dragoon.* New York: Wiley & Long, 1836.

Holden, W.C. *Rollie Burns.* Dallas: Southwest Press, 1932.

Hunter, J. Marvin. *The Trail Drivers of Texas: Interesting Sketches of Early Cowboys and their Experiences on the Range and on the Trail during the Days that Tried Men's Souls—True Narratives Related by Real Cow-Punchers and Men who Fathered the Cattle Industry in Texas.* 2d ed. Nashville: Cokesbury Press, 1925.

Israel, Fred L., ed. *1897 Sears Roebuck Catalogue.* New York: Chelsea House Publishers, 1976.

Jacob, Heinrich Eduard. *The Saga of Coffee: The Biography of an Economic Product.* London, 1935.

Jay, Robert. *The Trade Card in Nineteeth-Century America.* Columbia: University of Missouri Press, 1987.

Johnson, Laurence A. *Over the Counter and on the Shelf: Country Storekeeping in America. 1620-1920.* New York: Bonanza Books, 1961.

Johnston, Abraham Robinson, Marcellus Ball Edwards, and Philip Gooch Ferguson. *Marching with the Army of the West, 1846-1848.* Glendale,

Calif.: Arthur H. Clark Co., 1936.

Jones, Mat Ennis. *Fiddlefooted.* Denver: Sage Books, 1966.

Josephson, Matthew. *The Robber Barons: The Great American Capitalists, 1861-1901.* New York: Harcourt, Brace and Co., 1934.

Keynes, Geoffrey. *The Life of Wiliam Harvey.* Oxford: Clarendon Press, 1966.

King, Frank M. *Pioneer Western Empire Builders: A True Story of the Men and Women of Pioneer Days.* Pasadena: Trail's End Publishing Co., 1946.

_____. *Wranglin' the Past.* Pasadena: Trail's End Publishing Co., 1946.

Koehler, Franz A. *Coffee for the Armed Forces: Military Development and Conversion to Industry Supply.* QMC Historical Studies, ser. 2, no. 5. Washington, D. C., 1958.

Kotschevar, Professor Lendal H. *Quantity Food Purchasing.* New York: John Wiley & Sons, Inc., 1961.

Landauer, Bella C. *The Indian Does Not Vanish in American Advertising.* New York: Privately printed, 1940.

Lillywhite, Bryant. *London Coffee Houses: a reference book of coffee houses of the seventeenth, eighteenth and nineteenth centuries.* London: George Allen and Unwin Ltd., 1963.

McConnell, H.H. *Five Years a Cavalryman: or Sketches of Army Life on the Texas Frontier.* Jacksboro, Tex.: J.N. Rogers & Co., 1889.

McRae, Wallace. *Cowboy Curmudgeon and Other Poems.* Layton, Utah: Gibbs Smith, Publisher, 1992.

Massey, Mary Elizabeth. *Ersatz in the Confederacy.* Columbia: University of South Carolina Press, 1952.

Morgan, Dale L., ed. *The West of William H. Ashley, 1822-1838.* Denver: Old West Publishing Co., 1964.

Morgan, Lewis. *The Indian Journals, 1859-62.* Ann Arbor: University of Michigan Press, 1959.

Moseley, Benjamin. *A Treatise Concerning the Properties and Effects of Coffee.* 5th ed. London: J. Sewell, 1792.

Mueller, Wolf. *Bibliograhie des Kaffee, des Kakao der Scholkolade, des tee und deren Surrogate bis zum Jahre 1900.* Bad Bocklet, Wein, Zurich, Florenz: Walter Krieg Verlag, 1960.

National Live Stock Association. *Prose and Poetry of the Live Stock Industry of the United States.* Kansas City: Franklin Hudson Publishing Co., 1905.

Newcomb, Charles. *Throw His Saddle Out.* Flagstaff: Northland Press, 1970.

Niebuhr, Carsten. *Travels through Arabia and other Countries in the East.* Translated by Robert Heron. Edinburgh, 1792.

Parry, William. *Sir Antonie Sherlies Travelles.* London, 1601.

Potter, Edgar R. *Cowboy Slang.* Phoenix: Golden West Publishers, 1986.

Raine, William MacLeod, and Will C. Barnes. *Cattle.* New York: Grosset & Dunlap, 1930.

Rauwolf, Leonard. *Eigentliche Beschreibung der Raisz so er vor diser Zeit gegen Auffgang in die Morgenänder vollbracht.* Laugingen, 1582.

Reude, Howard. *Sod-House Days: Letters from a Kansas Homesteader, 1877-78.* Edited by John Ise. New York: Cooper Square Publishers, Inc., 1966.

Richardson, Gladwell. *Navajo Trader.* Tucson: University of Arizona Press, 1986.

Schapira, Joel, David and Karl. *The Book of Coffee & Tea: A Guide to the Appreciation of Fine Coffees, Teas, and Herbal Beverages.* New York: St.

Martin's Press, 1975.

Schmedding, Joseph. *Cowboy and Indian Trader.* Caldwell, Idaho: Caxton Printers, Ltd., 1951

Sellers, Frank. *Sharps Firearms.* North Hollywood, Calif: Beinfeld Publishing, Inc., 1978.

Silvestre de Sacy, Antoine Isaac. *Chrestomathie arabes, ou extraits de divers écrivains arabes, tant en prose qu'en vers, A l'usage des El'eves de l'Ecole spéciale Langues Orientales vivantes.* Paris: de l'Imprimeries Impérile, 1806.

Smith, Henry Nash. *Virgin Land: The American West as Symbol and Myth.* Cambridge, Mass.: 1970

Smith, Page. *John Adams, I, 1735-1784.* Garden City: Doubleday & Co., Inc., 1962.

Swarthout, Glendon. *The Homespun.* New York: New American Library, 1988.

Tannahil, Reay. *Food in History.* New York: Stein and Day, Publishers, 1973.

Taylor, Rosemary. *Ridin' the Rainbow: Father's Life in Tucson.* New York: McGraw-Hill Book Co., 1944.

Tea, Coffee and Cocoa Preparations. Food and Food Adulterants, investigations made under the direction of W.H. Wiley. Bulletin no. 13, pt. 7, U.S. Department of Agriculture, Division of Chemistry. Washington, 1892.

Thane, Elswyth. *Potomac Squire.* New York: Duell, Sloan and Pearce, 1963.

Thorstad, Bruce H. *Deadwood Dick and the Code of the West.* New York: Pocket Books, 1991.

Thurber, Francis B. *Coffee: From Plantation to Cup.* 12th ed. New York: American Grocer Publishing Assn., 1886.

Thwaites, Reuben Gold. *Original Journals of the Lewis and Clark Expedition, 1804-1806.* New York: Antiquarian Press Ltd., 1959.

Tyree, Marion Cabell, ed. *Housekeeping in Old Virginia, containing Contributions from Two Hundred Fifty of Virginia's Noted Housewives, Distinguished for their Skill in the Culinary Art and other Branches of Domestic Economy.* Louisville, Ky.: John P. Morton and Co., 1879.

Ukers, William H. *All About Coffee.* 2d ed. New York: Tea & Coffee Trade Journal Co., 1935.

_____. *The Romance of Coffee: An Outline History of Coffee and Coffee-Drinking Through a Thousand Years.* New York: Tea and Coffee Trade Journal Co., 1948.

Uribe, C. Andres. *Brown Gold: The Amazing Story of Coffee.* New York: Random House, 1954.

Valle, Pietro della. *Viagi di Pietro della Valle, il Pellegrino, descritto da lui medesimi in lettere familiari all'erudito suo amico Mario Schipano , divisio in tre parti cioé; la turchia, la Persia e l'India colla vita e ritrattodell'autore.* Brighton: G. Gancia, 1843.

Walsh, Joseph M. Coffee: *Its History, Classification and Description.* Philadelphia: Henry T. Coates, & Co., 1894.

Ward, Albert E. *Navaho Graves: An Archaeological Reflection of Ethnological Reality.* Ethnological Report ser. no. 2. Albuquerque: Center for Anthropological Studies, 1980.

Washington, George. *The Diaries of George Washington 1748-1799.* Edited by John C. Fitzpatrick. Boston: Houghton Mifflin Co., 1925.

Washington, Gen. George, and Marvin Kitman. *George Washington's Expense Account.* New York: Simon and Schuster, 1970.

Watson, J.F. *Annals of Philadelphia and Pennsylvania in the oldentime.* Philadelphia: Leary, Stuart Co., 1927.

Webb, James Josiah. *Adventures in the Santa Fé Trade, 1844-1847.* Glendale, Calif.: Arthur H. Clark Co., 1931.

Wilbarger, J.W. *Indian Depredations in Texas.* Austin, Tex.: Hutchings Printing House, 1889.

Willison, George F. *Here They Dug Gold.* New York: Reynal & Hitchcock, 1946.

Articles

"Arbuckle, John." In *Dictionary of American Biography,* 1:336-37. New York: Charles Scribner's Sons, 1957.

"Arbuckle, John." In *National Cyclopaedia of American Biography,* 24-26. New York: James T. White & Co., 1914-1916.

Armytage, W.H.G. "Coffee-houses and Science." *British Medical Journal* (July 16,1960): 213

Brite, W.T. "When He Got Big Enough to Fight, the Indians Were Gone." In J. Marvin Hunter, ed., *The Trail Drivers of Texas,* 684-86. Nashville, Tenn.: Cokesbury Press, 1925.

Brown, Bryan W. "Boyhood in Early El Paso—1903." *Password* 15 (Spring 1970): 4-15; (Summer 1970): 42-57.

Coppin, Clayton A. "John Arbuckle: Entrepreneur, Trust Buster, and Humanitarian." *Market Press* (Spring 1939): 11-15

Cushman, Helen M. Baker. "Trade Cards—Records of the Advertising Department." *American Records Management Association Quarterly* (October 1970): 17-21

Dale, E.E. "Cowboy Cookery." *The Hereford Journal* (January 1, 1946): 37-38.

Dodge, Matt. "Arbuckles' Branded the West." *Real West* (May 1978): 48-52, 60.

Dyer, Robert. "Arbuckle's." *The National Tombstone Epitaph* (February 1988).

Fest, Henry. " Parents Were Among Early Colonists." In *Trail Drivers of Texas,* 419-23.

Fugate, Francis L. "Arbuckles': The Coffee That Won the West." *American West* (January-February 1984): 61-68.

_____. "Coffee: Soldiers' Liquid 'Ammo'." *Army* (August 1983): 57-61.

Goetzinger, M.E. "Arbuckle Brothers. A Sketch of Their History and Activities." *The Percolator* (February 1921).

Haley, J. Evetts. "Make Me a Cowboy Again." New York: Paull-Pioneer Music Corp., 1934.

"How Arbuckle Beat the Trusts." *The Literary Digest* (April 13,1912): 782-87.

Judd, Dr. B. Ira, and John Matthews. "Arbuckles' Ariosa': A Household Word."*Grain Producers News* (November 1974): 8-10.

Kildare, Maurice. "Mr. Arbuckle's Coffee." *True West* (May-June 1965): 16-18, 53-54.

Landauer, Bella C. "Tradecards: an Overlooked Asset." *Bulletin of The Business Historical Society* (May 1935): 33-38.

Lunde, Paul. "Wine of Arabia—1." *Aramco World Magazine* (September-

October 1973): 1-4.

Moffett, Samuel E. "John Arbuckle." *Cosmopolitan* (September 1902): 342-44.
"A New 'Home for the Homeless'." *The Literary Digest* (October 12, 1912): 624.

Norcross, Charles P. "The Trail of the Hunger Tax." *Cosmopolitan* (October 1909): 588-97.

Nuhn, Marilyn "Century-Old Arbuckle Trade Cards Once Given Away."
Hobbies (September 1984): 86-89

Reif, Rita. "The Brisk Trade In Old Trade Cards." *New York Times* (February, 18, 1979.)

"A Short History of Trade Cards." *Bulletin of The Business Historical Society* (April 1931): 1-6.

"They Called it the Card Craze." *Saturday Evening Post* (March 16, 1946).

Ward, Albert E. "The Arbuckle Coffee Canister: Unrespectable Artifacts as Archaeological Dating Devices." *El Palacio* (Fall 1977): 2-9.

_____. "Navaho Graves: Some Preliminary Considerations for Recording and Classifying Reservation Burials." *American Indian Quarterly* (November 1978): 329-46.

Interviews and Correspondence with Author

Bauslin, Leslie F. Columbia, Mo.

Belsher, Harold R. Scottsdale, Ariz.

Blair, D. Beloit, Kans.

Dandridge, Arthur. Kansas City, Mo.

General Foods Corp. White Plains, N.Y.

Goldwater, Barry. Washington, D.C.

Harris, Ron. Scottsdale, Ariz.

Gowen, Frederick A. Overland Park, Kans.

Pennington, Marvin. Cheyenne, Wyo.

Sherman, James E. Tucson, Ariz.

Ward, Albert E. Albuquerque, N.Mex.

Newspapers

The (Atlanta) *Southern Confederacy*

Boston Herald

Bradstreet's Journal

Brooklyn Daily Eagle

The Cheyenne (Wyo.) *Daily Star*

El Nuevo Mexicano (Santa Fe, N. Mex.)

(Fayette) *Missouri Democrat*

Laredo (Tex.) *News*

Lawrence (Kans.) *Republican*

New York Daily Advertiser

New York Gazette

New York Times

New York Tribune

*The Penny Magazine of the Society for the
    Diffusion of Useful Knowledge* (London)

(St. Louis) *Missouri Gazette & Public Advertiser*
The (Tucson) *Arizona Daily Star*
(Willett & Gray's) *Weekly Statistical Sugar Trade Journal*